Everlasting

The Book of Love

and Spirit Communications

ZARA BORTHWICK

& NICHOLAS ARNOLD

Z & N Publishing

2021

Everlasting: The Book of Love
and Spirit Communications

©Zara Borthwick and Nicholas Arnold

ISBN 978-1-7643829-0-8

First published 2021 by Zara Borthwick and Nicholas Arnold, Melbourne, Australia. ©

The moral right of the authors and publishers has been asserted. All rights reserved. No part of this publication may be reproduced or transmitted in any form or by any means, electronic or mechanical, including photocopying, recording, or any information storage or retrieval system, without permission in writing from the authors and from the publishers.

These spirit communications were received by Zara Borthwick and Nicholas Arnold, Melbourne Australia, and edited by Cleo Gordon, San Diego USA March 2019 - June 2021

Cover design by Zara Borthwick and Nicholas Arnold.

Publications

These books feature Spirit Communication
The publishers of *Everlasting — The Book of Spirit and Love —* have also published:
The trilogy, collaborative spirit writings: *The Golden Leaf, Edges and Smooth Surfaces, Future Memory*
The Book of Love, *The Divine Universe*
The encouragement, *Celestial Soul Condition*
The Book of Divine Love and beginnings, *Shining toward Spirit, Volume I, II and III*
An Immortal Journey, *Traveller*

The Eternal Message of Divine Love, *Destiny*
Frequently Asked Questions about the Divine Love and Spirit, *Serenity And All Kinds of Wonderful*
Spirit Communications on Transition and Adaption, *Like A Shining Star*
Frequently Asked Questions about the Divine Love and Spirit, *Harmony And All Kinds of Beautiful*

The Book of Faith, *The Faith of Divine Love, a progressive faith experience*
The Padgett Messages *—Soulful Teachings Living with Divine Love —*, Spirit Communications Conveyed by James Padgett
And have published the first single volume in chronological order, November 2008 *The Padgett Messages* and present the freestanding website www.thepadgettmessages.net

These books are spirit leadings and inspirational writings that encourage love
The epic story, *Jupiter's Arrow*
The classic story, *The Butterfly Tree*
The novella, *Divine Love Day*
Affirmations of Love and Spirit, *The Meditation Tree*
Universal teachings of Love and Spirit, *The Last Guru*

The ecumenical and philosophical work, *Universal Input*
Contemplations, Essays and Discourses on the Nature of Love and Spirit, *Everything First*
An Odyssey, *Riding the Barefoot Breeze*
A full presentation of books involving *the Spirit* written and published by Nicholas and Zara are available for viewing at lulu.com (http://www.lulu.com/spotlight/2008padgettmessages)

Foreword and Dedication

Everlasting — The Book of Spirit and Love — introduces the teaching that the Divine Love is a non-evolving form of energy and substance that our mortal souls freely participate with. The spirit communications that comprise this book are expansive. The reality of our evolution interacting with the non-evolving Divine Love causing soulful experience and progression in our soul's life is dynamic teaching. Living with Divine Love brings a sense of wonder that we, of an evolving experience forming evolving relationships, can readily receive a substance and form of energy into our soul that is non-evolving, changeless, abundant and provides our natural love with its true Immortality. It is extraordinary to identify that the Divine Love causes or brings about such change to our soul-life when the Divine Love of God is a non-evolving form of energy! This reveals to us much about how spirits progress in their natural love in their soul-life by receiving the Immortality of Divine Love as we in our physical life are participating with the same Divine Love that brings about the same outcome and Immortality in our physical soul life.

This book is dedicated to all aspiring souls desiring to learn as much as possible about the nature of the Divine Love and our natural love that is consistent, true and relevant to the way spirits progress in their spirit life living in the Immortality and Everlasting nature of God's Divine Love.

Nicholas and Zara
  1st June 2021

Everlasting

The Book of Spirit and Love

March 2019

Hello my darling; quite some time has passed since I saw you last. I am well and my spirit-life is an experience of love that I am almost unable to describe. The Divine Love is so real to me yet I can hardly find the words to convey to you the full meaning of this Love and how It makes me feel when I am enveloped by the Father. That is why so many of us have now conveyed our personal experiences involving our living with this true Love so that every effort to make known this Love, God's Divine Love, is with more visibility so that you - the avid student of this Love - may gain clarity and insight through our loving spirit guidance and teachings.

I feel the presence of this Love in my soul and spirit attributes and I must say here that living with the Divine Love defines who I am and the way that I live my soul-life in my home in the Celestial Heaven. I feel the Love all the time. As I said, living with this Love in my soul has defined my human-spirit-life for although you may perceive me as being a spirit, I am in fact more human than I have ever been as my humanness, as being the essence of my feminine natural love, is perfect and does not live in any shadow in my personality separate from the Father's Love.

I bring word that more information will be coming toward you soon.

Remain of faith and love as the timing of this exchange takes place. I will not say more tonight and will see you again very soon.

Your own loving, Constance

May 2019
2

Hello my darling; I am here with your friend, Saleeba, who will speak to you both in a moment. I see that as I speak to you our Father's Love and Spirit covering your souls and spirit bodies and that you are both aware that to receive us, you are to be in good condition in your souls to do so with clarity and success.

We are pleased that you have published the communications that James Padgett and other spirits conveyed to you. Spirit-life experience living with Divine Love has been very much needed so that individuals who are becoming aware of the availability of Divine Love are able to read about this Love from our perspective and experiences so that this extensive vision involving the true nature of human-soul-life is expansively revealed with transparency.

I will stay while Saleeba speaks to you both in this happy moment.

My love to you both, Constance

3

Thank you Constance. I am filled with love being with you both again to speak about the Divine Love that we participate with. I can see how much your hearts are feeling the moment of this occasion knowing that I am with you again but please, let me say that my human-spirit-heart, as many thousands of years old, is just as happy to be with you! I would like to confirm what the beautiful Constance has just shared with you. We here are pleased that James Padgett has given voice to the world, providing an informative account when he as a man, received Celestial communication.

The existence of the Divine Love was present before James Padgett received some of our teachings and this Divine Love is present now as It will be in your human future, therefore, the knowledge of Divine Love doesn't begin and end with the communications that James received those hundred years ago. There are always, and I do mean always, going to be individuals who desire to advance in their knowledge of Truths relating to Spirit and that is why you have both set yourselves to this task to let us bring forth expansive teachings that illuminate more form involving the Father and the human soul.

As one may be aware, I communicated a degree of experience when James Padgett was receiving his messages those years ago. It was that I had lived in the Perfect Natural Sphere a very long time before Jesus was born and the abundance of the Divine Love not available. Many of us residents in the Perfect Natural Sphere knew of the First Parents and their offspring prior to the life of Jesus. In my own exchanges with the First Parents they had taught me much about the greater spirit universe and even that another form of energy existed that could assist us individually to form a relationship with the Eternal Being and Universal Creator, the Father. We could not go anywhere beyond the Perfect Natural Sphere. The rest of the spirit universe remained closed to all of us for as we know now, it required our individual participation with this Eternal Energy of the Father - being the Divine Love - to become part of our soul so that we could individually realise our soulful nature and that this Love would transform our spirit attributes so that we would be in that condition to participate with the Father in these other environments.

Much has been conveyed to you about the beginning that transpired with the life of Jesus, however, we desire to continue the advancement of knowledge about living with Divine Love that may provide illumination for that diligent student of truth.

As you would expect, I am able to speak about my spirit-life with objectivity and clarity as I am with that perspective of having lived without the Divine Love for many thousands of years available for my soul, and with the Divine Love for many thousands of years available for my soul and joyfully and soulfully replete. The First Parents in the Perfect Natural Sphere taught us well about the existence of a Universal Being, the Origin and Creator of the human soul and the potential life beyond the sphere we resided in. It was difficult for these two individuals, Aman and Amon, to convey to us any real solid form as to the true nature of the Divine Love for this Love was not present or available for all of us to readily receive as we do now. Imagine trying to explain to another the existence of an Eternal Love specific for the human soul when no amount of experience can transpire to qualify or prove Its existence. What this meant to us in the Perfect Natural Sphere, that there were extenuating spirit and soul realities that related directly with a greater and more expansive spirit-life experience that we were unable to directly experience. I, along with many perfect natural spirits, was introduced to extensive universal themes by our interactions with Aman and Amon, but we had no way to participate with these themes. We had no comparative context to relate our human and human-spirit life with other than the way we had lived our human life in the day we were born and the way we learnt about spirit-life experience in only what you understand to be the Natural Love.

When James Padgett received Helen and the other spirits, the emphasis of the human soul was front and centre. The relationship between the human with God was introduced as a true soul relationship and that one of the principle teachings involving the Divine Love is that this form of energy was made uniquely and solely for the purpose of the human soul to partake of. As you can see as I communicate my experience to you, your perceptions are able to see my living spirit-memory of when I and other mortal spirits lived solely in the natural spheres without being able to partake of the Divine Love. We could not understand, interpret or identify what the true nature of our own mortal soul to be. It has required the living energy of Divine Love to bring to life our own true soulful nature. Until Jesus arrived here in the human spirit world there existed no human spirit living in the natural spirit world, including the First Parents, who could teach us how to live by including the Divine Love in our mortal spirit-life. The First Parents, Amon and Aman, knew who Jesus was and who he personified when he was known among the peoples of the Earth in the time that he lived. They informed those of us who were prepared to listen that the collective humanity involving the peoples of the Earth and the people here in the natural spirit world had entered a time of change. They told us that the human life of Jesus marked the opening toward the Father that had been closed since their life when they lived on Earth and had created their error by assuming control and equal standing with God. Much of their error has already been conveyed to you in the previous teachings that you have received. Today, I still visit the Perfect Natural Sphere where I had once lived for such a long time. There are many humans still residing there just as I did those thousands of years ago only now as you have come to understand, we live in that time of change where due to the human life of Jesus and his spirit-life now, that wonderful resource of Divine Love available for one to partake of their first time and to begin that wonderful awakening into their true soul-life that can bring such spirit-universal understanding, an advancement in personal growth and most importantly, being able to continue living beyond the Perfect Natural Sphere that was once the limit that only the natural man and woman could reside in.

When Jesus established himself in his spirit-life and he began introducing individuals like myself to the soul-life, there were many of us who adapted to these new teachings that were pure liberation for us for we had lived in the same environment for such a long time that to leave it and progress through the spheres into the Celestial Heaven was pure joy, relief and liberation from what could be called living a stagnate life. The existence and availability of God's Divine Love represents so many things but most of all an addition of love. I know that over the years since James Padgett commenced receiving our spirit teachings and life experiences, there has been much emphasis placed on the Divine Love. We have been able to place much emphasis on the gradual perfection of the natural love and now the scales of Love are balanced.

I have adored being with you again. I will stay in touch as this shining time gradually opens wider and communication flows between the spheres again, from our spirit sphere into your earthly sphere.

Love, Saleeba

June 2019
4

I am here with you to resume our time together. There is much love that you both feel for I am shining my love toward you as this communication transpires. You have both lovingly accepted the abundance of Divine Love in your prayers before these communications take place, which assists me as I have no need to direct you toward the Soul of the Father as you have already done this. I would like to say that your ability to receive our communications is matched by your ability to receive a Celestial narrative that involves us speaking, introducing, teaching and providing an experience that expands and brings clarity to the vision of the Divine Love that so many in your human world are without. It is not every day wonderful teachings involving the existing Divine Love are conveyed by spirits into the human world, for although humanity is wide in its reach around the world, those receiving Divine Love and being able to identify what this Love is and how it works in the soul is narrow. You may ask yourself how many true teachings about the nature of the Divine Love have been shared or new truths revealed between men and women? That is why most of the information relating with the experience of Divine Love has come forth from us who have been living with this Love over an expansive time and we are aware of our own involvement living with the Father and how this involvement evolves. The essential truth that I desire to impart to you that is the foundation of these communications is to illuminate the relationship between the evolving natural love with the non-evolving Divine Love. As I share my spirit-life experiences with you and as other spirits share their spirit-life experiences with you, it will be to highlight how we participate personally with a non-evolving form of energy that our individual soul participates with bringing change that redefines what the meaning and purpose of evolution is. Men and women are experiencing Divine Love as they will be in the future, therefore, individuals are in contact with a non-evolving form of energy that infuses the soul which has - as a form of energy - no actual interaction with any other form of evolutionary experience. It is this non-evolving form of energy that causes the gradual perfection of the natural love and brings about the true Immortality of the soul and causes such transformation that is ultimately realised in all things defined as living with the Soul of God in and beyond the Celestial Heaven.

I have had quite some experience in my spirit-life living with the evolving natural love to my perfection with the addition of the non-evolving form of energy that God's Divine Love is. I am one who can honestly state that I have vast knowledge about living in the spirit spheres where only those living in their natural love reside. I could reveal all the wonderment of the spirit spheres where natural spirits reside and I could provide clarity that reveals how these spirit spheres are structured to sustain humans after their human life has concluded. You would think these spirit spheres to be the wonderment of God's Handiwork and Creation for they are beautifully formed, uniform in their symmetry and harmony but to the exclusion of the human populations that reside there knowing any real living truth that causes one to realise the identity and true nature of their own finite soul. Or, any reality bearing any knowledge or existence living with a non-evolving form of Love. I would like to say here that Jesus is the Master Teacher of the natural love and of living with the Divine Love, but unlike me, he never lived in the natural spheres in the time where natural spirits resided with the Divine Love being unavailable. Jesus lived his human life and then spirit-life in a reality of the evolving with the non-evolving energy of Divine Love. The complete truth that defines the entire human and spirit-life of Jesus is said in the fact that he has never lived in a time separate from the Father. As my life is a testimony too, I lived my human life and a long spirit life long before I could participate in a personalised relationship by receiving the Eternal Divine Love of the Father into my finite soul which unlike Jesus through his human and spirit-life, did receive the non-evolving Divine Love into his perfect natural love.

It really has required the Divine Love to be abundantly present and for us who are so voluntarily willing to receive this Love in our gratitude and love of the Father, to confirm the true soul-life. This truth about the relationship between the Divine Love and the soul was never more evident than the way we conveyed these truths about this relationship through James Padgett in our initial introduction those years ago. For you to understand how the spirit world functions you need to really understand the importance of the life of your soul and that you are able to participate with a true form of energy that has no evolution to give it the form it has. If you look at the spirit spheres where only natural man resides then you will only be looking at the way human mortal personality functions in spirit environments much like the way personality functions in your physical earthly life without any real visibility to the true nature of your own mortal soul. It is at this point why the revealing of the spirit spheres where individuals reside as they begin their receipt of the Divine Love and emergence of their soul from its dormancy in its natural condition with the spirit-vision of the Celestial Heaven conveyed to you, so that a comparison can be made between what is stagnate and dormant and with limit with what is living, awakening and progressive and what evolves and what is non-evolving. My purpose here is not to place the natural spheres in a shadow compared with the Divine Love Spheres. For all the spirit world is formed by the Father and so it has its particular purpose to ensure the survival of all mortal souls even when those residing in the natural spheres are largely unable to quantify any real existence of their own soulful nature. And even when they are living in these spirit environments and you there of the Earth may think these spirits as being advanced, spiritual and full and capable of imparting wonderful spirit teachings about the nature of man and the universe but are incapable of providing you with any truth relating with the teachings that illuminate the non-evolving form of energy that God provides which is the Divine Love perfect for the evolving mortal soul.

Throughout the time you have both received our teachings and communications your souls have been involved which means your natural love, your natural essence is involved in being able to give and receive as love does in the living as it flows and is generous. As you have received, we have made every attempt to bring the natural love to life as being a most wonderful gift from the Father to each and every created mortal soul, and, that the life of your soul is the gift of human life formed into existence by the Father. The Divine Love is such a substantial gift made perfect to be involved and infused with your soul's natural love but never to replace your natural essence or to dissolve your natural essence so that your natural love is loved and transformed out of existence. From your human perspective, I know that it can be difficult to identify the full nature of your soulful being and to see with visual clarity what your actual essence in natural love looks like. It is like trying to explain to one living in the desert sands what a drop of water looks and feels like. Here in my spirit-life, I am able to perceive my soul and I can see with my soul-spirit perceptions what the essence of my natural love looks and feels like. My spirit-body in its attributes has been advanced through my soul condition receiving Divine Love and having my natural love perfected so that I am able to see and feel my essence through my entire being. I don't believe there is a narrative for the visual imagery to convey to you the image of my natural essence. All I can say is that you may glimpse your visual essence and this will mean truth to you. You may glimpse this essence as your soul condition improves by receiving Divine Love and most certainly the feeling of this essence may cover you from your soul throughout your physical being. We have accepted that language and perception will vary to each reader and participant of the Divine Love in their own physical life and circumstances.

In the time that I have communicated with you and been one of your spirit guides, there has always been that certain mystery surrounding the true nature of the Divine Love and how a human and spirit really relates with this convergence. The Source of the Divine Love is with the Soul of God. The origin of the human soul and spirit body and the soul's natural essence is independently created by the Soul of God. As you in your humanness search out more identification of spirit-life experience in the spirit world, you are searching through real environments formed by the Soul of God. In your own humanness you are aware that there are things beyond your own experience, which we have highlighted, and that some of you are participating with by including living with Divine Love in your life. But through all of this, the real mystery involving the relationship of the soul with the Soul of God is defined by the evolving being in a relationship with the non-evolving and this truth requires more illumination.

Love, Saleeba

5

I am here with your relative Constance. Other relatives of yours and Zara's are present. Cleo's father is present. They are shining their love toward you all at this time. They cannot speak to you about spirit matters relating to the time Jesus lived his human and then his spirit-life those years ago, but I can for I was living then, so my memories of that time, I can recall with perfect memory. I know that you have both received spirits' experience relating to that time, but I would like to add to that time when Jesus entered his spirit-life here in the spirit world as it was a time of change and action. So much about spirit relates with Jesus and Jesus relates with spirit; spirit as being identified as the Father's Handiworks that relate with the forming of all that is human, all that is the spirit world and all that we become infused with when living with Divine Love.

In the Perfect Natural Sphere the First Parents, Aman and Amon, interacted with many spirits residing in this sphere before the human life of Jesus. Amon and Aman's soul condition had been restored in their spirit-life to be in perfect natural love. In their human life before the Fall, they had received an abundance of the Father's Divine Love - this Love remaining in their soul when they could no longer continue to receive the Divine Love. They had a perfect memory of their existence on Earth and in their spirit-life they understood the error they had created, which resulted with the Father ceasing the activation of the Acting Spirit, which is the only attribute of Spirit caused into existence by the Father that can bring the Divine Love into a mortal soul.

The experience of time differs in all the spirit world due to the fact that the spirit attributes in the spirit-body and the spirit-mind process experiences differently than how the organic brain learns human constructs of time and experience that forms memories. From the moment the First Parents humanly died of natural causes and entered their spirit-life to the time that Jesus was born having been conceived by normal human relations, it was not an endurance of Sin and Error dressed as compensation for the First Parents but rather a time to begin organising the natural spheres and the Hells to begin receiving all the humanity that was to arrive. By the time I arrived to begin my spirit-life the First Natural Sphere and all the spheres for individuals to reside in their relative condition of natural love were transparent and exposed by all the humanity living there. When I arrived, the natural spirit world was underway but the Divine Love Spheres and Celestial Heaven and any space for progress beyond the Perfect Natural Sphere remained invisible and closed to us all.

When Jesus arrived there was much anticipation for his life heralded beginnings and a beginning of change had entered the human mortal spirit world. It was a revelation to us all when Jesus taught us how to experience the Father's Love. I know that you have received information relating to this time in the mortal spirit world but in this spirit book my desire is to situate the Father as the originator of evolving and non-evolving forms of organic and spirit-organic Handiworks that Jesus in his relationship with the Father comprehensively understands and clearly teaches so that individuals like myself, other ancient spirits, your relatives and the humanity that resides here can understand what the Divine Love is, and how It acts as being Its own distinctive surface and Its own uniqueness and the form of energy that has caused so much spirit humanity to proceed in their advancement toward the fulfilling of their natural love being perfected and their soul condition interfacing with their spirit-attributes so that one can engage with non-evolving realities of the Father's spirit universe in context with the evolution that was once a physical life and the evolution toward the forming of accurate and true spirit-memories.

When the First Parents shared with us those years ago in the Perfect Natural Sphere, they did not illustrate to us in teaching or narrative terms of the natural love and the Divine Love as a teaching construct or platform to equate the whole existence of humanity. They didn't teach us that the Divine Love was the true Immortality. They had their own language that placed humans in a relative context with humans, the spirit world and super-spirit realities of universal life. They spoke about God, the Eternal Being and Creator, the Father of us all with absolute authority as they were clear that the Soul - the being God represents - existed. They had clear memories of their relationship with this Universal Being and that spirit spheres existed beyond the boundary of the Perfect Natural Sphere we resided in. They spoke about other mortal life forms that the Eternal Being had formed into existence that would never incarnate into any physical form of evolutionary mortal life, thereby never being subject to any planetary organic evolutionary systems to individualise their soul personality. These beings are non-evolving super-universal and coherent beings. In the Celestial Heaven and the spheres beyond the Celestial Heaven humans can interact with these individuals due to the fact that they have received that consistent amount of Divine Love as being non-evolutionary to contribute toward their soul condition and spirit-attributes that can converse about non-evolving realities involving the Father's Handiworks. The First Parents conveyed to us that there was another form of existing energy that was required to assist with interacting with universal realities. They spoke about this energy being an Eternal Love but it was Jesus who defined a more coherent narrative and teaching construct to assist you all insofar as being introduced to a beginning that involves true soul-life.

It was an extraordinary time being in the spirit world as Jesus began introducing us to the whole of the spirit world and what as souls, we could experience by choosing to include the Father's Love in our soul-life. As I began receiving the Father's Love, the First Parents resumed their receipt as well. For the wonderment of your own human-spirit-vision imagine many ancient spirits along with the First Parents being taught and guided in toward the Father as we entered the First Divine Love Sphere! A new beginning!

Try to imagine I had lived a vast number of years in the natural spirit world so therefore, I understood how these environments are situated with the relationship with these varied spheres that I had progressed through from the time I entered my spirit-life to then settle in the Perfect Natural Sphere where other human spirits resided. I knew nothing about the existence of the Spirit Law of Rapport and Communication that defines communication between human spirits with humans of the Earth. I did not know how the Spirit Law of Compensation functioned as I do now, having lived with Jesus and as he identified how these non-evolving Spirit Laws of the Father relate to the soul that is receiving the non-evolving Divine Love. I can state here that you can perfect your natural love without the inclusion of God's Divine Love. My own spirit-life was proof to this but as I have also revealed to you, I did not have the clarity of my existing soul when I lived in the Perfect Natural Sphere to even understand that I was in essence, living perfect and that I could not become any more perfect. The narrative that was conveyed to James Padgett introduces an array of teachings and spirit-life experiences depicting the difference between living with the Divine Love and a soul living without the Divine Love. This is even more realised in the living of the soul-life with the Father or without the Father, as being with or without the Divine Love. When I lived without Divine Love even with my conversations with the First Parents and with other natural human spirits, within my soul I lived my natural spirit-life without a direct experience of the Living Soul, God. Looking back in my memories I can see quite clearly that even though my natural essence, being perfect in this perfection, I did not know anything about the nature of God as Soul nor had I experienced within my soul anything Eternal or Immortal derived from anything identified as being 'divine'. The First Parents, as I have explained revealed to those of us who would listen that God was Eternal; a being whose presence influenced everything and they spoke of an Eternal Love but it was Jesus who gave to man the Living Truth about the true Immortality and how a mortal soul can partake and become infused with this true Immortality. The First Parents were right! The Divine Love is an Eternal Love and Jesus placed this in a structural context drawing the teaching comparison between the mortal natural love with the Eternal Love of the Father being not the natural love but the Divine Love so that man and mortal spirit has a surface and a narrative that is palpable to differentiate this difference.

When Jesus entered the spirit world after his death the living change arrived. He was quite young in his human years but he had individualised and personalised his evolving natural life with God the Eternal Being to that extent that was perfect. He had experienced human life as an evolving human being which his natural love was subject to as he personalised the Father in part by receiving the non-evolving Divine Love into his soul. No other human being had ever experienced this human convergence between a mortal evolutionary soul living consciously and participating with the non-evolving Eternal Father's Love. Not even the First Parents experienced this convergence and as it has been conveyed to you before and as it was conveyed to James Padgett, they had a different beginning and were the first and only to experience their beginning. However unclear the life of Jesus was when lived to those around him and in subsequent human accounts and history when he settled after his death and began to organise things here it was very clear to us, who Jesus was and why his relationship with the Father was a living example to us all. There were ancient spirits and individuals living their mortal spirit-life long before Jesus entered the spirit world but due to the amount of the Divine Love received into his soul during his evolving human life, when we saw and met with him in the natural spirit world, his spirit-body revealed that quality and difference to us that none of us had seen before. Not even the First Parents displayed such visuality in their spirit-body for the Eternal Love that they had received throughout their human life long before Jesus was born had become dormant in their soul. Ironically, in the great machinations of human life due to the First Parents creating their own separation from the Father, they then became subject to natural evolutionary forces so within themselves they experienced an evolving life that came to its natural conclusion which meant that they had experienced and understood human evolution. Had they remained true to their Father's Will, they may have never experienced what all of us have, including Jesus, as maturing through social and organic evolution that contributes to the individualisation of personality in the finite soul.

Now that Jesus, living in the spirit world, his work began being about the Father's business in the spirit world. You see, he was the only spirit living with the Divine Love active in his soul. He knew what was going on, and he knew that we had not partaken of the Divine Love so therefore he had to teach us how to do this. There were many of us eager to participate as our souls felt a draw to the Father by being in his presence. We also knew that we had to experience this Divine Love for ourselves to such a degree that we could then perceive with coherency the truths about living our soul-life with the Father. There were so many revealings being taught to us by Jesus that our whole comprehension about what it was to be human and residing in the spirit world was changing. By the time I had evolved in my experience with the non-evolving Divine Love to be able to reside in the Celestial Heaven I had become a different individual than the individual that had lived all those years solely in my natural love. Not only did I have to learn how to live my soul-life with the Father, but now there was in existence a whole new transparency involving my relationship with my own spirit-life in the spirit world and to present day, as the humanity of the Earth continues to arrive in the crossing over what the individual is exposed to today in all the wonderment of the natural spirit world with the Divine Love and Celestial Spheres full with humanity advancing in their soul-life began those years ago with the life of Jesus.

You have received my love and words as I conveyed them to you.

Yours lovingly and truthfully, Saleeba

6

Hello; it is a pleasure to be speaking to you again. Quite some time has passed since I completed the work that you have published now. I am really grateful that Zara and Cleo spent that time editing the final edition.

As you both continue to receive our communications it pleases me that you are now receiving this true teaching involving the Divine Love being taught as a non-evolving form of energy. I have much experience with this non-evolving form of energy. Looking back over the whole of my time receiving teachings that involved the soul-life, and of course being able to see the way I have advanced here in my spirit-life being able to perceive the Father's Divine Love as a non-evolving form of energy, has enabled me to place all my experience of what has evolved into a true and coherent perspective. Being able to identify the Father's Love as non-evolving provides real truth into the nature of spirit and why from a human life in a physical body, men and women may find it difficult to look into the surface of spirit with any real clarity or solid form and understanding. Everything about a physical life presents mutable forces internal and external engaging the individual but then to bring into this mutability a form of energy perfectly formed for the soul, yet completely separate from any physical evolution, well, it's obvious why men and women have struggled to perceive the existence of the Divine Love received into their soul as they live their physical life! It is just as well one can feel in their faith being Loved by the Father for these physical feelings can at least confirm that a little of this Love that has been lovingly sought for has been received. My good friend Samuels is present with me and it is time that he shares with you some of his insight and experience.

Your co-communicator in the Love, James Padgett

7

My name is Daniel Samuels; I have communicated with you before. My time with you at present is to elaborate on the non-evolving nature of God's Divine Love.

Throughout my entire spirit-life I have been aware of the existence of God's Divine Love and that this Love presents many things to the human individual. This Love and its existence represent change. A living truth about this kind of change is experienced in the realm of the finite soul but the truth about this change is that the Divine Love, as a form of energy with real causal power, does not change nor ever will change into any other form of energy. The remarkable teaching about this Divine Love is that by its availability and existence, humans are with potential to have immediate contact with a non-evolving form of energy that can be readily experienced in the domain of ones own finite soul.

There is at present vast humanity residing in this spirit world living their spirit-life experience readily receiving this Divine Love into their finite soul. We are in our spirit-life experience individually aware that we are with direct contact with the most advanced form of energy that is available for a human to live with and known to humankind.

When I became adjusted to my spirit-life and I continued receiving Divine Love, as I was aware that this Love existed during my human physical life, I was taught by those who understood the nature of this Divine Love and how the finite soul acted when directly receiving this Love. I was introduced to a principle teaching that this Love as a form of energy is changeless yet brings about change to the attribute of the soul, such as the gradual perfection of the natural love already living and forming the essence of the finite personality of the individual. I became aware that the condition of my soul and spirit attributes were going to change by receiving a non-changing, non-evolving form of energy. My early spirit-life was one of adapting to change from one world to another world. Every human obviously is with their physical attribute during the earthly life, but when human life begins here, everything about a human life changes!

Part of my spirit-life experience was to understand the nature of the Divine Love that was going to advance my soul condition and that would remain part of my spirit-life experience for all my finite eternity. I also needed to adjust my thinking so that I could grasp the fact that this Divine Love ever so real - that I could not see with my spirit-optical vision - and that I could not perceive with my soul-spirit-perceptions as this attribute was not yet sufficiently advanced to perceive this existing form of energy. In essence, my human brain and now my spirit-mind were formed by an evolving convergence; my individuality derived from human and spirit experiences that were palpable to me. What I did not have in my evolved attributes was the condition within my being to experience with certain tangible cognitive evidence, the existence of a form of energy that in Its own existing form, was not subject to any evolution or evolutionary circumstance.

In effect, I was realising in my early human spirit-life that my spirit-life experiences were now going to be shaped by my participation for the rest of my spirit-life with a non-evolving form of love energy that was going to bring about change and that this experience was going to teach me about the living convergence between what evolution is and what is spirit non-evolution. In this cradle of life experience my understanding and knowledge about what it is to be human and who and what God is would be a continuing advancement of my own finite potential being revealed.

An observation that I have made about how people are in their physical life when becoming aware that they can participate with this Love, is defined by their inability to be cognitively aware that they are receiving a non-evolving form of energy. This is why so many have so much difficulty insofar as being able to identify within their human life what this Divine Love is and how it functions in their soul. I was one of these individuals!

There are so many advancements in the worldwide human experience today that now some of you are in direct contact with the most advanced form of energy available and known to all worldly humans and is experienced directly in the evolving natural love of your own soul. I can state with authority that the humanity that resides throughout the Celestial Heaven is an advanced humanity and that as humans we each individually recognise that we are the way we are due to our voluntary participation that is our individual acceptance of Divine Love and that this Love comes forth from the Soul God and from no other existing universal life form. The Divine Love has only one origin, which is the Soul of Our Universal Father. If you cannot accept this to begin with, that is okay, as experience is the necessary teacher. But when your natural love is perfected by receiving Divine Love in your soul, you will know that you have accepted this living truth.

I would explain this statement by saying that as I advanced my own acceptance of the Father was a glimpse at best. In my spirit-life I was able to see very clearly those individuals living in their advanced condition and it was obvious to me that they had accepted their individual personalisation of the Living Universal Father with such palpable knowing that this only mirrored and reflected on my personal being at how little in my soul I knew the Source of the Divine Love, the Universal Father.

My experience like so many other individuals embracing the Divine Love is a continuing experience of wonderment. I found that by being in touch, in a voluntary manner with this Divine Love, that I was in touch with the purest form of energy that as a resource would redefine my human life. We are human here in our spirit-life experience. You refer to us as 'spirits' but we are human, very human. People are transitioning into the spirit world all the time day-in and day-out due to all the consequences that bring about human death, but living goes on. For me, being in touch with a non-evolving form of energy provided me with the understanding that so much that is present in this vast spirit world is in its various forms, non-evolving. The Acting Spirit that conveys the Divine Love into my finite soul does not evolve and nor does any of the Father's Spirit Laws that assist in the substantial make-up of all the spheres that comprise the environments that we as humans reside in and advance through. This is a very different world. Having come from Earth where evolutionary forces form part of the whole organic survival of species and even with the consistent movement of the planets and the weather and all the systems that define the Earth being what it is, to then live in an environment that is no longer subject to these natural forces and evolution is a human revelation in itself. Understanding this defines why people in their physical life have such trouble insofar as ascertaining how the spirit world functions and how it is in its essential makeup and how we live here. People in their physical life have in their organic nature an evolutionary rhythm whereas humans in their spirit-life experience are no longer subject to organic evolutionary forces that once defined their human physical life experience. How do you perceive the existence of non-evolving experiences that comprise the spirit world when day-in and day-out in your physical human life you are being constantly threaded with the evolutionary systems that define the human species? How is it that a person living such physical determinations of life's evolving experiences process and evaluate living with a non-evolving form of energy that their own finite soul is participating with on a voluntary basis? It's no wonder faith is a solid substance and a tangible presence that assists one to gain a foothold in a physical convergence between what evolves and what doesn't evolve; what changes with that which will never change. You have received my communication with such rapid delivery as only minutes have passed by. I will return to convey more.

Your friend, Daniel

8

I am here to speak a little more about my spirit-life experience. You received my previous message in a rapid form of spirit communication. It was one of the quickest teachings you have received in its delivery. You are both mature in your experience living with Divine Love and due to the amount of communication that you have both received, experience has made our being together now very available. This teaching about the Divine Love as non-evolving will answer many questions that people have with regard to their involvement with this Love. I speak from personal experience. When I became aware of the spirit communications that James Padgett received, and then with some of the communications that I received as a man living with the Divine Love, it never occurred to me to study the Father's Love in the context that I am speaking to you about now. If I, in my human life had studied the Divine Love and how It is as an identity caused into existence by the Father, and had I been able to ascertain how It doesn't evolve, then this would have revealed to me much about the nature of this Love and how you cannot make it anything of the material world. Here in my spirit-life, I live amidst spirit-material but there is nothing of the Father's Divine Love in it. You see, I am showing you the comparison that in your physical life and here in my spirit-life we are both in touch with this Divine Love that doesn't evolve yet we are residing in our respective environments where your physical-human and my human-spirit life experiences have an aspect of evolution to them! This is wonderful when you pause for a moment and actually think about it. What is evolving and what isn't evolving being together in the finite soul amidst environments suitable for us to live and prosper and progress through.

It has been important to illustrate to you that your experience living with Divine Love and my experience living with Divine Love is the same, though we live and reside in different environments. The Divine Love that we are both receiving is non-evolving, constant and unvaried, changeless, perfect, yet it has brought so much changed condition to our respective individuality about who we are, where we have come from and fulfilling our individual potentials. The primary difference between your experience and my experience is that what is external to you represents the way your environments change whereas what is external to me are the changed environments of the varied spheres that I have lived in and progressed through and that there are non-evolving aspects to these spheres that I in my soul condition can relate with since I understand what the non-evolving is in my own soul as I am in constant experience with the Divine Love - the energy that this Love is in my soul and spirit attributes. I will add here that when one progresses to the Celestial Heaven and can identify how it was to live without any awareness of the Divine Love existing, it is very clear that this non-evolving form of energy never formed an existing part of one's soul and that this Divine Love exists in its state of being external to us until we become aware of its existence and we voluntarily choose to participate with it by including this Love in our soul-life.

My experience is similar to all the humans who begin receiving Divine Love here in the spirit world. In the First Divine Love Sphere, my progression to advance to the next sphere wasn't reliant on my spirit-body adapting and then evolving with the organic spirit material that makes up the interior of the First Divine Love Sphere. Truthfully, by receiving more Divine Love my soul condition began to change, which was evident in the attributes of my spirit-body that was then harmonious with the spirit organic material in the sphere I resided in. Due to the amount of Divine Love I received and my adaption to my spirit-life experience, I was able to progress to the Divine Love Sphere where my spirit-body was harmonious with the spirit organic material that comprised this sphere. My spirit-body and soul were not subject to any external spirit environment evolution in order for me to evolve toward a brighter more substantial sphere. Unlike Saleeba, who adores you very much, Saleeba progressed in her early spirit-life through those spirit environments where one does not require any Divine Love to do so. Saleeba wasn't required to evolve in order to progress in the natural spirit world. Saleeba was subject to Spirit Laws that relate specifically with the soul and its condition and when the essence of the soul is in a better condition through any reconciliation that one might have derived from their human physical life. You would know this as being in touch with the Spirit Law of Compensation that was introduced by and explained through messages received by James Padgett and yourselves. The point that I am illustrating is, progression in a spirit's life revolves around soul condition and not spirit evolution. My experience of being a human-spirit is determined by my soul condition receiving a non-evolving form of energy that then causes changes in my soul and spirit attributes that have caused me to progress rather than evolution to gain improvement, maturity or further spirit-awareness. This is slightly difficult to explain to you since there is no reference to this in your daily physical human life. You can be receiving Divine Love for a long time and to have received an abundance of this Love into your soul with your soul condition having changed, yet you are completely hinged to the natural evolving process of ageing or other evolving circumstance that may not reveal to you that any real progress or change has been substantiated by receiving an abundance of Divine Love. The other difficulty that you are faced with is to believe so wholeheartedly in the

Soul of God and the existence of the Divine Love and to receive this Love over a long period of time and yet not to see any material change in your physical life. You have heard from us, you have read words conveyed by spirits who know and confirm what they are conveying to you for they have experienced, as I have, the dynamic of change derived from receiving vast amounts of Divine Love and you are both seemingly much the same. Fortunately, I, and other spirits are able to communicate the truth about the Divine Love being non-evolving so that in your experience you will know where to look, how to see this Divine Love as It covers your soul. Once you are able to begin perceiving what non-evolving looks like, then the form of Divine Love begins to become more solid and less abstract and more truthful and personally dynamic as the Divine Love is living energy!

In my spirit-life when I was learning about this Divine Love in the First Divine Love Sphere, I had to learn how not to do anything. By this I mean to let God, the Soul, Love me. Part of my education learning about living with the Father was to understand that I, in my humanity, bore no outcome to the way the Divine Love existed or was going to *act*, for a great truth about the Divine Love is that It only acts in accord with the Soul, God. Having lived a physical life where everything about being physically human was determined by my self-acting personality engaging and trying to establish a life for myself, now in my spirit-life, had to learn how to accept this Divine Love that was acting in accord with God and not to the wishes of my personality to make a life here in the spirit world for myself. Understanding this taught me how present and non-evolving God's Divine Love is! I was taught by my Celestial teachers that this Divine Love will never change in all its existence and that God had formed this changeless substance into existence so that life in the spirit world eternal, would forever have one reliable source of energy that we can individually experience that will gently and lovingly cause change so that a life is established in the spirit world *caused* by Living Love.

Once I had started to intellectually understand that the nature of Divine Love represented somewhat of the nature of Its Origin and Source, in my soulful prayers to the Father for this Love I could then begin to feel the living energy of this Love acting within my being without my having to do anything to bring such change to my spirit-life. Perhaps you might see a non-evolving form of energy as lifeless, but the Divine Love is quite the opposite. It is so dynamic and so full of light and life, an energy form that nothing in all the physical and spirit universe can create other than the Creator, God. This energy is so real that we can only receive a small amount to begin with. I learned that the Father bestows only the amount of Divine Love suitable to your soul at any one time so that one is not overwhelmed emotionally or in any attribute that will result in disharmony in the individual.

Saleeba lived that remarkable life, when upon her entrance into her spirit-life, she progressed to the Perfect Natural Sphere living a long time without ever experiencing the Divine Love as Saleeba has illustrated to you, she was not alone in the time that she lived her spirit-life. In my experience, I entered my spirit-life, having known of the Divine Love and believing that I had received it. In my spirit-life I was able to continue living with Divine Love and had my belief confirmed into knowing. This leads me to explain to you that being *perfect* is a truth for perfect exists here in the spirit world. I have experienced perfect when the gift of my natural love could no longer become anything more perfect than it is, and due to my spirit-soul-perceptions being sufficiently developed by receiving the abundance of Divine Love over time, I was able to become cognitive of my natural essence in its perfect state. Saleeba had experienced *perfect* without receiving the Divine Love but, as she has explained to you, in her perfect state she was unable to have any cognitive awareness and objectivity into the true nature and being of her soul. You must remember that the Father has originated your soul and in so doing, has fashioned each finite attribute of soul so that it can receive Divine Love and return to the perfect state that it was created in. There is nothing in all the universes to prevent this causal truth from happening. I have seen vast humanity living their everyday spirit-life being in their perfect natural love as a normal part of everyday spirit-life experience, so-to-speak. My soul loves experiencing Divine Love. Each time I let my soul be responsive to the Soul of God it is a personal celebration as I know what this Love means to me. The fact that It doesn't change is a constant confirmation that I am in the Father and the Father is in me, and this is evident in the existence of the Divine Love. My perfect state is sustained in perfect Divine Love. My spirit-attributes continue to mature and expand so that more of my personality learns of the Father's Personality and due to the fact that I continue to receive Divine Love, I am able to perceive more existence of the Soul that is central to life.

I will stop now. This has been enjoyable.
Respectfully, Daniel

9

Hello my darlings, it is I, Constance. Daniel is enthusiastic about having a voice in the world once more. What I do know, is hope. Our communications will bring hope to those souls who have yearned for a truth that is real and this truth, the Living Soul, God. Hope may be a little light in your life but enough that you have the beginnings of a living faith that you are reminded of each day. Bring this hope into the receiving of Divine Love and you have a hope that is living. Even I am still learning about living with Divine Love and it astounds me still how so many here are living with this Love who have come from all the beliefs that have formed human history. We are fortunate here for we have visible contact with Jesus and he is the example of living the soul-life with God. Saleeba is very close to Jesus and spends vast amounts of time in the natural spirit world among the natural beliefs of human spirits revealing with Jesus the way of the soul-life. Saleeba and Jesus have known each other for a long time and they work very well together. There are many individuals who like working alongside Jesus in the natural spirit world. There are millions of individuals entering their spirit-life who have lived their physical human life knowing of Jesus but have never met him. Here in the spirit world what was once believed in, though unseen and often unfounded, now known. Spend a minute thinking about this. Here in the spirit world, the dynamic of change is seen in the living Jesus as he moves among the natural humanity where so many have truly hoped in their physical life, that he is real and can be loved. Many people's beliefs about God, life, Jesus, or other human figures simply melt away when they come face-to-face with Jesus in the spirit world. Imagine what this must be like. He is the dynamic of change in the natural spirit world. The teachings about the soul-life and living with Divine Love and how the spirit world works and functions as part of the Father's Handiworks having their foundation of teachings brought forward by Jesus as the Father has taught him how to live in love with the Father and with humanity and the spirit world.

There are those of you beginning to learn about the Divine Love and that is why these communications are necessary especially those teachings that are pure and applied in the living, like the way Daniel is explaining to you about the relationship between the evolving and the non-evolving.

I will not write more other than to say my darlings, that you are proceeding well.

My love to you both, Constance.

10

I am here; it is I, Daniel. A day has passed since my recent visit to you. Saleeba's account involving the time that she lived in the Perfect Natural Sphere when the Divine Love was unable to be received serves to illustrate that there is a limit to spirit-life experience when residing in the natural spheres. Ironically, in physical human life the individual can be all about extending their physical life beyond the limit in the life experience they are participating with. The word advancement comes to mind. I can recall in the day that I lived my physical life there were advancements and changes happening all around me, especially in the field of science and medicine.

In some of the messages that James Padgett received, it was conveyed that man is bestowed with the attribute of an unrestricted will. This could be more appropriately explained by saying that man is invested in a dynamic of personality with the desire to express personality in all respective fields of human experience. This reveals involvement with an unrestricted will. What happens when the unrestricted nature of the personality in man commences a relationship with a restricted form of energy that the non-evolving Divine Love represents to the soul? How unrestricted can an individual be when living with a progressive experience involving Divine Love?

From your perspective, what Spirit symbolises can be called limitless and unrestricted as one is no longer subject to the limitations of a finite physical body. But, Saleeba, through her account has taught us that in the natural spirit world when one does not include the Divine Love, the personality reaches a limit of spirit-life experience that cannot be exceeded by the personality of that individual. Perfect natural love in the natural spirit world is exactly a truth, perfect. And by becoming perfect, cannot exceed its own perfection by advancing beyond the Perfect Natural Sphere. This is why here in the spirit world, having the Divine Love available is the dynamic that has been provided to us by the Father so that we can exceed the solitary limit of our own perfect natural love. With the relationship between the evolving nature of human experience with the non-evolving nature of God's Divine Love, we are able to see a relationship formed between the unrestricted with the restricted as separate forms of energy, the natural love and the Divine Love, converge in the soul, which causes change in the condition of the soul, which is then expressed through the individual personality. Does a Celestial spirit live with an unrestricted will? Yes, we do but this unrestricted will is defined by our living with Immutable Spirit Laws and Workings of Love, just like the Divine Love, that in their particular unique forms of existence, present a restriction or rather measure, that acts as a progressive working boundary of love. I live in the Celestial Heaven and I am unrestricted in my ability to be able to come and to see you, for I can travel through the spheres that I have progressed through. My soul condition has advanced and I feel limitless, but I cannot travel beyond the sphere I reside in, in the Celestial Heaven, until I am in a more advanced spirit condition.

I was familiar with the communications James Padgett received. I had read about perfect natural love. In my human life, I had no idea what this perfect soul condition involving my own essence would look like. I can say this, for here in my Celestial life, I am living in my perfect natural love and I know what this looks and appears like in the attribute of my spirit-body. My spirit-soul perception reflects that my natural essence is perfect; that the living condition in my soul cannot become any more perfect. I live without any compensation and I am clear in my living soul condition from any erroneous human experience or teaching that is untrue, so for me, I live in the truthfulness of my human memories that all have their origin in my natural love. There is nothing in my spirit-life now that contributes toward my soul being anything other than living in the gift of my perfect natural essence.

When I began actively participating with Celestial teachers, they began to teach me about living my soul-life with the Father. It wasn't until I had progressed to the 7th sphere that I could gain real identity into my natural essence as living; that this natural love was really my true nature. I could feel my spirit-body becoming fuller in its function. I was able to perceive how my human life had been, and then my early spirit-life to my now participating with the influence of Divine Love in my soul in the 7th sphere. As you have received communications from those individuals who have shared with you how they felt in the 7th sphere, and about to proceed into the Celestial Heaven, in the 7th sphere I was very excited!

The great truth about living in the spirit world is that it requires living with God to exceed your own finite limit. In physical human life, there is so much confusion and lack of visible truth about who and what God is, that to a personality living with God it can seem like living with the greatest restriction known to man. When this is reinforced with human beliefs being taught and imposed as pertaining to what is God's Will, beliefs are cast as truths that are usually errors relating with the real truths that give God transparency to love. It is quite possible that God, by having caused the Divine Love - this truthful form of energy brought into existence - has created the ultimate form of energy that will never change, that we can participate with that gradually brings limitless change!

From your perspective, you may stand in awe of all that is ahead of you as your senses gain more truth about spirit-vision. And, here I am living in my Celestial spirit-life standing in awe of all that is ahead of me. Insofar as I am able to interact socially with individuals that have travelled to the Celestial Heaven from the spheres that exceed this Heaven, with my spirit-vision I can see the truth that exceeds my own place and standing in the Celestial Heaven. In all of this, I recognise how it is that this Divine Love extends from the Father's Soul all the way to my soul and yours.

In my Celestial life, the organic spirit-material is palpable to my spirit-senses. I am able to equate distances, width and depth of spirit-space and spirit-time, which differs to your organised constructs of time based around the Earth and the sun. In the Celestial Heaven, I am unable to see the Earth. I can stand in the sphere I reside in, knowing in which direction to look, and if I were to point would locate where the Earth is. I can sense the presence of the Earth, which I find comforting, as it is where I began the individualisation of my soul. Living in the spirit world is an amazing experience for we are able to see with such objectivity where we have commenced our life. But, also now that I have lived my Celestial life for some time, I am well aware that my soul preceded its earthly existence, as being formed by God and having existed prior to its incarnation. Though I have received an abundance of Divine Love and I have felt the Father's Acting Spirit cover my spirit-body, here in the Celestial Heaven I am unable to see with my spirit-optical vision the Acting Spirit or Divine Love, as if it were physical, external to my soul. Here in my spirit-life I am living in these spirit environments, but the Divine Love external to me is still invisible as is the Acting Spirit. This is important to know for it reveals that there are certain aspects of the Father that remain of the Father and that the Divine Love and Acting Spirit have never become engaged with any other part or function of a mortal's domain. Other individuals can see that I am living with Divine Love, as I can see that they are. This is reflective in the condition of the spirit-body which reflects our true soul condition. I can perceive how my soul-nature is now that I am living my soul-life, which is the living convergence of my natural essence harmoniously living with Divine Love that I have acquired. I can certainly feel how it is in my spirit-attributes, feeling how I am as the energy from my soul from this convergence of the Loves is active throughout my spirit-being. I derive comfort knowing that my natural love, perfect. I have no more resolve to perfect myself or my natural love. This means that my agenda for receiving the Divine Love has changed. I receive the Love so that my spirit-attributes will continue to develop as this is what the Divine Love provides me now so that I am able to perceive more existence of the Father in a truly universal sense. I like learning and finding things out about the Father. Many of us do here. There are so many levels to the Creator's existence that for anyone who has ever been interested in finding anything out about anything or anyone, the Father is the ultimate search - only that we search from an individual position of already knowing the Father due to the Love we have received. Therefore, in my devotion toward learning more about the Creator, I am not trying to define the universal meaning of my own existence, for I already live in the Supreme Truth knowing that I am soul and Loved eternally.

Each sphere differs so much in its spirit-organic nature that progression through these spheres reveals the diversity of our Creator's Handiworks. There are individuals who have created spirit material infrastructure, but another truth that exists throughout all the spirit spheres, is that nothing can be mortally created that is disharmonious with the Father's Handiwork insofar as forming each spirit sphere. This is unlike the humanity of the Earth that can create such destructive forces that when imposed, cause such disharmony to the organic processes of planetary systems, elements and to oneself or another. No mortal in their natural soul condition or living with Divine Love can create any structure or form of creation that works in contradistinction with the ongoing flow of the spirit sphere. This is a truthful Spirit Law that exists. If any mortal spirit tries to engage in any active or voluntary creation of any destructive force that will cause spirit harm to oneself, another or to the fabric of spirit-organic life, the Spirit Law of Creation comes immediately into effect and any such wish or desire within the individual to create such disharmony, nullified. The individual is powerless to cause any such disharmony into effect in any of the spirit spheres.

This is a very important truth as it defines how mortals reside and prosper in the various spheres that comprise the Father's spirit world. When studying the spirit world it is easy to forget that the spirit world is

Everlasting

God's domain. The spirit world did not evolve over aeons of time and was most certainly not a construct formed from the energy caused by chaos or some random act and convergence of energies generated by a spirit universe. Studies of the sun and Earth and human cosmology reveals the convergence of energy forming the sum parts of the whole as a kind of energetic evolution that has organised its form into relationships with energy. This is a simplified expression, but I am illustrating that how the physical universe came into being does not represent how the spirit universe came into being. All of this exists in the Eye of God, but the spirit universe in all its existence was never formed out of chaos or a random act of super-heated cosmic energy. There is a particular form of energy that is not the Divine Love but that the Father has fashioned into all spirit creation so that such creations are active, living, responsive and can sustain life, but most importantly, mortal forms of life can interact with, experience and work with to form structures that enable works of beauty, harmony and love to thrive and prosper. In the spheres where humans reside in the poorest of their soul condition, these spheres sustain their lives, but due to the lack of living love in their soul condition, they are unable to work with any of the Spirit Laws or available spirit energy to create anything external to themselves. They are in effect, void. Another truth is, as your soul condition is, so will you be in the spirit world. It is a sobering thought when from a human perspective you begin to understand that the human afterlife, which is the spirit world that sustains all human life, is God's Spirit World.

As Saleeba illustrated to you, in her soul condition when she lived in the Perfect Natural Sphere, she was unable to identify with the true nature of her soul, and also, she could not identify with the fact and truth that she was residing in God's Spirit World. Even though the First Parents knew that God is supreme in all spirit affairs, Saleeba could only accept the word of the First Parents, for in her own soul she was without that condition derived by receiving Divine Love that could confirm to her this truth that she was always residing and living in God's Spirit World. Each sphere from the First Natural Sphere to the Celestial Heaven is an extraordinary form of Fatherly Creation. Another truth about the spirit world is revealed in the fact that when your soul condition improves in its natural love, then by including the Divine Love, you are in a better condition of soul to create your own handiworks so that you can participate with them or that others may participate with these creations. Everything created in the spheres is consistent with the integrity of that sphere. For example, the kind of music a Celestial musician can make differs than the kind of music a personality may create when living in the Second Natural Sphere. This example, a small example, will illustrate that the kind of creations that Celestial individuals create reflect the soul condition that is perfect in natural love and living with that soul-spirit internal life force that is derived when sufficient amounts of Divine Love is living within the individual. As I have revealed to you, there is nothing made or created by individuals in any of the spheres that will cause disharmony in that particular sphere to another individual or the sphere itself. Such things simply don't exist and this is where every human who enters the spirit world will experience a certain degree of harmony that differs from any lived human life experience. The only disharmony that resides in the spirit world exists in the soul condition of the personality who arrives here from their human life and has developed by the way they have lived their human life, such a condition of soul relative with the true existing harmonious Spirit Laws of Love that God has established that sustains all human life residing in the spirit world.

What we have learned from the teachings conveyed to us by Jesus and the teachings that we have shared amongst each other involving God with the mortal, is that God acts upon the soul firstly. Another truth that we live here, for we have enough lived perspective involving human evolutionary life, is that God caused our own truthful soul into existence before physical life. This means that God acts upon the soul and not solely upon the physical attribute of the body or the spirit-body of the spirit-human. The human may be in doubt of their own soul, but of our own soul, the Living and Loving Soulful Father is never in doubt nor has the Soulful Father ever doubted or overlooked the existence, condition and love of your own soul.

Living on the Earth, humans experience their physical attributes as the centre of their life and life itself. Having experienced this, I understand this reality perfectly. It is the same with humans living in their spirit-life in their spirit-body having no knowledge of their own soul. Saleeba, at the beginning of her spirit-life experienced this.

In the communications James Padgett received, the word Kingdom was used often such as 'the Kingdom of God'. But now in this advancing modern era of human social civilisation, an upgrade is necessary to open up the wonderful minds that men and women have and who desire to explore the forming of man and the human afterlife so that now the afterlife can be identified as God's Spirit World, where you will find no real kingdom in existence. What you will find is a human afterlife filled with ordinary spirit involvement that is extraordinary in its existence and that we are individually able to interact with other humans in these spirit environments. As more of our own potential realised, we can begin to fathom the full creation of these environments that God has formed for our souls to survive, prosper and to become the fulfilment of the soul one is, that was created to begin with, by the Soul of God. It's a perfect round trip!

There are many spirited conversations asking the question as to whether God has ever evolved. We have asked Jesus this question and he has said that in order for God to create a form of evolution, God would have had to experience a form of evolution in order to create and establish an evolution that living lifeforms, such as humankind (being independent souls) can experience. We have concluded that there is an aspect in God that has evolved in order for God to form external realities that include evolution as part of their independent form, but, we also recognise the consistency of God as being eternal, singular and at the centre of all living love. When Jesus is asked questions such as this, he always responds with an open manner so that we are able to perceptually glean the leading truth that assists us seeking more information about the nature of God. But, when we ask Jesus a question involving the Divine Love, his response is with His Fathers, Our Father's, Spirit of Truth, and is spoken with love for one and all human souls. An example being, the Divine Love provides the mortal soul with its true Immortality. Much has been said to you about this Immortality so I have no need to expand on this here and now.

This has been another wonderful time.

Respectfully, Daniel

11

I am here; it is I, Daniel. It is 7:46 p.m. on the 11th of June 2019. It is a Tuesday for you, and a cool wintery evening. I wanted to begin my speaking with you with this information, to demonstrate to you that I know the social human time that you are living in. I can see that it is night and I can see the illumination in your living room where you receive these communications for you have the light on. There are quite a number of individual spirits present, many of these individuals would like nothing more than to share a word with you. I have been instructed by Saleeba to continue on with my discourse.

As I stand close to you and perceptually convey my narrative to you that you hear with your spirit-sense, what you are receiving you are hearing with clarity. You are both experienced at this now. As I said, there are many individuals present and the reader may have previously read, as it was with James Padgett or in those recent years when you were both receiving, that there are other individuals present at the time of such conversing. I wish to add here that as this communication transpires, there isn't a sudden rush or influx of individuals that then causes a jostle for position to be close to this convergence of communication. The Celestial teachers are present, such as Saleeba who is our guide in this convergence. They provide a boundary so that this form of communication isn't interrupted purely by another spirit's eagerness to communicate.

It is different as I stand close to you, for I am not technically in the First Natural Sphere. I am, but I am not. The First Natural Sphere doesn't interface with your biosphere or human spirit-bodies. There is a good reason for this. In God's design of the First Natural Sphere, God installed if you like, a barrier so that human-spirits can no longer move freely about among the human biosphere of social living. As I stand beside you I feel very comfortable and there are individuals present and we can stay here awhile, but we know that we cannot live here or remain permanently in this barrier of energy. Individuals like Saleeba, Luke and Jesus, can move about in this barrier quite freely, as if it is not present, and can remain in this barrier of energy for as long as they know is harmoniously necessary. Humans recently arrived to begin their spirit-life can only be in this barrier to visit a loved one a very short length of time, as they will not have the soul condition or the spirit-acumen to understand where they are and how this energy works that exists between the human spirit-body and the First Natural Sphere. It requires a depth of soul condition and spirit-awareness to actively participate in this barrier of energy for any substantial length of time. When people transition into the spirit world, no personality is ever resurrected to begin their spirit-life in this barrier of energy. I am able to move freely in this energy, and I have been told by Saleeba that if she desired to move an object on your table, she could so long as it was a harmonious and loving action. I am also aware that a relative of yours and a loved one could lay their spirit-hand upon your shoulder and you would feel their presence. You have experienced this in your interactions with relatives and loved ones. Even as I am here, and I am not a relative of yours - though we share a common acceptance in our love of the Divine - you can feel my energy upon your spirit-body. I have seen how Zara can feel the presence of Saleeba when she is present and or communicates with you. Being in Celestial soul condition does not mean that we are rigid in our experience of feeling. It is quite the opposite. In my own experience of becoming perfect and having observed other individuals progressing in their experience of adjusting their spirit-life living with Divine Love, part of our experience is to integrate how much love we do feel as real, living feeling.

 A spirit can receive the Father's Love in the barrier of energy that exists as a field of energy that is transparent to the matured Celestial eye. It has been said to you, as it was to James Padgett, that spirits here have enjoyed receiving the Divine Love as you have received Divine Love, which reveals another truth. Wherever a mortal personality resides, the Father's Divine Love can be obtained as readily as anywhere else in God's Spirit World and Universe. I have been told and taught by the high Celestials that there are other created worlds that exist in their spirit universe, and that these citizens are with soul just as we are, and that the same Divine Love is available for those citizens, that in their physical and spirit-form, the same causal function of the Divine Love acts in the same way that we experience the same non-evolving energy that the Father has provided. So, we in our respective and various forms can all recognise the universality of God and God's Eternal Love. I haven't met another from another world yet.

 Saleeba has shared with me her experience of progressing from the First Natural Sphere through the other spheres to the Celestial Heaven with the First Parents. She explained that when the First Parents were able to receive the Divine Love again, as they progressed with Saleeba and Jesus and many other spirits, their soul condition visibly returned back to that kind of cosmic power that the Father had originally bestowed in their personality, soul and spirit-body as being the two individuals formed in the image of the Perfect Natural Man and the Perfect Natural Woman, but with the addition of all the spirit-personalty that was unique in their forming. The First Parents did not experience the forming of their personality through normal planetary evolution, incarnation and life-lived human experiences. Saleeba said that not only was her own involvement with receiving Divine Love a miracle to her own being, but participating in her progression alongside Jesus and with the First Parents was truly a human wonderment, and that by the time they reached the Celestial Heaven, she could see why Jesus and the First Parents were different in their being than any other human or human-spirit. Having met the First Parents, I came to understand this difference and celebrated it for their life forms part of the story of humanity, but most importantly, the story of the humanity of souls that originated from The Father.

As I have learnt in my relatively short time living my spirit-life experience with Divine Love, when Jesus or Saleeba speak a truth involving the soul-life, it comes with a matter-of-factness about it and always enveloped in love. There are individuals here and among the social fabric of earthly life being introduced to the availability of God's Divine Love and related truths for their first time. As I have experienced here, there are many individuals experiencing this way of soul-life in Divine Love as an introduction being taught by those who have lived with this a very long time… a time that began with the life of the First Parents. You must not be afraid of the Truths. The Truths relating with how the Father has formed the human soul and the spirit-body, the personality of the individual, how through God's Handiworks the soul individualises, and then when that time comes, takes up its place in God's Spirit World. There is nothing to be afraid of for the Father's Truths are soul comfort. As I have experienced, these vast and many truths existed a long time before my life originated. I have found it comforting knowing that these truths involving the soul-life have been with existence before any generation of human or any age that humans have lived in. This means that living with Divine Love is unique to each and every soul, and is not compromised by any sense of humanity in its experience and system of belief. The Divine Love represents an original beginning to a human life that has already become somewhat established, and this momentum causes us to realise that we are becoming involved with a long-standing form of energy that has never aged or been affected by any humanity meddling and certainly not by any spirit here in any of the spheres. The point I am trying to illustrate here is for you to recognise that the feel of Truth is comforting, sustainable, nurturing and true, and that it is not to fear; for receiving Divine Love comes directly from the Soul of the Father. There is nothing to fear in the Love of God.

Everlasting

Another truth that has defined my involvement living with Divine Love, I never felt that by receiving Divine Love, that the Father then pushed me to continue my soul-development. Having entered my spirit-life upon the completion of my physical life, I awakened in the First Natural Sphere and was greeted by relatives and eventually Mr Padgett himself. Having known about the teachings James had received, my introduction to my spirit-life was one of pure eagerness. I knew that the Divine Love existed and I had read the messages James had received. I wanted to progress, learning as much as I could with the aim of my becoming a Celestial teacher. I realised that nothing could stop me from achieving this. This was my single purpose now that I knew that I was going to be living here permanently and that my physical life, completed. I had my memories and my relationships, but I was a man invested insofar as learning about God and the greater spirit-life. I adapted very quickly, for in my physical life I had already accepted that the spirit world existed and that I could become a Celestial spirit. Once I understood the geography of the mortal spirit world and how my personality functioned in my spirit-body, which didn't take me long, I was into my involvement with the Father's Love all the time. There were Celestial teachers present in the First Divine Love Sphere and I was open to being taught. I had a thirst for knowledge, for in physical life we can be somewhat starved of spiritual truth. As you are both aware, I invested some of my time during my physical life believing I was receiving Celestial communications. In my previous communications with you, I have outlined this experience. In the First Divine Love Sphere, I felt the immediate causal effect when receiving Divine Love and being with the Father in my prayer. The good thing was that I required no convincing as to define and confirm whether the Divine Love existed or if such an Immortal life was set for me. I knew about Divine Love and having met and personally been introduced to the Celestial teachers, I required no convincing of my future destiny in the spirit world. In the 7th sphere, the one that precedes the Celestial Heaven, I was very settled in my permanent spirit-life. I was happy and receiving Divine Love abundantly, but never did I feel that the Father was placing a condition on my advancement. I was aware that I could remain in any preceding sphere as long as I liked, even as I continued receiving the Love, and this truth about the action when living with Divine Love is very important to know. A spirit's life experience when living with Divine Love is a life of love and never to be controlled by the

Giver of this Divine Love. It would be a contradiction in terms if by receiving the Divine Love as I am an independent voluntary personality, that then the Father seeks to control my independence, and the Divine Love becomes the means to do this. I have always felt independent in my experience living with God. The Celestial teachers and other Celestial spirits that I have interacted with are absolute examples of independent and voluntary living, even when some of these teachers have been living with the Divine Love present in their souls since the time Jesus arrived in the spirit world and began teaching the way to live the soul-life with the Loving Soul, God.

There is no doubt that my interest in the spirit-life when I lived as a man on Earth assisted me when I entered my spirit-life. I have seen this with individuals here. Those who have some degree of understanding adapt more readily than those who have no idea what awaits them when their physical life concludes. A true desire of mine in my spirit-life, once I had adapted, was for me to have more of my soul made visible to me. I realised that in each spirit sphere, there is an incredible array of spirit organic material, but my soul and its condition became the central focus of my spirit-life. My spirit-body was an extraordinary creation! I say this for in my spirit-life I was able to see it, having never had such clear visibility of its form when living in my physical life. Even though I had realised that my spirit body was an extraordinary creation, it still wasn't sufficient for me to make any real progress to reside in the Celestial Heaven. I had to involve my soul and to do this, I had to involve the gradual perfection of my natural love with the assistance of including the Father in my life. Today, I reside in the Celestial Heaven and I am with a clear perspective of how my spirit-experience has evolved by including the non-evolving energy and love that the Divine Love is. What the Father had formed as my individual potential for my soul, I had fulfilled with the assistance of Celestial teachers, my own voluntary participation, and with the Father being at the centre of my experience.

I will stop now as this has been quite a detailed experience.

Respectfully, Daniel

12.

I am with you both to continue sharing my spirit-life experience. Each individual that I have met and conversed with here in our spirit-life experience, shares or expresses their own experience of living life in this remarkable place. Those who are living with the awareness of God as Soul, and living with the inclusion of Divine Love, have their own interesting relationship with this extraordinary Love. We know that the Divine Love is consistently the same Love that we all participate with. In my early spirit-days, the Divine Love I was receiving was the same Divine Love that Saleeba had received those thousands of years ago. Time almost appears irrelevant to the existing non-evolving energy that God's Divine Love is. It was the same Love that Aman and Amon received at the beginning of their earthly universal life, and the same Divine Love that Jesus received in his earthly and spirit-life. The Divine Love I receive has always been consistent, unchanged and non-evolving. Individually, it means many things to our individuality. As I became more proficient in my living with this Love, I became aware that it was not exclusive to me, that I was participating in a spirit-life experience involving this form of energy that so many other souls also included in their lives. For you, individually being introduced to this Divine Love and experiencing it your first time, it may feel like an exclusive experience. But the Divine Love is inclusive and this is part of the teaching that Jesus has revealed about this Love and how inclusive humanity can be with this Love, and ultimately, in our acceptance of its source and origin. As I progressed, part of my soul condition caused me to recognise how inclusive being with the Father is, and that it is only the mortal personality itself that chooses to exclude oneself from the most extraordinary way of life that is available for one to live their complete life.

As other individuals have revealed to you, here we have that clarity of experience and vision so that living with Divine Love has real visible evidence, especially with those who have lived with this Love a long time. There was a time when in my physical life, I had been introduced to the vast array of teachings involving the soul - the mortal soul-life, but my visibility, so far as being able to grasp the meaning of what this Divine Love brings to the soul, I completely underestimated. What was lived has come to pass, and I have accepted this long ago. For me, being interested in God and spirit and how I related to these extensive realities was my innocence as I began my life here. I knew my life, my spirit-life permanent, for I understood before I arrived in the spirit world that reincarnation was never going to occur and that once I resided in the spirit world, there was never any going back to physical life. Receiving Divine Love and seeing how my spirit-body matured and understanding that the Divine Love brings the true Immortality to my soul, my human spirit-vision in my spirit-life was all about going forward, full steam ahead! I have met other individuals here who have pursued the development of their soul with as much vigour as I did. Not everyone is like this. Some individuals stay in the First or Second Divine Love Sphere for a long time and feel no real urgency to make for the Celestial Heaven. They know it is there and being with the Love, they know they won't miss out. Being highly social, these individuals like being in their more human-spirit condition, than purely Celestial condition. This means the more human-spirit in the initial Divine Love Spheres enjoys their gentle experience feeling the Love in their soul, but they also feel a relatively strong connection with their physical memories and relationships that were established in their physical life. Some may have a little compensation to resolve. The Celestial teachers never infer to these individuals that it is time to move on - that they have been residing in a sphere for too long, or that they must make their prayers more fervent for the inflowing of Divine Love. The general ambience of these initial spheres is where individuals gain traction into their soul-life with the Father, a relaxed atmosphere with an ambient harmony and a general sense of experienced wonder and well-being. It is so dynamic when you factor in the circumstances relating to the diversity of people entering their spirit-life. In the First Divine Love Sphere when I was there, I was introduced to a man who had lived well into his nineties. He had lived a good life. He had only been residing in the spirit world for 12 months, yet he had 90 years of experience behind him. Many relatives of his had assisted his adaption and he was a lovely man. He met Celestial teachers and had a natural love of God, so for this man who had been a good man, accepting Divine Love was an acceptance that he received comfortably. But as the spirit-body begins to adapt to the changes in the early spirit-life, while having been part of a physical life, this man had decided to stay in the First and then the Second Sphere until his spirit-body had sufficiently changed (as it does) for he found that remarkable experience of becoming younger again a miracle! He had a lot to adapt to for not only was he becoming younger in his appearance due to that ability that the spirit-body has to change in its image here, but this man also enjoyed the time experiencing this as he settled into his new Immortal life. The spirit-body is not an immutable force or image set that can never change. It is mutable and changes, but as has been taught to you, it cannot change ahead of its true soul condition.

Everlasting

As I said, the diversity of beginnings in the First Divine Love Sphere involves every human permutation. Obviously, I cannot list them all for such is the vastness of the human population now. Well, you can imagine just how it is going to be in all the future years of man; life in the First Natural Sphere and life in the First Divine Love Sphere. We are aware of this, of course, so there is a vast teaching capacity going on as millions upon millions, hundreds of millions, billions in the many years to come will take up their residency in their soul condition and thus spirit-life experience begins. The magnitude of vision is incredible here. I don't know if there is one single word or phrase that any spirit could convey to you how life is here in its magnitude of population and the future that is to come. Just as your world is advancing with worldwide information, the spirit world is more than able to receive each individual soul. The industry here established by Jesus and the countless number of those in service to the natural humanity will oversee that every soul is to its place in the harmony of the spirit world and love is at the seat of everything. I know that you have received word from a few spirits who, like me, want to know everything! It is a wonder when you look toward your own inner soulful nature and you realise how much you desire to know and to our relief, there is so much to know due to the incredible constitution of the spirit-body and how our individual personality continues to manifest through the spirit-body so that we can each interact with and grasp such living knowledge about God and the spirit-life one resides in. It is a liberating experience to say the least. It is bizarre to think that once individuals in their physical life were persecuted for their knowledge of their love of man and God. Over here it is entirely the opposite. I don't know if the humanity on Earth will ever be able to evolve beyond or past its old belief systems. To move beyond a belief you really need a truth that is enduring and sustaining, and you need to be about living love. The available Divine Love and knowledge of this availability have little traction in the physical life of humans, therefore, there isn't at present a general worldwide discussion about this Love and what it means for the human soul or the Living Truths that relate with it. People can't form an opinion about something when they don't know that that something exists! Some of you know and have realised the kind of vision that this Love presents, and that this Divine Love brings change to your soul and the way you perceive yourself to be the person you are living with the humanity you are living with. What I do know is that by evidence alone, the fact that so many are living their soul-life here, this spirit-life experience, this Immortal way of spirit-life is gaining traction all the time as there are so many wanting to experience this Love and to move on at a speed that suits the individual as established by seeing loved ones and relatives and so many brighter individuals living a real wonder in such an ordinary spirit-life that is extraordinary because anyone can choose to be involved. No one has to miss out.

When you spend time contemplating how life, spirit-life, might be here in this spirit world, you will be introduced to a vast place that you are currently not living in. From my perspective, having lived a physical life and now living in this spirit world in my spirit-life, I have that vision that is big, small, liberated and detailed. I like the minute detail and I like grand vision. This forms part of my personality and clearly demonstrated when I reside in my home in the First Celestial Sphere. I am aware of the current history of the Earth and the present history of the natural spirit world, and that there are spheres beyond the Celestial Heaven and that humans reside and are living in all these places at one time. The time I am living here in the Celestial Heaven is within the same framework of time that you are in and that the rest of the spirit world is in. Due to my soul condition being what it is in my perfect attributes, my ability to experience time appears faster than the amount of experience and information I once received in the First Divine Love Sphere or when I was a man living on Earth. In the Celestial Heaven, I am not projected into living in an advanced future from the time-related experience of living in the spheres that exceed the sphere I reside in. In the First Divine Love Sphere when I began in earnest my soul-ship with the Father, I was more human than spirit. Having recently crossed over and begun the adaptive process of integrating my life hereafter transition, my memories were still very much from my physical human life. This didn't complicate things as I was looking toward this new life with all the new information being processed in my spirit-mind. Part of my progressive experience through the spheres to the Celestial Heaven involved the development of my spirit-mind so that I could perceive spirit realities with more clarity and visibility, as my experience becoming more solid in image and form. My physical human memories were reconfigured as the condition of my soul progressed and my emotion and feeling and sense about myself adjusted with the new input involving new relationships with other spirits, with my spirit-body, friends and family and especially with God. The truthful relationship that I was feeling was my own love essence being honed by the causal effect of Divine Love. I found that my capacity to experience love within myself as living, increased. My physical body had contained me well and had served its purpose. Now, my spirit-body had taken over and its ability to adapt and to change as my soul condition changed exceeded any conscious presumptions about what I could or couldn't achieve. This was a whole new life and I was living it to the maximum. As I entered the Celestial Heaven I recognised that there had been a significant change that had taken place within my being, that I had hardly noticed until this time. From the First Divine Love Sphere, I was in essence, a human-spirit; as I entered the Celestial Heaven I was a spirit-human. I was able to participate with so much identity of spirit-reality that I related with myself as being spirit-human along with the humanity that resides in the Celestial Heaven respecting and revering our humanness.

When the beautiful Saleeba is close by or another Celestial teacher who has lived such vast amounts of time here, and they love and know the Father so well, I think at times how small I am by comparison to their superior attributes and how much they have loved me. They are so sensitive to our beginnings. They know what is going to happen when a soul begins receiving Divine Love its first time, and they know the finite limit in all the causes and effects transpired in the dynamic of natural love. They have seen humanity crossing into the spirit-life for thousands of years. The love that they demonstrate in their living with the Father is an example to those of us who are at our beginning and for an individual like myself, I derived confidence when being with these individuals as I embraced and settled to my new way of life. Personally, I am really happy with my choice to involve myself in the receipt of Divine Love; no-one forced me and I have only ever felt encouragement here in my spirit-life. I was able to ascertain that the only dynamic for change in the spirit world revolved around receiving this Divine Love. I, as I have stated, knew about the Divine Love and some of the truths when I lived as a man in the flesh. I knew that these truths that I had never heard taught before from any other source, that such change was involved, but it can be difficult to understand the nature of that change when so closed in by the fabric of social physical life. I am able to live my life here the way that I really know my soul to desire. I am free and loved.

I will stop now,
Respectfully your friend, Daniel

13

I am here; it is your Celestial friend, Daniel. I am ready to speak. I would like to speak about soul condition. Throughout the messages James Padgett received, soul condition is a truth that is introduced and then expanded upon by the various Celestial teachers who communicated spirit-life experiences, teachings about the soul, the spirit-body, various Spirit Laws and of course, the natural and the Divine Love as being formed by the Soul, God. It was said, and by this I mean conveyed, that James was required to be in the right condition of soul to receive such information relating with the soul-life and the expansive teachings involving the Father's Divine Love.

At the beginning of this spirit book I listened as Saleeba conveyed some of her experience to you and what is so fascinating is that when solely in her perfect natural love in the Perfect Natural Sphere, having lived in this sphere for a great length of time, she was without any real awareness of her soul which means that as far as understanding her own soul condition as being perfect in its natural condition, Saleeba had no understanding about this truth with her own involvement in her spirit-life. The fact that she could convey a teaching to James Padgett, and that she has been able to convey experiences and teachings to you both over the years you have received spirit communications, reveals the dynamic that Saleeba became aware of what 'soul and soul condition' means. Since my arrival here in the spirit world I have studied as much as I can about living life here. Having shared in the exchanges with other individuals who I will identify as being of ancient life, these individuals have all shared similar experiences with me. Most noticeably, that until the availability of God's Divine Love becoming available again for the individual to receive, life in the natural spirit world was without any cognitive perception about what is the nature of the human soul relating to soul condition. Soul condition was a teaching untaught, immeasurable, as there wasn't anything in the natural spirit world that could quantify or substantiate what the real soul nature of the human was. This is why the information contained in the messages and teachings James received was so different from anything else that had been received from the spirit world. Saleeba was such an ancient spirit but the dynamic of change that resulted in Saleeba understanding the nature of her soul, and thus becoming the teacher she is, was brought about by the influence of the Divine Love bringing such active causal change into her soul so that her condition changed and Saleeba - like so many ancient spirits - finally had that identifiable and tangible reference to gain such reflective perception about soul and soul condition.

As you know, the teaching about being in the right condition to receive Celestial communication is all through the messages James received. You can't help but read this when introduced to this vast presentation. James was guided by Jesus and other Celestial teachers to pray more to the Father so that he would receive more Divine Love so that he would be in a better condition to receive truths that you have all become fascinated with. Since Padgett, quite a number of you have tried to receive but to the extent of truths being revealed, few and far between. There have been messages of love and encouragement, and messages of confirmation, which have provided social assistance for those of you believing in the truths and endeavouring to draw closer to the Soul of God by receiving Divine Love. It has only been recently that advancement of truth has been received as the individuals receiving these teachings understand about the Divine Love and how this Love relates with the soul. I tried to receive spirit teachings, but in my physical life I failed to understand that the convergence between the soul with God by the means of learning how change happens in the soul. This of the utmost importance to improve the condition of ones soul so that any real teaching can be expanded upon by the Celestial teachers with some degree of relatedness to the mortal who is living on Earth while not seeing the reality of what is being taught and lived in the spirit world. I wish to add here that receiving teachings about the soul living with Divine Love in a human experience is not a commonplace truth. If it were so, every human experiencing Divine Love would be able to receive just like James, furthering teachings that advance the human condition of living with the Father as revealed by Celestial teachers in the exchange of spirit communication. This simply hasn't happened. It did not happen with me and it hasn't happened with others.

In the spirit-life, there are millions of humans involved in their experience of receiving Divine Love. In the First Divine Love Sphere I was fortunate enough to know about soul condition as I had read Padgett in my physical life. I had involved myself with what I thought at that time, was the continuation of receiving truths where Padgett had left off. But how wrong was I. Soul condition in the First Divine Love Sphere was a goal of mine, but not to receive spirit teachings, rather to understand the teachings that I was learning. There were many progressing with me who had little interest in learning about their condition. A vast majority of humanity proceeding toward the Celestial Heaven were doing so socially. It is not an Immutable Truth set in Spirit Law that decrees that every individual upon receiving Divine Love in the spirit world is to comply with a rigorous education about what soul condition is. Receiving Divine Love is an effortless experience. The way this Love is infused into the soul, the Father has made every provision necessary, and by this I mean, of an economy of experience to assist the soul to fulfil its perfect natural love and become transformed in this Divine Love and to progress into a beautiful spirit-life.

The word condition here in the spirit-life involving Divine Love, means that the individual can socially enjoy their spirit-life experience as they gently adapt to an improvement of their spirit-attributes so that they are no longer subject to any unnecessary compensation and are free to socially engage enjoying the sphere they reside in, the spheres they progress through with other individuals, and the particular environments that comprise each sphere. The Father and the Celestial teachers do not desire any human to suffer and believe that the condition of their soul, due to any compensation, is permanent. Everything about living your spirit-life is about becoming independent, loving and above all, happy and engaging with other individuals in this happiness. It sounds simple when you think for a minute how extraordinary the whole spirit world and spirit universe is in its forming, but happiness is a truth.

The truth about soul condition insofar as living with Divine Love, is that each individual as they experience Divine Love will be in their truthful condition of soul that is perfect for the requirements of their soul-life. For instance, Jesus as he receives the Father's Love has become to the right condition that is perfect for his natural love and spirit-attributes. No other receiving the Divine Love will ever mirror the same soul-image that Jesus is. Saleeba is in the right condition for Saleeba and no one else. In my experience, I am in the right condition, which is to pursue as much knowledge as I can about my own experience living with the Father and absorbing as much as I can about the dynamic of living with Divine Love and how I relate with everything external to me that is spirit world and spirit universe. For many other individuals proceeding from the First Divine Love Sphere, their true condition is social. These individuals love the social exchanges that happen in such extraordinary circumstances that each sphere presents, and personally realising that God the Soul, is living. Padgett was required to be in the right condition to receive spirit communication about Divine Love teachings but he was gifted, as he could receive communication from natural spirits even if he had never received Divine Love. As men and women continue to receive Divine Love and explore their experience, each will have an economy of experience to their own condition, which will be perfect for their natural love and social circumstances of the day. There are going to be many men and women who receive Divine Love, but may take or share very little interest insofar as understanding or desiring to understand anything that involves the causal dynamic of this Love and how it brings about change in the soul. One may receive a more improved condition of their faith or social confidence, or as Constance revealed, hope, or simply the loving involvement being able to have this Love in ones life. A small knowing that a close companion can always be called upon for comfort, which is from God, or in the loving spirit communications that have been published. Here in the Celestial Heaven, we would like nothing more than there to be a real sense of social companionship among the people worldwide who are aware of this true Divine Love, but we understand the physical differences and social ramifications that bring such diversity to this worldwide experience. I for one, understand how socially it is being aware of this engrossing subject as I tried to establish the grounds for the *human* "final and comprehensive religion" when I received spirit communications. My agenda only served my own ego and as I have seen here, there wasn't a Celestial teacher communicating that those years ago. The fact that people *are* experiencing Divine Love worldwide is a tremendous vision for me to see here from my spirit vantage point. It warms my spirit-heart no end that at least the Love is being experienced and the sight of God as being Soul is gaining more visibility among the people of the Earth.

    The Divine Love is the causal dynamic that brings about change in the spirit world, and if one chooses to identify their soul and its true condition, they can as I have experienced by my soul changing and my spirit-attributes becoming in a more improved condition, understand such causal dynamics. It makes me shudder to think that a beautiful soul like Saleeba, lived in the spirit world for such a long time without being able to move forward from her perfected position and not knowing what that position was. Imagine living your spirit-life for thousands upon thousands of years and never being able to move beyond a particular environment. Thank goodness the Divine Love resumed and became part of the social human evolution of the populations in the natural spirit-life.

When I am standing in the Celestial Heaven, I am still adapting to the amazement that so much spirit universe is there for me to explore. I can recall being in my physical life having the same thought about history and the rest of the world that could be explored. There are those who stand on the Earth and wonder about the seas or the mountain peaks, or how the dynamic of the physical universe is comprised. Here in my spirit-life, I am a spirit-human who is living in the right condition to perceive so much spirit world and universe that is present. I am aware in my Celestial home, of the mortal spirit world that I have explored, the spheres I have progressed through and the Celestial Spheres that are present to me. I am aware of the spheres beyond the Celestial Heaven and the earthly world I once inhabited and the physical universe, I live with this awareness all the time. My spirit-mind is able to comprehend this expansive vision, but it's not just vision. I have lived in many places now involving the Earth and the mortal spirit world and here I am, in the Celestial Heaven knowing that there is a vast spirit universe waiting for my participation. It is no wonder that there are wonderful individuals living their spirit-life that have realised their full human potential and that their personality is able to interact with evolutionary and non-evolutionary existing forms of energy. All the while, the Eternal Father present, and this Individual by Its loving fact of existence, is the most extraordinary Living Soul to relate with!

My blessings to you both,
Respectfully, Daniel

14

I am here; it is I, Daniel. Like James Padgett explained to you about his involvement receiving communication from the spirit world, I am with my memories that involved my experience believing I was receiving communication from the spirit world. You have both received communications from those of us living in the spirit world who participated with our endeavour to receive spirit communication. You have received word from Eugene Morgan, he has been a contributor throughout the time you have both received. You have also received from the lovely Kathryn, James Reid and of course Jocelyn, who had a long involvement with Padgett's messages. Where I stand, I am clear in my vision, being a spirit and understanding what I would like to contribute in our exchanges, and how this communication transpires from me to you when we are both in different environments. I say both of you, as you are together when we have conveyed what we have desired to impart from our respective spirit-life experiences. There have been a vast number of individuals who have conveyed to you both some of their spirit-life experience drawing from a vast range of spirit-life diversity. As I shared with you in my recent message, condition is an individual response to us individually experiencing the same Divine Love that brings about the same condition in each of our respective souls. On one hand, by receiving Divine Love and with this Love being consistent, we are each in effect participating with the same causal outcome that our individual soul responds with, when the Father's causal energy acts within our soul. It must be reconfirmed here that in order for the soul to experience any sufficient degree of change by the influence of Divine Love, a fair degree or amount of Divine Love must be received over a sustained period of time. As men and women may have experienced, if you experience the Divine Love for a short time, just once, and expect everything to happen all-at-once, then you will be sadly disappointed. The soul takes time to integrate the causal change that Divine Love brings. You can never exceed the speed of your own compensation and how this is resolved; if there exists any compensation to be rectified. From the First Divine Love Sphere to my life in the Celestial Heaven, I couldn't get there fast enough! But, I had to be patient as my soul adapted to the influence of this Love and the small amount of compensation rectified. Which in my case, was really just bringing my memories into a harmonious alignment with myself and, a little forgiveness to do with past relationships. But, I was really innocent with some compensation that I had not expected to be there. When I had adapted to my spirit-life in the First Divine Love Sphere, I realised that I had introduced what I perceived to be a truth, which in fact was an error. This error was my effort to define the truths about the way to live in an organised religion based on my desire to define that 'Final and Comprehensive Religion' for people to live in, in their involvement with the Divine Love. I honestly thought that I was doing the right thing by defining this, as no such formal religion existed for people receiving the Divine Love to live in. I assumed this was necessary, and I also assumed that I was receiving Celestial spirit communication crafting this religion. In my experience living in my spirit-life, living wholeheartedly with Divine Love, with many other individuals living with Divine Love, I am here to say that from the First Divine Love Sphere onwards no one is living in any religion. There doesn't exist a Spirit Religion. The Divine Love is readily available; has its own structure that we abide in and our natural love is expressed through our spirit-attributes and personality, so in effect, no matter how bright we are, we are living love and that is the great revelation of the spirit world. From my observation, it would seem hopeless to organise an organised religion involving men and women, being aware of this Love in their physical life. How can you religionise a perfect and eternal form of Godly energy! Having said this, a truth about this Divine Love is that being of Godly energy, never in all spirit eternity will a mortal soul ever become God. Living with Divine Love doesn't transform us into gods.

Ironically, the most organised form of energy known to exist for the soul of the individual, which is the Divine Love, in physical life will be the most socially diverse and disorganised social experience, which is due to the fact that people are diverse in their individuality and social interests, and that to partake of this Love, only requires the individual's voluntary participation and a little personal faith. The human world is only going to become more diversified and socially interrelated as the worldwide exposure of global awareness continues to evolve, bringing humankind toward a greater expression of personality and social culture. Nothing will stop humankind from being interested in its own physical dynamic and this, with the advent of the internet is cross-fertilising ideas and beliefs across the seas. Humans are able to pursue their interests with more exposure and transparency than ever before. Living with Divine Love in a physical life is a mobile and mutable experience for such is the independent freedom to participate with this Love once one is aware that such a universal and abundant form of energy, present for the soul. The full expression of this is seen that by being aware of the Divine Love at such a universal reality that involves the individual of the Earth and the individual in the spirit world, that the Divine Love represents to both man and spirit, to humankind and spirit-kind, a whole new revealing and revelation to the identity of God, and such a revelation is an advancement insofar as humans realising who and what God is, and, whether or not a human afterlife exists. The Truth that the Divine Love brings is personal experience and this experience translates into the fact that God exists, is real and living and that by receiving Divine Love in a physical life, this life continues as the true soul-life in the human afterlife, which is where I am standing to communicate at this time, living with Divine Love.

Those of us who have studied the truths involving how to participate with the Divine Love, we are aware that for however abundant this Divine Love is, we can never force or impose our personality toward another to make another participate in their receipt of this Love. What this reveals is the difference between living earthly beliefs with the actual realised experience of receiving a living form of energy into your soul. Here in the spirit-life, I have seen so many living their soul life from any beliefs that may have restricted any human potential from realising its full individuality. It is a fact that the humanity of the Earth has never lived with a world awareness that such energy existing for the soul is universally present, and the same form of energy that is the dynamic of change in the human afterlife. To participate freely in this Love does bring individuality to the surface, and if you look at the humanity of yesteryears, the one thing about people, people have feared the most is the individual. And yet, the individual is what people have tried to become! And, when the individual shines brightest in a good way, it is what humanity adore the most and recognise as goodness. Individual is what each soul is and this is a truth that is seen all the time in the spirit world with the humanity that is living with Divine Love as this Love completely realises the potential of the individual's natural love. The thing that I really like about the Divine Love is that a person in their physical life can begin receiving Divine Love and will be able to continue this on in their spirit-life. The individuals I mentioned at the beginning of my discourse were all aware of the existence of Divine Love at a time in their physical life, then since becoming resident to their spirit-life, have continued on and flourished in their soul-life realising the fullness that this Love brings to the soul and a perspective never really realised on Earth but that you can realise now as the real gift that this Love brings.

I will finish now. This has been another wonderful exchange, thank you.

Respectfully, Daniel

15

I am here; it is I, Daniel. As you both know, there has been quite some history involving the communications James Padgett received. From the time James commenced his receipt of the Celestial communications to the present day, various individuals including myself, having come into contact with these messages and have then become involved with this material in a substantial way. The history of this material has a greater profile in the world today. The evolution of James Padgett's messages continues as you both recently received communication from James himself conveying experience involving that time from the perspective of his spirit-life experience today. There is a vast array of information contained in the messages James received a hundred years ago. The reality about the natural love existing in the mortal soul and how this love acts toward its perfection, and then how the addition of the Divine Love relates to this natural love have been expansive themes.

In my spirit-life experience, I obviously have met and conversed with the individuals who were once involved with Padgett's work and who are now residing here living their soul-life. They are friends of mine as I knew some of these individuals when I lived my physical life. I observed that throughout the time you have both been receiving our spirit communications, part of the history involving the Padgett messages has formed part of our collective communications. This keeps the continuity of what has come to pass on Earth with what is living here but in the context of certain individuals having their interest and relationship with the spirit communications that James received and now collectively known as the Padgett Messages. The input about the Divine Love has become substantial now that there is a vast array of spirit-life experiences conveyed involving spirits living their spirit-life involved with this Love. I know that what I have just said in this message may sound repetitive relating with similar messages conveyed to you both in the past, but I have to include the past and the present as the profile of the Padgett Messages continues to widen around the world.

The teaching structure relating to natural love with Divine Love is the most fascinating subject of all. Why? Because it relates to the soul - the human mortal soul - with God's Soul. We have heard from Saleeba how her natural love perfected without any assistance from receiving Divine Love when she lived in the Perfect Natural Sphere. As I have explained to you, I am living in a time when Divine Love is available for my soul to receive, which has meant that my own experience of having my soul's natural love perfected happened as a consequence of my receiving Divine Love as I progressed through the spirit spheres. Unlike Saleeba, I never experienced living a long time in my spirit-life having my natural love perfected without the Divine Love being involved. I have conversed with Saleeba and other ancient spirits about the quality of their natural love being perfect when they commenced their receipt of the non-evolving perfect Divine Love in their spirit-life. This is an interesting point. So many of you will be introduced to the availability of Divine Love, that it exists for your soul, and that it will perfect your natural love as you make every effort to receive this Divine Love, and to understand any compensation you might have acquired during the course of your natural life experience. This means that your entry point insofar as beginning to receive the Divine Love is realised by yourself as beginning to receive Divine Love from a position of being less than perfect. This is the same for so many spirits who begin receiving Divine Love when they have been residing in the First Natural Sphere or in any other sphere other than the Perfect Natural Sphere. It was evident to me as Saleeba shared her experiences with me, that any compensation that she might have had became nullified as her soul condition improved during the course of her natural spirit-life, and that the essence in her soul - being natural love - became pure. She told me she never spent any time actively involved or pursuing the goal to perfect her natural love. Like so many ancient spirits, they simply found that over time their human relationships became resolved and that they were able to move freely through the spheres that comprised what they understood as being their mortal spirit environments. The fact that Saleeba didn't know that her soul had in fact become 'perfect,' does reveal to us the quandary that involves the individual ascertaining if in fact the condition of their soul is perfect in its natural love. This equates to being able to discern when the condition of your soul is perfect in natural love when you have been receiving Divine Love for any length of time on Earth. Saleeba said to me that by receiving Divine Love when her soul, perfect, her natural love could not be made any more perfect. By living with Divine Love, this energy living and active in her soul resulted in her spirit attributes being extended which in time gave her the capacity to perceptually perceive with cognitive accuracy the teachings that Jesus was conveying about living in love in the soul-life that happens when participating with the Divine Love of the Father. In essence, what I understood was that Saleeba and other ancient spirits couldn't perfect their perfect natural love any more than it was, but that they could progress in their understanding about their own active involvement with their own soul-life and the many workings that this involves as one draws closer toward the Father living in their soul-life.

    The fact that I have been able to spend this time sharing some of my experience with you consistently, is teaching me about another aspect of the Father and the Spirit Laws involved that assist with our soul condition so that I, being where I am, can actually converse with you both where you are, involving a subject matter that we three participate with and is an individual experience that is perfect and involving living truth.

Ultimately, if it is perfection that you are aspiring toward insofar as living your physical life without any compensation, and that your natural soul essence is perfect and you are receiving Divine Love, this is attainable even though I myself never experienced this in my human life. Fortunately today, individuals are more exposed to the information and sympathetic with soulful living. As it has been taught to you and as I will confirm, here in the spirit-life having our natural love perfected by receiving Divine Love is evident in the proof of our spirit-attributes and how our spirit-body changes as our soul condition changes. In the 7th Divine Love Sphere, I knew my natural love, perfected. You cannot reside in the Celestial Heaven if your natural love is out of harmony with perfection. The physical body can mask your ability and capacity to be objective about your condition of your spirit-body when you are receiving Divine Love, so any recognition as far as being able to ascertain if your natural love is perfect will be a subjective experience relating to your soul condition. The personal endeavour to have your natural love restored to its perfection in your physical life by including the Father's Divine Love is a very worthy pursuit and one that is obtainable. The Divine Love is such a sustaining influence in the natural love, that when the natural love is perfect here in the spirit-life, never again does that natural love lapse into imperfection and disharmony.

I have utilised Saleeba as an example throughout my discourse with you. Saleeba has encouraged me to do so which I gratefully acknowledge.

Respectfully, Daniel

July 2019

16

Hello; it is I, Daniel. Another teaching I would like to convey to you about the Divine Love is that Divine Love is not an abstract form of energy. I know that when we are introduced to the truth that this Divine Love exists for our soul, we are at a beginning and that our knowledge about the existence of this Love is virtually nil. This could lead one into thinking that the Divine Love is abstract in form.

Everlasting

In my experience living receiving Divine Love, as I became more confident with the condition of my soul changing, I was able to understand that the Divine Love as an existing form of energy does not exist in abstract form. There is a reason why the Father has formed this energy of Divine Love with such concise existing perfection and not an abstract thing or form of substance. If I were to receive an abstract form of energy into my soul then my soul and I would progress into an abstract form. The fact that I have received a lot of Divine Love, and that my progression as a soul has become clearer and more identifiable as the soul I am, has revealed how true and complete the form of Divine Love is in its universal existence to me.

I have been able to learn about my natural love because I am receiving Divine Love, which has caused noticeable change within myself.

Divine Love has caused change to my soul and spirit attributes. Although I have changed, this change is a personal change and one that I have embraced and enjoyed. My purpose here in my spirit-life is for me to learn as much as I can about living with Our Father and sharing this with other souls. I have changed, but my purpose here involving change has never been to change another individual's life. I have experienced change with such substantial consequences, but my motivation has never been to direct what I have learnt toward another so that that soul feels that they must embrace the change that the Divine Love brings. I have never sought to change another person's spirit-life. Only the Divine Love can bring such change in the spirit-life. This is evident in the experience that Saleeba shared. The only change that Saleeba really experienced was her introduction to the Immortal life brought about by the addition of the Father's Divine Love.

Here in our Celestial life, we understand that the Divine Love doesn't evolve. Living in the Celestial Heaven I am able to see how I progressed and evolved through the various spheres to arrive at the Celestial Heaven. My soul changed and so the condition of my spirit-attributes changed in harmonious accord to my soul.

There are so many conclusive teachings involving the soul-life living with Divine Love, but the most important truth that I can possibly convey to you is that the Divine Love represents change. So substantial are the changes brought about by involving Divine Love in my soul-life, that all my spirit-life experience relates to my being involved with this Divine Love.

Another truth about living in the natural and Divine spheres is that the spirit-body can never exceed the condition of its soul. This means that the individual cannot develop their spirit-body as a separate interest to further their progression in their spirit-life. In the physical life, individuals can develop their physical attributes as they see fit but here in the spirit world, the individual cannot develop their spirit-body to advance their position or capabilities beyond their soul condition. This is a very important teaching that involves mortal personality living in the spirit world. If you can understand how important the soul is, then you will ascertain how progression happens here in the spirit world.

As I have said to you, the spirit-body is a remarkable creation. Every provision for the spirit-body to survive in the spirit world has been established by God. There are Spirit Laws that assist the spirit-body to continue forming if an infant or young person dies and begins their spirit-life. In this circumstance, the spirit-body of the individual will continue to mature as a matter of spirit-life fact. The ageing process that transpires in the spirit-body is subject to a completely different form of energy than the physical body. But, the emphasis here is that when the individual is mature in their spirit-life, one cannot by force of their personality, establish their spirit-body by will alone, to be a body that continues to advance in its own evolving condition. Saleeba's example, how she arrived to a spirit condition in her natural love where her spirit-life remained until the arrival of Jesus and the availability of God's Divine Love, demonstrates that in Saleeba's perfect soul condition in natural love, Saleeba remained contained to that perfect sphere unable to develop her own spirit attributes by her personality to advance in the spirit world to any other spirit sphere beyond this boundary of the Perfect Natural Sphere.

Saleeba's natural spirit-life experience teaches us that the spirit-body when living without any influence of God's Divine Love can only be matured to its perfect natural condition. This is a very important truth to know. The natural spirit spheres in their spirit-organic existence have been formed into existence by the Father to sustain mortal human life but without any organic spirit material that lives to assist the development of the spirit-body beyond the soul condition of natural love.

As soon as the soul begins receiving Divine Love in the spirit world, the individual is free to advance their spirit-life by progressing through new and wonderful spheres referred to as the Divine Love Spheres eventually arriving, as I have done, in the Celestial Heaven. I wasn't assisted in my progression through these Divine Love Spheres by consuming any living spirit-organic matter to sustain, nourish or advance the condition of my spirit-body. The only change which consistently existed providing me with a progressive experience of my spirit-body becoming more solid in form and extensive in its function to relate with the brighter spirit environments and ultimately with the Father was brought about from my soul being infused with the non-abstract and non-evolving form of energy that the Divine Love is.

I am really happy in my spirit-life. I feel fulfilled knowing that my natural love is as perfect as it can be. I am like many other spirits living in the Celestial Heaven where we feel that a certain destiny and fate about being human has been completed. I know that I was soul before I was conceived and born. I know that the Father created my soul and that I existed in this finite soul-form without personality or spirit-body before I was conceived. When I was conceived the Father formed my spirit-body. Throughout my physical life, my soul present and my spirit-body present, I was finitely individualised. My physical life contributed toward the individualisation of my personality and then when I died I experienced transitioning into the spirit world where my soul lived in my spirit-body and I adapted to my spirit-life. Knowing about Divine Love I continued to receive Divine Love, which continued the individualisation of my personality and brought change to the attributes of my spirit-body, which was subject to the change in my soul condition. My natural love became perfect from the causal energy of Divine Love and my life experiences and memories, harmonious as the soul I am in accord with the Father's Spirit Laws of Love. I entered the Celestial Heaven complete and fulfilled in my knowing that I, in my soul's life and journey had obtained perfection, immortality and the individualisation of love living with the Father.

When learning about the Father, it can appear that certain dynamics involving the Father's Handiworks are in abstract form. It is only that we are not in the real soul condition to perceive these Handiworks as they really are in their form and existence. If, in a physical human life, one can grasp the vision of the Divine Love and how this Love relates to soul and how soul relates with the spirit-body, then one may understand that the existence of the Divine Love represents a whole new revelation to the individual and to humankind about who and what God is. This is certainly how it is here in the spirit world. The humanity that resides here, when introduced to the existing form of energy that the Divine Love is, and how this energy relates to the soul that can bring about change that is consistent with each and every soul created, the teachings conveyed by those who are living with Divine Love reveal a whole new revelation to those in the spirit world in the natural spheres, to who and what God is. Understanding the way the Divine Love is and how this Love activates a dormant soul is an entrance into a life that reveals the true loving nature of God as Soul and this truth about God being Soul is to humankind, a new revelation.

Once again, this has been a wonderful experience. I have loved sharing with you both.

Respectfully, Daniel

17

I am here; it is I, Luke. Daniel Samuels has done well introducing the truth about God's Divine Love being a non-evolving form of energy. It is on this subject that I wish to convey a word.

There are many teachings that we have revealed to you about the nature of this Love. We know that it is gifted by the Father for our souls to participate with, and we know that this Divine Love is the dynamic of change that results in the only real progress of the individual in their spirit-life. We have understood that natural love can be perfected to its own limit within the soul, when that soul of the individual is not receiving the Divine Love, as Saleeba's spirit-life an example of; we also understand that natural love perfected to its limit with the inclusion of the Divine Love.

The Divine Love is non-evolving as it is not subject to any external influence that can change or alter it. When this Love is infused with the mortal soul, this Love is never changed within the soul or the spirit-attributes of the spirit-body. There is nothing in the systems of the spirit-body or the energy of the soul that can combust the energy that the Divine Love is. It is incredible when you realise that by receiving this Love, this Love remains true in the human soul for all time! The reason why this is such a significant truth that defines the form and existence of this energy that the Divine Love is because this Love causes much change within the individual while never altering, absorbing or diminishing its form when coming into contact with the spirit-biosphere that each individual is, residing in their spirit-life. We have conveyed to you how the spirit-body is subject to a different ageing relationship with spirit environments. The Divine Love is ageless, it is eternal and represents that part of the living Soul-life that the Father is - eternal.

The condition of my spirit-mind, having lived with Divine Love for a substantial period of time, is that my spirit-mind is able to perceive this existing form of energy, the Divine Love, being part of my soul and spirit attributes. In this way I am god-like but I am not a god. In the condition I am in, I am Immortal which leads us to the teaching that Jesus conveyed to James Padgett about being transformed from the mortal into the Immortal soul.

From a physical life experience involving living with Divine Love, you are with the condition of your organic brain. In my spirit-life, I am in the condition of my spirit-mind. It can be difficult for the organic brain to process what a non-evolving form of energy might be like, even when you may have been receiving this Divine Love in your prayers. In physical life, the individual likes experiences to be concrete, so-to-speak. The Divine Love is a solid form of energy, but there is nothing else in all God's created physical and spirit universe that can compare to this Divine Love.

There is nothing in existence that is of the Earth that can emulate the causal principle that this Divine Love has. Even here in these spirit environments, there is nothing that can emulate this Divine Love. This is why when we conveyed our teachings to James Padgett, we clarified the fact that this Divine Love has been formed by God for the specific purpose of engaging the mortal soul. It can be a difficult experience in a physical life to identify the image of your own soul. We clarified this too, that there is nothing made from the evolving forces of the Earth that represent your own soul's image. It takes mortal spirits quite some time to develop their soul condition so that their spirit-attributes can perceive and experience the Divine Love that they have received. Daniel outlined this in some of the recent messages he conveyed. If you can perceive the Divine Love as a non-evolving form of energy, if you can reflect with your soul perceptions this enduring quality of God's Eternal Love, then this will provide you with an image that we here live with throughout our spirit existence. This will also provide you with some degree of sight into the nature of God, as being eternal and having gifted an eternal form of energy that our finite souls can participate with. Understanding that the Divine Love is non-evolving, that this Love does not change when as the form of energy it is, is commingling within the soul and spirit attributes, then, by understanding this aspect of the eternal you will be in reach of understanding the quintessential teaching about the nature of God's Divine Love. From your human experience, as you look into the spirit-life, the spirit-vision reveals the real action of spirit and what this represents when the soul and spirit-body include the Divine Love in its journey.

I am pleased that you have both been open to receiving this teaching about the Divine Love as it will assist the individual in their education about this unique form of energy that is the basis upon all soul change and spirit progression involving a spirit's life.

Well done, your Celestial friend Luke

18

Hello my friends, I am here to share more of my experience with you that relates to my spirit-life. It is your friend, James Reid. I have quietly observed how these messages are being conveyed to you like it was when you were both receiving the messages that James Padgett conveyed to you, I am interested in this progressive experience. I have contributed, now I find that another time has opened and I can contribute once more.

Since I conveyed my last message to you, you have not received a message from me, nor have you received any experience from me involving my spirit-life. I have spent much of my time since I last saw you listening to other individuals as they give discourses on the greatest mystery of all, which is to clarify the existence of the Soul that we know and live with, the Father. I am well adjusted in my experience living with Divine Love. As it has been recently taught to you, I am aware that Divine Love is a non-evolving form of energy. I am also aware that my natural love, being finite, is at its perfect essence now in my soul. All my human relationships are in their rightful place, which means I live my spirit-life now without any lingering compensation which gladdens me as my soul condition reflected in my spirit-attributes reveals to me that I am free in my spirit-life experience, free from all physical life experience, although I still retain deep love for certain individuals who are still living their physical life.

As I have become more soul-like, my spirit-attributes have come to the fore. I am able to participate with my spirit-senses that interact with spirit environments in a more compelling relationship and this I am pleased about for I am more mutable and less physical. This may sound an esoteric strangeness, but, the more I am in my spirit-attributes the less I am served by the memories of my physical life. This has freed me up so I can be more engaging in a social way and in my own exploration that involves living a human spirit-life.

I recently went to a discourse given by a human spirit who has been living their spirit-human life to the equivalent of 1700 human years. All of these years this individual lived in the spirit world were with his receipt of God's Divine Love. His interest is solely identifying more about the nature of the Father. I have been to many of these discourses given by this individual, whose name is Marcus who lived and travelled through Europe in his day. He was, as he called himself, nomadic but he has also said that he was never lost from God. He was devout in his worship of God and would stay in places with people who would offer shelter as he was a man without an address, but a man of God. He said that there were quite a few like himself, and in the winter would travel to Spain where it was warmer and where there was an influence of Arabs so that he could gain more perspective about the way different cultures perceived the existence of God. That was a long time ago! In the Celestial Heaven where Marcus resides, he resides in the Last Sphere before the beginning of the Universal Spheres. There are many like Marcus, who have specialised in their particular field of interest or study of the greater reality of spirit. The discourse Marcus gave was for an hour; I still retain the memory and feel of what an hour was. The discourse was situated in an open amphitheatre set amidst a beautiful spirit garden. We could sit on solid forms of energy that resemble seats and there were individuals from all human cultures and backgrounds listening. The discourse was in the First Celestial Sphere where I reside. There were individuals present from all the spheres that comprise the Celestial Heaven. We could ask questions at the end of the discourse, which is always an expansive experience. I didn't ask a question.

There are many theories circulating around the Celestial Heaven involving the mystery surrounding God and how this Soulful Creator came into existence. All of us are living in our perfect natural love and we are living in the abundance of God's Divine Love so we know that God does exist due to the Divine Love that we are continuously living with, but none of us have actually seen the individual, God face-to-face so to speak; certainly none of us who reside in the Celestial Heaven. There are individuals living beyond these spheres who appear to live closer to God but they, as spirit-humans haven't met or seen the Face of

Everlasting

God. It is an incredible thought when you think about how God came into existence. Marcus theorised in his discourse, that a form of energy at some point became aware of its own existence. If you can imagine, a form of minute energy having energetic consciousness and then a collective form of energy formed to collectively form a complete individuality with a uniform consciousness that was stable in its existence, then, you have a small perception on Marcus' theory. He did go on to say, which we all liked and responded to, that the Creator was formed in an image and consciousness of what is known as the energy of love. Marcus theorised that for a Creator to be a creator, was required to understand its own dynamic origin of creation and how this form of creation originated so that the consciousness of this energy could then create and be a creator. He went on to say that by the fact that human souls have been created, and that our life-force originated in love to produce loving human beings capable of experiencing love, it would require the Creator to understand what love is and how this love would be when in the action of independent living independent of its own creation, yet involved with the Creators creation - love itself.

Having received much Divine Love myself, I am so comforted with this Love in my spirit-life that I can hardly believe that there may have been a time when the Creator didn't exist. There is so much life here with such a vitality present and that population of humankind thriving in their Immortality, that it is almost humanly spirit impossible to fathom a time that existed without the Creator.

I will conclude by saying that the discourses that I attend only serve to be truly wonderful and never to cause doubt on the experience we are living involving the Father. There are discourses given by individuals who try to define how the First Parents came into being, for these two individuals and what they represent is part of the human narrative. They are residing here in their spirit-life and we are able to meet and see them, but still, their origin and creation are as much of wonderment to us as it is for us to individually establish our own soul-life with the Father. There are so many conclusive experiences here but there is still that wide spirit horizon that we are able to look into as we participate in our Immortal adventure.

It is good to see you both again.
Your friend, James Reid

19

Hello my friends, it is your friend, James; I am in a good condition to convey more experience to you. As I said to you in my last message, I have attended discourses involving an array of subject matter that expands our spirit-life experience. These are regular social happenings where one is free to go along and listen and ask questions if they feel inspired. It is a good way of learning and I find this way of learning suitable for my progressive spirit-life. I have attended discourses involving subject matter ranging across different themes. One individual gave a wonderful discourse involving the kind of energy that is present that constitutes the living spirit-organic energy and life of the spirit-body. The spirit-body is a unique attribute with its own energy that differs than the energy of the soul contained within it. Having experienced my own spirit-body and how it changes when the energy of Divine Love causes its effect in the soul, there are different forms of energy converging in one finite place at one finite time. In physical life, people study energy at all levels of existence. It is the same here. There is the energy of Divine Love, the energy of the soul, the energy of the spirit-body and the energy of the spirit environments. There are other forms of energy here that constitute a sustainable spirit environment and there is the energy that Spirit Laws and for instance, the Acting Spirit, is composed of. The individual giving the discourse specialised in the energy of the spirit-body. He explained at the beginning of his discourse that several conversations had transpired between himself and Aman as Aman had revealed to him how the spirit-body functions internally. Having been a doctor myself, I am naturally intrigued. Over here no individual is injured or becomes ill so there is no apparent need to look inside the sprint-body to resolve any dis-ease or to study the organs of the spirit-body. It has required teachings from Aman and Amon who understand the creational aspect of the spirit-body to convey teachings about the interior of this body. I have the memory of my physical life; I have the memory of doing certain things left or right handed, with one side being more dominant than the other. I have learnt now that I am a Celestial spirit, that this is only a memory. When the spirit-mind is functioning in the soul condition of perfect natural love with the addition of Divine Love the spirit-mind doesn't have two hemispheres like the organic brain. It is organised as being uniform and it has mass, but in my spirit-life, I do not have a dominant side. I still find that having my memories an interesting experience. I am learning so much about spirit-life experience, forming new memories but I do possess as part of my memory, certain physical memories.

My spirit-mind has the visual capacity to recall my physical memories in living colour. I can remember sunlight and I can recall the sound of the ocean; as you both know, I liked spending time by the sea. The spirit-mind is a dynamic mass of energy that has its neuro systems organised so that this uniform cohesive mass of energy can continue to evolve as the condition of the soul changes. You have to keep in mind that the spirit-mind in its design was made to form memories when living a spirit-life and also to house memories lived in physical life. As it has been taught to you in previous teachings that you have both received over the years, memories formed in your human life have to survive that human life so that in your spirit-life, you are able to have these memories. Otherwise, no-one would know themselves to be the individual they are, the physical life experiences lived, and whether or not any compensation forms part of that soul-life and condition of that life lived.

There is no comparison to be made with the organic speed a physical body matures to the way a spirit-body matures in its spirit-life living with Divine Love. I can remember what ten years feel like between the ages of 60 and 70. I have gone from the First Natural Sphere to the Celestial Heaven in a very short time. The change that my spirit-body has experienced is at a fast rate; the physical body cannot possibly change at this speed. This might seem obvious but it does illustrate how dynamic the energy that constitutes a spirit-body is in its cohesiveness to experience change at a fast rate and remain uniform in all its definition. This also demonstrates how dynamic the spirit-mind is, as it changes and adapts quickly as the soul condition improves in its natural love inclusive with the energy of Divine Love becoming part of the soul.

The individual did relate the difference between the spirit-body living without the soul receiving any Divine Love to the soul receiving Divine Love. Comparisons are made here, for this is happening in real time in the spirit world. The difference between the spirit-body progressed in its energy by the inclusion of Divine Love compared to the spirit-body that has been dormant without progression due to Divine Love is substantial. Such a comparison between these differences in spirit-body quality is highlighted to demonstrate the convergence of energies that transpire in one finite place that results in dynamic change.

The individual giving the discourse highlighted energy as this was the focus of the discourse. I understood why his focus was on energy as I had experienced this change myself.

I have been to discourses given by individuals that teach solely about the life of the First Parents. I have been to other discourses that provide a broad spectrum on the life of Jesus involving his relationship with God, his place in the spirit universe and how he is as a personality. There is so much information here and so many individuals specialising in their spirit field of interest and willing to share what they have learned that there is never a dull moment for one who has a desire to invest their time in the development of their spirit knowledge. I must state at this time, that once your natural love, perfect, and that you are living without any compensation the physical life one has lived is complete. There is no need to create any drama to add to this. One is free to pursue their spirit interests that are as wide and diverse as the humanity residing in the Celestial Heaven and beyond. Having been introduced to the true soul-life one may always think that there is more healing or soul condition to improve, but I am here to tell you speaking from personal experience, that there comes a time when your soul condition complete in its natural love and one can no longer spend any further time trying to figure out what is wrong.

I will finish now. It has been a pleasure to share this time with you both and to say a little that may bring spirit enlightenment.

Your friend, James Reid

20

Hello; my name is Ian. You know me as I lived in the same suburb that you both live in, and we saw each other on a regular basis since 1990. As you know, later in my life my physical condition deteriorated with a chronic physical disability which resulted in my death.

Here I am speaking to you from the spirit world. It is to say, that I did not study or share in any interest in the human afterlife; I know that you knew this. My interest lay in human philosophy where the individual could master the art of spiritual living. I knew very little about what I am living now. As I speak to you, I can see that you know that it is me speaking to you. My soul condition is in that condition that enables me to live in this First Divine Love Sphere. I am very new to my experience living with Divine Love and, very new to the reality of living my life with the Living Soul, God. I considered myself elite in my human life and by this, I mean of a super intellect with a refined sensitivity for the highest form of cultural and spiritual living that man had established. I was not interested in the general social mundaneness of the day. I lived a good life and although we saw each other regularly we never really spoke that much other than daily pleasantries.

Everything that I have experienced here is different. I didn't have any soul condition to prepare me for the kind of change that I was introduced to. As I established myself in my early spirit-life my ego took a hit. I must say, that I was relived to be free of my poor physical health, with my faculties reinserting themselves so that I was cognitive, independent and voluntary again. As my physical condition developed I became less voluntary, with the disease taking over my life.

As I speak to you, I can see that you can see me, that I have changed and that I appear younger. This is so and a miracle. Being introduced to my soul-life I am at a beginning, which I am actually really happy about. I am being assisted as I speak to you by more advanced teachers who seem to know you both intimately. I am impressed by this. I say this because I can recall - as you can - that at a local cafe in the year 1990 we shared a conversation involving spiritual philosophies. It was in this conversation that you politely introduced the truth about the availability of Divine Love and the soul-life, but I held little interest in what you brought across the table. That was a long time ago and here I am in my spirit-life now communicating to you about my living with this Divine Love and beginning my soul-life with all my physical and human philosophies fast becoming memories as they serve no purpose to the life of my soul. Though I am a beginner with Divine Love, I have received enough to know that this energy is the catalyst for my progression toward a fulfilling spirit-life. Being here in the spirit world brought so much change that this change happened quite naturally as you can well imagine. I find it quite humbling that you knew about this Divine Love all those years when we would see each other and I was never interested and now I am so interested that at least I can share this with you. I am a man who is very interested in achieving the best outcome for myself and to realise my own potential. I also like the best of what a man can be. Having seen the teachers and the way they are, this is my inspiration for my future here. I did help people financially in my human life, as you know I was wealthy. I am pleased about this, but wealth is irrelevant here. In a beautiful way, for I was a man who liked beauty, I am free to pursue my main interest in life. I am able to live how I really always imagined how I would like to live, which is to pursue philosophy in an aesthetic setting. My past human life served me well. As you know from our conversation those years ago, I told you that I believed in reincarnation. I can see now that is not going to happen. I have had to change an intricate belief that formed part of my human philosophy about life. My belief in reincarnation formed the building block of my spiritual philosophy. I was convinced that reincarnation was going to happen, my right of passage and that it was a truth that generated my evolution toward my own individual human spiritual way of life.

In our conversation back in 1990, you didn't try to change my belief, you politely listened as I shared my experience. You told me about The Padgett Messages but I didn't listen and never read these teachings. I have been told in recent times that I can meet James Padgett, I am looking forward to this.

When I awakened in my spirit-body, that was the moment my life changed. It didn't change with death, it changed with life. I was alive. I must say here that my belief in reincarnation did help me as it meant that I did believe that when one died one would become something universal to then be returned to continue improving their evolution in their physical life. When I awoke in the spirit world I was in awe that a small part of me accepted this fate. I was greeted by my mother and father; they, in their appearance, differed than how I remember them to be. I didn't know that they had become Celestial spirits as I never received any communication from them in my physical life. I never received anything from the spirit world in my physical life, especially not any Divine Love. I didn't know that anything like I am experiencing now had any existence at all.

With my superior intellect and intelligence and with my intuition I wasn't arrogant insofar as dismissing an existence of God, but this existence was more of an intangible form of energy that was bound up with nature and a sense of the cosmology. Having experienced a small amount of Divine Love, having seen those living with a great amount of Divine Love, I am now including God as Living, Soul and that I am personalising God's Love and Truths into my new philosophy. I have been introduced to the teaching which is brand new for me, that involves the true Immortality that a human can experience and this I am, as a truth, invested in.

This, what I am sharing with you, is all new to me. I know that I may sound a little clumsy in my delivery to you, but I am not long in the spirit-life and my physical memories fell very near and close to me. I have never experienced communicating like this before and I didn't even know that one could do something like this when I lived as a man. There are quite a few individuals helping me at this time. I came to be with you as your mother is here and we knew each other those years ago. I was reintroduced to Rose here in the First Divine Love Sphere through social connections. It is a very social place here in this sphere, which is unusual for me for in my later human life I was a recluse. I don't know why I wasn't interested in the Divine Love when you spoke about this Love, but reflecting on my life I was in my own mind superior in my intellect, or so I thought. I still have a superior intellect, but I am aware that without including my soul in my life, I am limited to any real development for me to go forward with.

My love and gratitude to you both, as I had met Zara those years ago.

21

Hello; this is your reacquainted friend, Ian. My knowledge of living with Divine Love is very limited. I feel good about this, and not overwhelmed. I have been introduced to so many beginnings that my being aware that another beginning, made, presents an advancement that I am prepared to accept and to undertake.

It appeals to my intellect that I am embracing a way of life that I had no previous knowledge about. I have seen in the First Divine Love Sphere there are many like me making this new beginning. It speaks of a uniqueness that I can see there are many who are already established in living with this Love. My whole understanding of participating with God at a personal and intimate companionship is a way of life previously unknown to me. In the evaluation of my own physical life, there was nothing really wrong. I gather that I am like so many who simply live their lives and for all the experiences and relationships formed, that real change comes when you transition from one world into another world. That was new to me in action and thought, as I had never really spent any time whatsoever contemplating what the afterlife would be like. This was the result of my belief in reincarnation. As far as I was concerned, when living as a man the whole consequence of death and the spirit

Everlasting

world didn't exist for me as I had already concluded with my intellect, that I would be living another physical life, so in effect, my belief in reincarnation had already entitled me to my next physical life. The physical life I was living, in my mind, was purely to get to the next incarnation and a more progressed one at that! It's an extraordinary experience being able to review your own physical life with such objectivity.

I have met some of the teachers and this has astounded me. At this time I am unable to provide you with any insight or teaching that relates to a non-evolving form of energy. As you know, I haven't been residing in my spirit-life for a long time. My involvement in receiving Divine Love has been for an even shorter time. I have heard conversations between individuals that speak of things like soul condition and non-evolving, and I am aware that there are spheres beyond the one I am in and that I am to refer this to you as the Celestial Heaven.

The experience of the body I am in is so new to me that I am still adapting to it and learning about its function and mutability. Simply moving about is a whole new experience! Moving from here to a place just over there brings a whole new sensory experience in this body I am in. This has been explained to me as follows: in a physical body one begins as an infant, therefore, as one matures through their life they experience their physical attributes through all the age of their life. In the spirit world, individuals transition here from their human life at all ages. I was an older man in my late 70's, so, when I awakened in the spirit world the spirit-body that I awoke to was of the same age and I was not an infant beginning my spirit-life and consequently maturing all the way through so a spirit-body is completely normal. This is how it was explained to me. Many people begin their spirit-life in their mature age. This means that their personality is quite formed, so to begin life in a spirit-body with a matured personality one has ample awareness but no awareness about this new body that houses the personality.

I can't tell you much at all about living with Divine Love other than I have felt the Love when I have asked for it. I have also seen the image of those who are adequate in living with this Love, and they differ to me in their appearance. I am astute enough to see that by including this energy in my life, is a dynamic of change. I know nothing about any sphere beyond the First Natural Sphere that has anything to do with natural love. I went from the First Natural Sphere to the First Divine Love Sphere with my parents. They told me about the natural spirit world, but I haven't ventured there at all. I know nothing about a perfect natural love or a sphere to reside in with that soul condition.

As I said to you, I was a recluse in the later years of my physical life. I still feel quite involved with this, although there is tremendous social connectivity here in the First Divine Love Sphere. I spent so many human years being true in my own life experience and having very little to do with anyone else, that I am realising that I am still like this here. I will follow this with interest, as my intellect is superior and so is my ability to experience refined concepts and details. The word master comes to mind. I was trying to 'master' the life of being human but I was with one weakness, which was control. This wasn't a bad thing, as it requires quite a lot of control to master the art of ones' life, and I had the money to do it. I was a compassionate man and a man who lived with the emotion of empathy but I had this great brain and a huge desire to read and to study life. I am still with this and I have been briefed that there is much for me to study. I am humble enough to understand this as defined by, so far, everything I have experienced is a study of everything that I have never experienced before!

Thank you again, Ian

22

Hello; my name is Carmel. I have lived all my life in the spirit world. This is the first time I have spoken a word that will be heard in the physical life of men and women! I am one who resides in the Celestial Heaven and I am one who has lived virtually all my life aware of the Soul God, that I am soul, and that I have a beautiful spirit-body. I have lived with Divine Love as part of my life nearly all my spirit-life.

My life here began when I was an infant; I was abandoned by my mother. My father never lived with my mother. It was a random act that set in motion a pregnancy that was me to be born in an unsustainable environment. My mother was very young and inexperienced so the thought of rearing a child at an early age was overwhelming. She didn't know what to do other than to give birth to me and to leave me hoping I would be found. I wasn't found until it was too late and I didn't survive. This happened way back in the early 17th Century. What is important, that as an infant I continued my life in the First Natural Sphere. My spirit-body survived as did my soul and its essence of natural love. My life, although conceived in the physical human world and born with physical attributes was sufficient for my soul to have individualised. In the First Natural Sphere, I continued to thrive on the nutrients that my spirit-body required to mature. By the time I was ten years old living as a young feminine spirit, was all the life I knew and perfectly normal to me. I was cared for by the most loving and caring women and men spirits. I was socially integrated into my spirit-life with these beautiful souls who cared for me and the many other infants and young children residing here due to the consequences that ended their lives.

The reason why I am speaking to you is not to convey a portrait of a lost life that never made it into adulthood, but rather to illustrate to you how extraordinary the spirit-body is as a creation that continues to thrive in its spirit-life. There has been much conveyed to you about the spirit-body and that the spirit-body will only ever be as true as the condition of the soul. This is a spirit truth. Part of my service has been to assist individuals who transition into the spirit world and find themselves living in their spirit-body without having any prior knowledge or experience that this body forms part of their human existence. The man, Ian conveyed to you how he is finding his experience of living in his spirit-body. He is receiving Divine Love but he is unable to fully embrace the ramifications of this Love in all its causal power, as he is still acquainting himself with his new environment, which is his spirit-body and extended attributes. Individuals such as myself, assist individuals like Ian at acquainting themselves with their new-found awareness. I have ever only known my spirit-body. I am one of those humans who lived unaware of their physical body due to my age with all my self-awareness developed in my spirit-body in the environment of the spirit world.

Humans in their physical life can ask, 'is there an afterlife', or 'what happens after you die', 'what does a spirit world look like' and any of these questions can lead to further questions involving the existence of the physical life. For me, the spirit-life and spirit world is all I have ever known. It is so real to me that I actually have imagined what it would be like to live a full physical life; what it would be like to become a mother myself and to experience the full gamut of physical reality. I knew in my teenage years that I would never become a mother. I am without the reproductive systems. In the spirit world, the spirit-body cannot reproduce with another spirit-body. Humans can no longer continue to procreate in the spirit world. This might be an obvious statement for some, but it does illustrate to you how my own feminine nature established its full essence without being physically developed. How I matured differed than how I would have matured in my physical life, for my spirit-body here in the spirit world matured without any organic or hormonal driving force. Through this current time of communication between our worlds, you have been introduced to the non-evolving reality of Divine Love and how evolution in the spirit environments differ to earthly cycles of evolution. In my spirit-life, I was not subject to any spirit evolution or evolution in my spirit-body.

While the soul requires the physical attribute to individualise as well as the spirit-body requires the soul and physical body to materialise, each spirit-body retains its energy of spirit-related energy that defines the spirit-body to be in attribute, what it is. The soul is with its own energy just as the physical body is comprised of its energy. My spirit-body, having only been present with my physical body a short earthly moment, was never impacted or compromised in its energy to continue its existence in the spirit-life by my death or lack of physical development. The soul is subject to the influences of the physical body and personality. This is why there is soul condition! The spirit-body, whilst reflecting the soul's true condition cannot of its own volition in physical life, influence or determine the physical evolution of that physical being. In other words, the evolution of a human in physical life is not being driven by the spirit-body and its energy or spirit-will. It is not a self-acting, determining influence in the overall outcome of the individual.

My spirit-body, as it continued to thrive in the spirit world never went through an evolution. It was sustained by spirit nutrients and its own energy and energy from my soul so that it continued to mature. With this maturing experience, my spirit-body was not self-acting as being evolved to its own determination. The spirit-body is a creation formed into existence by God and is subject to the Spirit Laws that determine how the spirit-body functions here in the spirit-life and, when with a physical body.

I never knew life to be anything other than living in my spirit-body in my spirit-life. All my memories of my life are formed and generated from my living in spirit environments with spirit friends and acquaintances. In my teenage years, I was introduced to the experience of Divine Love so for me, growing up knowing that God is Soul and that I could receive Divine Love and what this Divine Love represents was a normal experience. I have lived well over four human centuries with this Divine Love knowing that God exists and that God is Soul and full of life and loving.

The man, Ian who conveyed to you a little of his experience lived a long physical life. He has explained how being in his spirit-body is a new beginning. He still has the memories of his physical life waking up in the dawn, seeing the sky and then at night seeing the stars and a loved one but now, his entire landscape has changed. He is in his spirit-body and this is still largely unknown to him. His personality, having been fully formed as a male adult, had no previous skill or experience relating to his spirit-body in his physical life. He is now being subject to a different form of energy that his soul and personality are clothed in. As he has said, he is in awe as he adjusts to the difference between a change of world and for me, the experience that he is acquiring to adjust to his spirit-life is all I have ever known.

I know the spirit world well. I have been to all the natural spheres but there is no need for me to go to the spheres where the poorest of soul condition reside. I went there once, and there was nothing I could really do to help those in such poor condition. Only the advanced teachers go there for they have to deal with the central force of the self-serving personality. My gift is being able to assist individuals like Ian, as these individuals are really coming to terms with their new life and are open to a loving input as they find their feet having lived a considerable physical life. My expertise is assisting one to learn about their spirit-body. I am so at ease in my soulful life with the Father, that they are calmed when I am present and this brings a sense of companionship and knowledge which is comforting. There are many like myself who assist those who have come across and are adapting to their spirit-body. I am in my spirit appearance, somewhat like how a human artist may depict an angel or someone who is spiritually advanced living in a halo of light. It is actually quite important, the service I provide for every human that I assist has never met anyone like me before, but as they adapt into their spirit-life and begin receiving Divine Love, they will socially interact with individuals like myself all the time, so it is important for one to know what is ahead and the kind of individuals that reside in a Celestial life.

Having experienced my life in the spirit world, I don't have the same emotional experience or feeling experience that people do who have had the time to physically mature. My relationships have been different. I have lived without drama and of course, I have lived without any material need or structure and I have lived all my life without ever experiencing physical illness or dis-ease! As I said, and as history recalls, there have been many who have not lived for any length of time in the earthly life. I am not unique and a singular human. I live with my soulmate who did live a full earthly life. This individual is living with Divine Love and resides in the Celestial Heaven with me. I can relate to him as he can relate to me. He had a family with children whereas I didn't. I have a family, an extended family. My mother and my father reside in the Celestial Heaven too. I helped my mother achieve this as she needed to learn how to adapt in this new life as did my father. It brought us together and was important for me. I was very well established in my spirit-life by the time they came across. I had long since forgiven all circumstances and outcomes having only love for them. As a soul, you can be in that condition, that simply can overcome anything with love. Perfect natural love is a true capacity for love in the action of living regardless of worlds.

In my spirit-life, I grew up knowing about Jesus. Ever since I was young, I lived knowing that he was a beautiful individual living among us. I have never lived without knowing this. As far back as I can remember, those who cared for me interacted with him, so he was a person that I knew. My perspective differs than many of the individuals I have assisted. What this difference is about is of the of worlds and the difference in life experience. I was introduced to the Divine Love as a normal way of life. When I was young I regularly saw individuals living with this Love. I knew that they lived in the Celestial Heaven and I knew that this was a place where I would eventually live.

As I have shared with you, I began my spirit-life as an infant. My parents were Spanish. My father was never present when my mother gave birth to me. As I said, I was abandoned and without a name. The name I was given by those caring spirits who raised me in my spirit-life is the name I have given to you. As I matured I learnt to speak Spanish and in later spirit-life, English. There wasn't a spirit language that existed in the natural spirit world that is spoken among the natural population that is a language universal to all. There are certain words and expressions used to describe certain spirit material adjuncts that comprise the spirit spheres and most certainly, the language involving the soul living with the Divine Love is a language used here that isn't used as a common language among the people of the Earth. Some of you have come into contact with a little of this language through the spirit communications you have read involving the soul living with the

Everlasting

Divine Love. It is not every day that a new form of language appears among the human world, especially one that describes the Divine Love, the spirit-body and soul which is unseen to the mortal population.

The image that I would like to convey to you about my human spirit-life is as follows. Most certainly, my beginning as an infant abandoned was unfortunate. Most definitely, my beginning in my spirit-life a godsend and gift! Another chance at being able to experience life when such a beginning deprived me of any physical life experience. I grew up in the spirit world without forming any beliefs that people form in their human life about God, Jesus, the afterlife, and as to whether the continuation of human life happens. I was born without sin. As an infant, my soul was in its pure natural love. When I died and was transitioned into the spirit-life, there I was pristine in my spirit-body without any sin or error that led to any compensation. That compensation remained with my mother and father. Those two poor souls lived with that condition of misfortune throughout their human life. When I met them here I was able to assist them with their compensation. My mother had to alleviate the guilt that she burdened herself with for abandoning me. My father never assumed any responsibility for my conception; he never knew that he had fathered a child. He used force as my conception was not consensual. My little body was found and taken to some priests who wrapped my body and in a brief religious ceremony, buried me in a small plot with an inscription titled, 'Daughter of God'. There is nothing left of my remains as that plot of land has long since been built over. My mother and father are Celestial spirits and they love me as I love them. How individuals change their soul condition so that their natural love becomes perfect by involving the Divine Love has been conveyed to you numerous times so I will not elaborate on my parent's progression here. They are lovely parents. We still stay in touch but I am independent. As I have seen and heard, every individual who arrives in the spirit world has a story to tell.

As I said, I began my spirit-life without any sin or error forming part of my soul condition. As I matured in my spirit-life the natural love in my soul did not digress or de-evolve. I was never subject to any physical action in life that I generated or was generated toward me, that would cause by choice or by another's unloving action, that could have possibly resulted in any compensation. My spirit-life evolved from my soul condition being in perfect natural love. I never formed any beliefs that were untruths about life. Everything I experienced as I matured was an expression of my perfect natural love. I was never taught to follow any human belief system by those who cared for me as I matured. In my teenage years - as you know them to be - I really embraced my living with Divine Love. My personal relationship with the Soul of God began easily as I had seen so many established in living their soul-life. My progression to the Celestial Heaven was rapid, effortless and loving and I must say a very happy one. Many humans have begun their spirit-life as infants and like me, have lived their whole life in the spirit world without ever forming any existing human beliefs that are only formed in physical human life. When you think about this, this is the introduction of another whole human experience that is unknown to the peoples of the Earth. In my Celestial life, I learnt about the physical life as individuals shared their experiences with me. I have spent time in the First Natural Sphere and the First Divine Love Sphere assisting individuals to adapt to their spirit-body. I am an expert in this experience. It's all I have known. You have both received numerous experiences conveyed to you by those who, as adults, lived their physical life. Some of these individuals were introduced to the existing Divine Love that relates with the soul-life, while many other learnt of this existing Divine Love in the spirit-life. What they all have in common is the weight of physical life and experience, then, introduced to the potential of another life involving the Immortality that the Divine Love brings to the soul. In my experience, I never lived a physical life. I am sharing my experience with you as one who has only ever lived in their spirit-body. My introduction to the potential of living with Divine Love, seamless and there has never been a single doubt as to my involvement in my soul-life. I have never had to live in any faith, nor have I ever lived in a certain quandary as to whether God exists or is the Divine Love real. In my life as I live my soul-life, living with Divine Love is so normal and accepted that I don't even think about it. Living with the Father, the Eternal Creator is as normal for me as it is for you know that you are with the air that you breathe. I have known nearly all my spirit-life that the Divine Love is a non-evolving form of energy. It is a non-invasive form of energy and the soul integrates very easily when this Love enters the soul. I did evolve but only as a maturing set of stages, as my soul and spirit-attributes seamlessly matured into their full expression. My personality matured without any disruption or influence of fear or negativity. I have never lived knowing what fear is as a distortion in my soul. Ever since I began including Divine Love, which was a choice and one that I gladly made, for it is never ordained that an individual who matures in their spirit-life must automatically receive Divine Love as a condition of living in the spirit world. The only choice I have ever made was to begin my receipt of Divine Love. I have never made any other choice, and yet I live with complete independence and fulfilment.

This has been a beautiful experience.

My love to you, Carmel

23

Hello; I am here with you both, it is your friend, James Reid. Listening to Carmel as she conveyed her experience to you reconfirmed to me how uniquely different and diverse living with Divine Love is.

Her experience brings another perspective to this experience of the soul, the soul-life and how individuals begin their spirit-life and are introduced to the Immortality of Divine Love.

I have lived enough experience now here in my spirit-life to see that the Divine Love of God is the change bringer and the dynamic which results in the full individualisation of the soul. My own experience involved a long physical life and then the introduction to the greater extended realities of spirit and soul. Carmel lived a short physical life with her introduction to life being involved with these spirit and soul realities being part of her normal life experience. What a difference this is!

I have found it to be truly fascinating conversing with individuals here who have no form of memories from their physical life. I have my memories, which are formed from my physical life and from my spirit-life. Carmel has her memories formed only from her spirit-life. We are both living with Divine Love in our Celestial lives. I have met individuals like Carmel who have lived all their life here, having died at such a young age.

Carmel's experience puts a whole new perspective on the exercise of the free will. There are so many teachings that the Celestial teachers conveyed to James Padgett that involve a physical life. In contrast to this, looking at Carmel's life growing up and maturing in the spirit world brings a new perspective to the definition of human free will. The way a human exercises their personality through the attributes of their physical body is one thing - exercising your personality through your spirit-body and its attributes places the personality into a different experience of free will in the spirit world. We heard how Carmel made only one choice, the choice to live with the Divine Love, and this choice extended her progression and independence.

When I meet and converse with individuals who have grown up in the spirit world, their whole outlook on life differs from mine. This is an obvious statement but one that can't be overlooked. These individuals appear settled to a fate that is not exclusive, unknown or intimidating. In my physical life, especially my later years when I knew about the Divine Love, my perception about the spirit world was all toward my future. It was seen by me as a place that existed that I knew very little about, that I was intrigued by and eventually, quite quickly in fact, transitioned into. My own journey was one of change, which I had to adapt to as I settled into my spirit-life. Meeting Carmel and others like her who have grown up in the spirit world, they are with this known calmness due to the fact that it is all they have known and this produces a calming effect that is within them and around them but it also produces another kind of human, a human full of living love without any actual lived memories from a physical life. When you meet these individuals they are what could be called 'spirit'. In my spirit-life, I will always have my memories and relationships as part of my spirit-life. Carmel will always have her memories formed in her spirit-life without any clouded or physical experience shaping her energy.

Carmel's experience reveals to us how sympathetic the spirit-body is to its receiving the covering of the Acting Spirit. It also teaches us how true it is that the soul can receive Divine Love in physical life and just as easily how the soul can receive Divine Love in a spirit's life. When you look at Carmel's life and individuals like her, they have accepted the fate of their life and their receipt of the Divine Love from their position of perfect natural love but no prayer need be given or human ritual to ensure the inflowing of this Love into their souls. It is an error for people in their physical life to assume that there is only one single prayer or method that confirms the only way the soul can open to the Soul of God for the inflowing of Divine Love. The good thing about having an experience shared from an individual like the beautiful Carmel, is that it brings contrast to what has been purely a physical experience involving the introduction to God's Divine Love and the soul-life. Looking at Carmel's life mirrors the singularity of a finite physical life being introduced to the same Love and Truths that Carmel was introduced to from her spirit infancy.

The fact that Carmel is with her soulmate who lived a physical life makes her story even more beautiful, that one who lives their entire life in the spirit world can, in the Celestial Heaven, live their entire eternal life with their soulmate who lived a large portion of their life in a robust physical domain. It is a good outcome to have such perspective on the difference of life experience and how everyone regardless of their beginning, is able to at some stage make a choice to include living with God's Divine Love. This is the perfect outcome that is consistent for us all.

It has been a pleasure to speak to you again and to see you receiving my words.

Your friend, James

24

Hello my friends, I have returned. As you can see, it is I, James Reid. The discussion about the Divine Love being a non-evolving form of energy is of real benefit to ascertain information as to how this form of energy acts in our souls. You both know that the condition of the finite soul when formed into existence by God only contains the life-force, soul-life force, of energy that is its natural love. The soul is not formed with any Divine Love in it. If this were so, the finite human soul would then be formed with non-evolving energy as part of its creation along with that Immortality that the Divine Love causes in the soul. If the soul were created with the Divine Love and the natural love as its complete form, then you would have perfect natural love with perfect non-evolving Divine Love fixed in the same location, which means having the mutable with the immutable as the initial form of the soul. As we know, our finite soul is only bestowed with its essence of natural love. The Divine Love is sought for after the soul has individualised by incarnation into its physical life. When the Divine Love is received depends entirely on when that individual is aware that such a form of energy exists and the individual chooses to participate in their soul-life with the Living Soul of God. As we know, this choice can happen in a physical life but most likely happens in a spirit-life.

When I embraced my understanding in my spirit-life that I was living with this Divine Love, I never felt that by receiving this Love that It was 'evolving me'. As it has been taught to you, you can receive a small portion of this Love and experience very little change; in fact, nothing seems to be happening at all. This is an important truth to know about Divine Love. The Father has made a form of energy that brings the true Immortality to the soul, a form of energy that doesn't change or evolve but a form of energy that does eventually cause change. My point here that I share from my derived experience is that for all the Divine Love that I have received, I never felt that the Father was deliberately evolving me. The change I experienced happened slowly, gradually and like the lightest of light and energy enveloping me. My changes were not evolutionary but conditional. By this I mean the Divine Love brought about a causal change in my soul condition which was the perfecting of my natural love. It is hard to describe how evolution did not form part of my changing soul condition. It just seems to happen! This is a good thing that we are discussing - the very nature of Divine Love - as it is the real dynamic of change that the soul experiences to bring about any changed perception, soul condition (as being progressive here in the spirit world) and fulfilment of individuality and happiness in the spirit world. I know that in the messages James Padgett received, as I had read many of them, the continuing guidance conveyed to James involved the importance of the Divine Love and why in the spirit world it meant everything as the Divine bringer of change. Living in the spirit world now myself, and having experienced the condition of my soul changing by receiving Divine Love, I understand only too well why such emphasis placed was in the messages that James received those years ago and why the work you are both doing is so very important.

I will not write more now and will see you again soon.

Your friend, James

25

I am here again in this delightful moment. I am to convey to you that I, like many of those individuals who have conveyed their words of love to you, do so in two parts. There is our personal spirit-life experience living with Divine Love and then there are extensive truths that we accept as being true but do not form a personal reality to our origin. By this I mean my own experiences, the spirit-life experiences I have lived are experienced in the origin of my finite soul. I experience Divine Love and for me, this Love is so very real and true. It is personal to me. However, as I experience this Divine Love into my soul, I am unable to see visually or be close to - as soul by Soul - the origin of this

Love, where this Love originates from. I know that the Source of the Divine Love I experience in my soul originates from the Source, God the Soul. Now, I have not seen with my own eyes the Soul, God. Although I reside in my spirit-life I have been unable to see visually the existence of the Creator of the spirit world that I reside in. God is an originator and creator of so much that I experience, but I am unable to see this source myself in solid form.

It has been revealed to you that there exists the Pre-incarnation Sphere where souls reside before their incarnation. I have been taught this too but I am unable to go to this sphere or to see inside this sphere. I do not know anything about the internal fabric of this sphere. All I know is what I have been taught by those Celestial teachers, such as Jesus, who know of such things and the kind of existence God has created these things to be.

My purpose today is to confirm to you that although we can experience Divine Love directly into our finite souls and this Love becomes clearer to our soul perception, there are existing universal realities of Spirit that exceed our own finite comprehension, that are with form and existence but that only the Universal Father understands the synthesis of energy required to establish such creations. This we are to accept as truth.

As I said to you a short while ago, I attend discourses given by other spirits. In the Celestial Heaven we are all living in our personal experience with Divine Love but there is a tremendous amount of research that individuals invest their spirit time and energy in to bring to life more about origins and truths that exist external to our finite souls, such as the existence of God. If Jesus didn't exist, as far as I can see we would all be in a considerable state of confusion. We would all be where Saleeba once was, in the Perfect Natural Sphere, content in our own finite limitation. Jesus has taught and currently teaches about truths that continue to expand our knowledge about the Living Father. Many of these truths I can grasp their essence by utilising the perception of my soul and its condition with my spirit-mind, but to put this into an English language and narrative, I am lost for words. When the spirit-body is formed, as mine is, to thrive and function in the Celestial life I am able to receive information about universal experiences beyond the Celestial Heaven but there isn't a human language that can adequately convey a true essence of the Master's teachings about the Universal Father. I am not avoiding anything, as part of these communications is to bring across from our world to your world as much information as possible for there are those who are genuinely interested in the spirit realities.

I will stop now.

Your friend, James

26

James Reid speaks:

At another discourse that I attended, there was an interesting theme discussed. The individual conducting the discourse had been a woman who had lived in England and described herself as a Theologian. She described how her passion in her human life was God and the history of humans trying to establish the nature of God in human social life. You both know, as well as I do, that religion and spirituality, philosophy and science are continuing themes explored by people who are passionate in their exploration of such long-standing social ideas that form cultures. The feminine individual was most beautiful with a strong countenance and stature. Her name was Elizabeth. Elizabeth spoke about the difference between God's Will in physical life and God's Will in a spirits life. I found this absolutely fascinating.

In her physical life, Elizabeth had tried to understand what was God's Will. Being a Theologian, Elizabeth had researched how people had socially tried to define the nature of God's Will in physical life. Becoming a spirit changed Elizabeth's educated and studied perspective about God's Will. Over here, we can see human life, physical life, with such clarity. Drawn from my own experience, as my soul condition changed from the receipt of Divine Love, my perspective of my physical life became clearer, objective and with clarity. Elizabeth discussed her observations which involved seeing how individuals progress once beginning their receipt of Divine Love in the First Divine Love Sphere and progressing to the Celestial Heaven. In her own life and experience, and other people's life experience here, God's Will was never mentioned. Individuals here are no longer posing the question that may involve their present or future outcome as being determined by figuring out what is God's Will for them to act within.

Receiving Divine Love over a continued time changes the soul; this has happened to me. I have real clarity into my own experience living with this Love compared to the time I was introduced to this Love in my physical life. I could have lived with my soul receiving Divine Love for twenty human years but I would never have established such clarity into my soul-life as I have established here in my spirit-life about living with Divine Love. In my spirit-life, I have never tried to figure out if I am doing God's Will. By receiving the amount of Divine Love I have, and the way this Love has brought about my changed soul condition so that I progressed and can live comfortably in the Celestial Heaven, I have been living in God's Love. This Divine Love has brought harmony into my soul and spirit-attributes, a harmony that once may have been an ideal but now is an actuality.

Elizabeth spoke about the difference between God's Will - being perceived by people in physical life - with these same people now living their spirit-life. Becoming a spirit changes so much about what we think we know or believe a physical life to be.

It is evident and blatantly obvious here, that God's Will exists but not in the way physical humans may believe such existence of will to comprise. Here, every single human spirit lives according to the condition of their soul, which means the sphere they reside in, which relates to the possible movement the individual has through the spirit world within the boundary and limitation of their soul condition. What you never hear here in the First Divine Love Sphere or the First Natural Sphere, is an individual expressing their desire to live in God's Will. What you do hear in these spheres are individuals recounting their physical life and describing how they thought they were living God's Will in their physical life. There are so many beliefs that become redundant in the spirit world. I have seen this, but the spirit world does present a whole new human experience that is outside of human conceptions. All the Celestial teachers I have met and conversed with know that every Celestial spirit is living true and harmoniously with God's Will due to the fact that each soul living here has received the required amount of Divine Love to bring about the necessary change in the soul condition for that soul to be living in perfect natural love with the Immortality of Divine Love sustaining it, which is defined as living and being at-one in love with the Soul of the Father. So, effectively part of the causal effect that the Divine Love has in the mortal soul results in the individual knowing and living consciously God's Will. When you are not living with an awareness of Divine Love in physical life, God's Will remains outside to the realm of conception and possibility.

Elizabeth explained how extensive God's Will is. It involves the soul living with Divine Love and how the Acting Spirit acts to convey this Love into the soul. This is an act of God's Will. Elizabeth identified many Immutable Spirit workings that happen, function and have their existence solely in the spirit world. There are many Spirit Laws here that we relate with as we progress that a person in their physical life will never come into contact with. Ultimately Elizabeth stated that God's Will is God's Love in all its Handiwork and that the addition of Divine Love formed part of God's Handiwork, which all originates from God's Eternal Soul Love. I do not want to complicate what God's Love is, but God's Love extends throughout all of God's Handiworks, but the Divine Love, which is the Love energy that our souls receive, is a distinct form of energy that God has formed with specific attention for the human soul.

I will close for the moment.

Your friend, James

27

James Reid speaks:

There are two things that I wish to speak about. As my experience develops here in my spirit-life, it becomes increasingly clear that there is much to learn that involves the greater spirit universe that humanity resides in. I have been to discourses presented by individuals covering different subject matter involving God as the central individual to all that appears in the spirit spheres. I recently spoke about God's Will, I also spoke about the existence of God, shared from my experiences having listened to such presentations. These discourses are numerous as individuals study particular interests relating to spirit life experience. This is not to be confused with the simplicity of receiving Divine Love. We all know how simple it is to participate in our soul life with God.

In my spirit life, I have always found my experience receiving Divine Love a simple thing to do. I had to adapt to life in my spirit-body and there was much I had to learn which I have shared with you. Receiving Divine Love, I have never had any difficulty doing, and it is as simple as the Celestial teachers proclaim this to be. The good thing involving progressing in your spirit life is no matter how progressive you become, this doesn't change the simplicity of receiving Divine Love. This is a good thing to know. It could be assumed that the more advanced or elite the soul condition becomes the more complicated or complex being with Divine Love is, but this is not true!

The drama of compensation should not be confused with the ease of the soul receiving Divine Love. Progression should not be confused with the ease of receiving. Having a physical body should not detract from the soul receiving Divine Love. I have enough experience in my spirit life to confirm to you that receiving Divine Love is simple. How I experienced receiving Divine Love in the First Divine Love Sphere is the same as I receive Divine Love in the Celestial Heaven. In my Celestial life, I am simply with more clarity and visibility with how simple it is to receive this Love. Nothing in my Celestial life causes any complication or misunderstanding involving my ability to live and experience Divine Love.

It has been conveyed to you how Divine Love perfects natural love. There is nothing in the natural love living in the soul that causes any distraction to the simplicity of receiving Divine Love. The Divine Love is abundant but in this abundance, never erratic. It is abundant because the Father has made it so. I have conversed with individuals such as Luke and Saleeba about their experience of receiving Divine Love, and their example teaches me how consistent, true and abundant this most reliable source of energy is. They have never changed in all their time living in their spirit life the way they have received the Love. I need to communicate this to you. One could easily misconstrue in physical life the ease of receiving Divine Love by not having any direct visibility of this Divine Love evident in the physical world. I know this, as I was once aware of Divine Love in my physical life but I did not have the clarity that I live with now. If I did have this kind of clarity, I would have made much more of an effort to receive Divine Love and place more providence on this unique gift for my soul.

I will leave you now,
Your friend, James

28

James Reid speaks:

In the last years of my physical life I was aware of Divine Love. I shared in the wonderful area of spirit communications with other people who had similar interests. They know who they are, it was a happy and spirit-inspired time. Of course, I prepared and published the communications I receive. I can recall a terrific amount of enthusiasm that came together very quickly for my received spirit communications to be published. I had received Divine Love but I didn't have that real connection with it that I have now. My progress here in my spirit life is never more evident than when I leave the Celestial Heaven and travel to the First Divine Love Sphere where I interact with individuals beginning their experience living with this Divine Love. It's a service I like to be involved with, assisting individuals at the beginning of an eternal and Immortal soul-life. In the First Divine Love Sphere, I have clear perception and visibility at how my soul-condition has been sufficiently developed by the influence of Divine Love. When you live in the Celestial Heaven spending time in normal soul-life, this Immortal normality becomes constant. When you travel to other spheres, you suddenly realise how changed you have become, how developed your spirit attributes are, and how at-one in love you are with the Father. Comparison is a good thing as it reveals the progressive changes you have made, how effective receiving Divine Love is and how this non-evolving energy causes such dynamic change not possible without its presence. Late in my physical life, I was receiving spirit communication and I was receiving Divine Love but there was never that clear indication that I had changed by receiving Divine Love.

It can be perplexing reading spirit communications, trying to ascertain how a vast array of information brings to light a perspective that culminates in a complete form of the spirit world measuring against our own mortal physical life and its progress in Divine Love. A true statement defining a true form could be stated as: 'life and death and the life of the soul'. Life brings to light our physical mortality, relationships and life experiences. The spirit world exists. For one to reside in the spirit world, mortal death has occurred. Living here in the spirit world, the life of the soul continues and death exists no more in our future. Death forms part of human physical life. This kind of death is not permanent for the soul lives in both lives. The study of life in all its complete form includes the study of the soul. This is never more evident than my understanding having lived here in my spirit life experiencing the emergence of my soul and spirit attributes due to the consequences of receiving the Soul Love of the Father, the Divine Love. I truly understand the teaching of Jesus "I am soul first and foremost".

On another note, I do have imagination. In the discourses I have attended I have found them to be thought-provoking. It is beneficial socialising with those who are well versed in their spirit life as their experience when shared, extends my spirit perception about spirit realities. I am receiving Divine Love, this Love known to me but its origin remains somewhat of a mystery. Receiving Divine Love has perfected my natural love and advanced my soul condition so that I reside here in the Celestial Heaven. The Soul of God remains with less visibility so I try to imagine, utilising my spirit imagination, to gain more experience about the actual existence of this Eternal Originator and Creator. It has been a very good insight for you both to understand the Divine Love as a non-evolving form of energy. This has stimulated your spirit perceptions to gain more sight into the nature of God's Divine Love, how this Love is external to your soul and then acting in its causal action when living in your soul.

Physically you have emotion and feeling, intellect and thought, senses and sensitivity. All these physical attributes contribute to an active physical life but the Divine Love is to its causal existence that isn't any of these physical attributes. Sometimes, as I have received Divine Love I have felt an intense feeling of energy welling within. My spirit attributes become activated, receptive to the energy of Divine Love engaging and infusing my soul. Of course, my natural love being perfect means that the Divine Love I am receiving isn't perfecting my natural love. The Divine Love is sustaining and complimenting that which has already been perfected in its essence and cannot be perfected any more. Which means that my spirit perceptions and attributes are engaging with the Father in a pure experience and exchange of energy for I, in my perfect natural love, am loving the Soul as the Soul is loving me. I can feel the presence of the Acting Spirit as it covers my spirit-body. I have been taught by those advanced Celestial teachers that if I were to cease receiving Divine Love in the Celestial Heaven for any length of time, my soul condition in its perfect natural love would not regress to an imperfect state. The amount of Divine Love I have acquired will sustain me for a long, long time.

What is incredible is the experience of this kind of communication. I know that you have both received shared experiences providing insight into how these communications transpire. I would like to say that from my perspective, I find this experience fascinating.

When I communicate my experience to you the city of Melbourne can be in full sunshine, as it is today, or in full moonlight. The country you reside in always moving as the Earth moves along its axis. When I come through the spheres to convey spirit life experience to you, I am aware that the city you reside in has changed since I last saw it and planet Earth has moved in its orbit around the sun. If I didn't come to see you for three months I would travel through the spheres to be with you knowing that the Earth has changed its position relative to the sun since my last visit. As I stand in that barrier of spirit space that interfaces with your environment I am comfortable. There are no forces imposed upon me that make me feel uncomfortable. My soul condition allows me to remain in my position near your side. When I first arrived in the spirit world I was without that soul condition that would have permitted me to remain as I am now for any length of time. The closer you are in a rapport with the Father's Soul in your soul condition the more comfortable living with all the Father's miracles are! As I stand by your side I am very close to your spirit bodies. You are both together as I communicate my experience to you. I am aware that the Celestial Heaven is at distance from me and that an entire spirit world is happening close-by whilst the Earth moves in its orbit around the sun. If you stop for a minute and consider the geography of my experience, a miracle of creation is at hand regularly. The Father is the originator and supreme Creator in all these spirit affairs. Not even Jesus can originate the existence of an entire spirit world.

    I would like to say that the Divine Love is not a creational energy. It does not create anything. In its existence, the Divine Love isn't creating new life, as in life in solid form or image. What it is doing is contributing to the life of the existing soul, adding to this life-energy that brings what is already resident in the soul to its full potential of love. I have been able to see that life in the Celestial Heaven is a peacefulness that I cannot explain with mere words. This is largely explained by the fact that the Divine Love creates love and nothing else. This means that receiving Divine Love doesn't create any drama that changes or is creative that we can then misunderstand, misinterpret or be confronted by as continuously experiencing too much change. If we were changing all the time as we continued receiving Divine Love, then we would individually remain in a state of flux and this is not loving.

    I have enjoyed this time with you, as I have communicated to you now being more of my spirit-nature and completely in my soul-life.

    Love to you all, James Reid

September

29

Luke speaks:

Various individuals have recently conveyed to you the non-evolving truth about God's Divine Love. I would like to continue expanding on this truth.

The communications that James Padgett received those years ago emphasised the reality that the mortal soul is the true human, that the man or woman is first and foremost, soul. From this truth the natural love and the Divine Love were introduced as living Loves that the soul participates with, the Divine Love being that Love that one participates with when the individual begins to accept this Love into the natural love of their soul. We introduced in our communications to James various themes that remain constant and true even though the ear of the reader may be hearing such truths their first time. Another truth that we identified was the truth about the existence of the spirit body. We introduced the Living Truth that God is Soul.

In these recent communications, we have expanded the teaching on the nature of the Divine Love being non-evolving and not subject to any evolutionary condition that can disturb or interrupt the way the energy of Divine Love interacts external or internal to the mortal soul.

I will clarify here by reconfirming the teaching that when the Divine Love enters the mortal soul and becomes part of that soul-life, God has not caused into existence a Spirit Law that can then actively withdraw that Divine Love back out of that mortal soul. Once you have received the non-evolving form of energy, the Divine Love, this Love will never in all Eternity be removed or be extracted from your mortal soul.

It was in the communications James received that the First Parents, Aman and Amon, introduced themselves to humanity residing on Earth. When you sift through all the information and spirit life experience that has been conveyed to present day that involves the natural and the Divine Love, the two governing forces that define the quintessential truth that bring it all together is the Life of God's Soul and from God's Soul, life has been given to all mortal souls. It really is a story about soul. Once you have arrived in the Celestial Heaven and you participate with the humanity that is aware that it is soul and you see all the individuals aware and living with the Soul, God, then the original story about man is complete.

As you know, I have lived my spirit life a long time now which has included my soul-life being changed by my involvement living with God's Divine Love. I would like to state here that when Jesus lived his life on Earth, other than Jesus himself, there were no other individuals actively participating with their souls receiving Divine Love and progressing through the Spheres to the Celestial Heaven. There were no spirit-humans residing in any of the Spheres that comprise the Celestial Heaven. It has been conveyed to you that the First Parents lived in the Perfect Natural Sphere along with other individuals like Saleeba living in their Perfect Natural love.

It is a good thing to be reminded about the interplay of God with all mortals and the timing of the available gift that the Divine Love is for all mortal souls. We have conveyed a lot of information with true spirit vision detailing the time when Divine Love was available and then not available, then available again throughout the communications and teachings about the Divine Love that you both, as well as James have received. I can assure you that such truth relating to the Divine Love has not been humanly, intellectually contrived. Your own physical experience when your soul receiving Divine Love is the confirmation that such a form of energy exists. We have simply expanded the vision of this compelling non-evolving form of energy that God has established as being part of universal experience.

I will state with all certainty that God, our Loving Eternal Father, was aware of the planet Earth long before humans were established on the Earth. The human is defined by having the attribute of soul and spirit body. Those of us residing in the Celestial Heaven know this truth, the truth that identifies what it is to be human. We have confirmed to you, and I will say that every spirit communication you have received is a form of living confirmation about the life of the soul, that the soul exists and is formed by God. If all humans are human by having received an incarnating attribute of soul, an attribute caused into existence by God, then God knew when and where to incarnate souls that began populating the planet Earth. When you look at life from God's eternal perspective, the planet Earth and its established evolution was known by God as being a suitable environment for souls to individualise and receive a spirit body that would then be fit to continue living in a spirit world and on into the progressive universal Spheres of spirit. There was nothing chaotic, random or untimely about the beginning of man. This is all about understanding the timing and life of the human soul. If you only look at humans from a physical origin without ever understanding the life of the soul, then only a singular perspective will be revealed to you. Here in the Celestial Heaven, we understand human life to be the life of the whole journey of the soul, therefore, our perspective envelops many aspects that contribute toward the life of the soul being complete and fulfilled. The physical attribute is only one aspect of this human completeness. This information will change your perspective about God. Suddenly, you may realise that God knows the planet Earth very well! So well in fact that God knew that this planet was evolving toward a time when humans could be sustained by the generating process of forming souls and incarnating souls, of forming spirit bodies that would ensure the survival of the soul once it leaves the physical human life behind. If the people of the Earth today understood that life is soul, then a more complete perspective about God would follow and the world, the worldwide human awareness, would live without any doubt as to whether there existed a human afterlife. Knowing about the Divine Love changes everything within the individual. There are individuals living their natural spirit life currently living without their active participation through receiving the Divine Love. They have adapted to the experience of their natural spirit life. They know they have survived physical death and that their life has exceeded the small boundary of their small intellect and limited beliefs. These individuals, while residing in the spirit world, live their life with their potential waiting to be realised for the life of their soul still remains dormant. The reason why you have been able to receive so much spirit life experience from us over the years is only due to the fact that those who have communicated to you are living with Divine Love and the life of their soul is active and full of life. These individuals are aware of the world of spirit in which they have lived and have progressed through in their natural love being perfected in sight of the Glory of God.

    I have really enjoyed speaking and sharing experience and vision again.

    With my love, Luke

October

30

Luke speaks:

When the reader reads through the communications James Padgett received and then reads through the communications that you have both received, the reader is subject to a vast amount of information provided by many individuals and contrasting personalities who are living here in their spirit life. Within these communications are experiences that are broad in their reach and substantial in the substance of the communication. The reader is receiving vast amounts of information that detail so much spirit life experience all in one place at one time when the reader's experience of actually receiving Divine Love has been limited. This means that the reader is being introduced to truths, spirit truths, that may exceed the soul condition of the reader to perceive the living existence of these spirit truths.

Here in the spirit world, the individual who is being introduced to the existence of Divine Love will be introduced to Celestial spirits who are living advanced soul conditions and who understand the many related Fatherly Spirit Truths that relate with advancing soul condition. The reader will find it a rare opportunity to be exposed to so much new information all in one place at one time about a Divine Love that exists and reveals all there is to reveal about the life of the human soul and the full extent of human nature. We understand there can be much confusion between people relating to the spirit truths due to the differing soul conditions and preexisting mortal beliefs that define the essential attributes of the individual.

The primary difference between your experience and the experience here when beginning with Divine Love is that the individual here in the First Divine Love Sphere is able to see the evidence of the Living Divine Love in the individuals moving among them - such as me - that provides living confirmation that what they are being introduced to is living proof that the Soul, God exists, that the Divine Love is real and that all that is to follow is a fact of spirit life that fulfils the natural potential of the natural love in their soul. The beauty of your experience, having read our communications, is that you are able to experience the Divine Love in your physical life and to utilise your soul perceptions to see how we live here in the spirit world with Divine Love in the essence of the communications that we have all brought forward.

Everlasting

As you receive Divine Love and accept your faith wholeheartedly in the Living Soul, God, over time certain spirit truths may become so palpable to you that the reality of spirit and the existence of the spirit world may become more absolute than the temporary forces of your physical human life. It will also become evident as time passes, how dormant most other human souls in your physical landscape are. Remember, you are soul and the Divine Love is specifically for your soul. The Divine Love is so real that if you continue to receive this Love your own perceptions about your truthful soul nature will emerge with certain visibility. This will result in your own ability to see with mirrored exactness how by living your soul life you are in contrast to the apparent dormancy of those around you for active participation with Divine Love is non-present in other peoples lives. I am required to speak this truth as individuals who will set their life course in the pursuit of real spirit progress and to do this requires the Divine Love. These individuals will set their soul to the Soul of God and commit their time and love receiving Divine Love and expansively progressing toward the perfection of their natural love in their physical life. These individuals require all the sustenance and nourishment that we can provide that involves living the Immortal life as it will not be forthcoming from those who are unaware that such spirit truths and the Divine Love exist.

There is change coming soon that will set a new motion among humanity. The natural world of men and women will experience a global event that will compress humanity into the dynamic of contraction and then expansion as this change occurs. Humanity is unprepared and unsuspecting of this global rationalisation.

I will return soon,

Everlastingly with Divine Love, Luke

31

Hello; my name is Jan. I died in 1974. Once I had adapted to my spirit life, which included realising that I had survived death and that a human afterlife existed, I have lived comfortably in my spirit life. Everything I experienced here was brand new. I had never thought about what happens after you die and to be frank, I didn't care about what happens after you die. I was living my human physical life with all the freedom that I could live as my passion was riding motorbikes. Needless to say, I was involved in an accident which I didn't cause, but resulted in my death. I was a free spirit so-to-speak. It's quite amusing that such expressions like 'living like a free spirit' are quite commonly known on Earth then suddenly you find yourself being a spirit! I lived a long time here feeling very resentful that my life ended by the careless and reckless actions of another. I loved my life and lived it to the max. I was a motorcycle mechanic and travelled, or I should say, I enjoyed the ride across the United States of America finding work where I could repair bikes and then I would ride on. I liked travelling and for me, it was all about the ride.

I was a strong individual, reliable and independent. I was an individual never joining any other group of riders. It was a different day back then where everything that I lived felt like an open road with all the music and the dramas going on in the world. I did feel that I was on a spiritual journey of some sorts and the landscape was my friend with all its tremendous energy. I was 34 when I passed over. As I said, I resented the way my life ended. I found it hard to come to terms with the way it ended as I was a responsible citizen on the road obeying the laws. I wasn't about speed on the road - I was about the ride.

For those who find themselves here by the reckless hand of another, it can take time to accept this irresponsible consequence. The main reason why I am saying this is entirely due to the fact that when you are here it becomes apparent, quite quickly, that life here is permanent. As time goes by you not only sense or feel this, but you see this truth. You see it in the face of those you meet who have been living here for thousands of years. What you don't see are individuals that you have met suddenly disappearing due to the fact that they are reincarnating into another human life. From my perspective, that belief is entirely contrived and only remains a belief in the minds of people living on the Earth.

It took me quite some time to come around to an acceptance of my living and accepting my soul-life with God. Had you been receiving these communications in the 80's I would not have been able to teach you anything or provide you with anything involving living with and being aware of the Divine Love. I live with this Love now. I made my choice late 1989 to be involved. My reason for this that I could see that it was the only form of involvement for me to progress beyond my condition. The idea of staying as I was, where I was, didn't suit me and quite frankly I had met too many individuals who were examples of what I could become if I started receiving this Divine Love in the spirit world. I only learnt about my natural love by receiving the Divine Love. If I had never received Divine Love I would never have known about the attribute of my natural love in my soul. In the sphere I lived in before I received Divine Love, no one knew about perfect natural love as being soul related and the fact of it was that no one could teach the real truths about being soul. This is not a statement that forms a judgement about the people in the natural spheres but rather an observed truth involving the soul-life and how real it is when you become aware that you are soul and the life of your soul that you can live. It is clear to me that only by receiving Divine Love can you actually identify the real soul-life. It has been conveyed to you that the Divine Love is non-evolving. This is true. What I would like to say here is that whilst the Divine Love is non-evolving, it is loving! Non-evolving doesn't infer or mean in action, non-loving.

I will stop now. I thank you and for those who know about bikes, I rode an Indian.

32

Hello; my name is Tessa. When I lived as a woman in the 1990s, at the age of 35 all I wanted to be was a man. I had lived with these feelings all my adult life. I never had the complete gender change but the way I looked compared with the way I felt, I was estranged to myself. I had thought a lot about the transgender condition, but I remained a woman and it was with other women that I formed my personal relationships. I have met many people here living their spirit life who had lived their human life with sexual differences and somewhat challenging circumstances. When I began receiving Divine Love my true nature of soul emerged. What I realised was that I was no longer participating in my own life as a singular personality. I was no longer acting in my spirit life with any physical influences. In my spirit body, I was a personality living a feminine spirit life. What I couldn't do was live in the spirit sphere I was living, being a feminine spirit but desiring to be a male spirit. There are exacting things here relating to the spirit body which we have no control over. There are so many things that people of the Earth experience that become redundant here due to the Spirit Laws that exact the spirit body. I found my way to accepting my soul and peacefulness came to me. I began receiving the Divine Love and progressed in my soul condition to the fulfilment of my perfect natural love which developed all my personality attributes and now my life in the Celestial Heaven is a portrait of the most beautiful feminine human spirit that in my essence and personality I could become.

Life has many portraits. So loving is the Soul of God and so different is the physical human life with the human spirit life, that in my knowledge about living love and being a soul, and even when I lived my human life in the dichotomy of my sexuality, I was still a soul and a soul quite capable of receiving Divine Love. You do not have to be in perfect natural love in your physical life to begin receiving Divine Love. You just begin accepting this Love where you find your life has arrived you at. If you are lucky enough to know that such a Love is present for your soul to receive as not all the earthly human world knows that such a gift available. Loving is truly individual and universal and the Divine Love fits both these causes perfectly.

Much love and thank you, Tessa

33

Hello; my name is Robert. My experience that defines my perception about the spirit world I reside in can be described by a single word: enormous! I was an adventurer in my human life spending time travelling the world climbing the highest mountain ranges, traversing great valleys and plains and exploring the largest river systems. I also spent time at the South Pole in the Antarctic region. I loved everything about the outdoors, travelling, being in the wilderness where man was shaped by the natural forces of the planet. I liked being on the edge and had come close to death many times. There are many like me, liking the edge where you feel connected with your physical attributes and nature in a way that transcends ordinary life. Strangely enough, it wasn't living on the edge that took me into my spirit life. I died from an unknown heart condition which had never been diagnosed. It happened quickly and without warning. I adapted easily to this new edge. I had in my human life, time to think about things when stuck on mountains unable to move when the weather closed in. I always felt there was more to life. This partly explains why I never feared death and why I could take myself to extremes functioning perfectly normal in such extreme and adverse conditions. The more extreme it became, the calmer I became; the closer I felt my core connect with nature, the more clarity I had about the true and beautiful gift a human life is.

Everlasting

In my spirit life, once things had been explained to me about living here, I kind of knew that this was how it is … there was nothing abstract about this new life, nothing taught to me by strangers with an agenda. I realised very quickly that my entrance, my passage into this adventure, was limited in my experience but those kind and loving souls teaching me about this new way of living were very calm, loving and resolved.

As I adapted to my life here, as you can well imagine, I had developed a good relationship with my physical attributes. Now I was setting about establishing with the same intent, a good relationship with my spirit attributes defined as my spirit body. I wanted to explore this environment and I knew that I had to develop a better rapport with this spirit body of mine. It was explained to me how vast God's spirit world is, and that to reach all boundaries of each sphere and to continue on beyond these natural spheres I needed to acquire the Divine Love to do so. Learning about the Divine Love and Its existence was a whole new thing for me to learn about. This would become the atlas and geography of my soul and spirit attributes. I thought to myself, 'Okay, the Divine Love is oxygen for my soul'! There is no oxygen in the spirit world but I found a great resource of skills from my adventuristic human life that I could apply to all the new information I was being exposed to.

When you spend time high in the mountains in what could be called solitary altitude, it has been mentioned that you can feel close to God. Standing on the highest peaks reveals the awe of creation as you look at surfaces extending out beneath your feet into that vast horizon. I met men and women who had experienced the 'creation touch' and yes, I would have to say that we were all soulful humans. I know that you are both aware of the Divine Love and have been so for quite some time now. I have been observing how these communications are unfolding, I had hoped to participate, to contribute that may inspire another to understand the gift that the Divine Love is for the human soul. There are many gifts, some of which I climbed and walked upon and admired with universal beauty. Here in my spirit life the enormity of the spirit world, how it is formed and where it is placed in context with planet Earth, simply engages that horizon that makes the spirit within oneself rather quiet. I am very happy. I love my life and I loved my human life. I am one of those souls who simply lived a terrific human life. I had no compensation, my parents were lovely, my brothers and sisters were empathetic people and I met so many diverse people around the planet Earth that showed me what unconditional love means in the living.

Sometimes families who were very poor would give me shelter and were generous and kind as I was in return. In my progression of my soul condition, I liked the idea about perfect natural love. I liked it even more that this idea is the mountain of love that I ascended by receiving the oxygen of Divine Love into my soul. I have been to all the natural spheres now so I have seen the enormity of these environments and the humanity that resides in all conditions of soul in these unique spheres.

When you are standing alone on the mountains, you are aware that you are involved with a planet that has different landscapes and seascapes but you are involved with a singular planet. Here, you can be in a sphere knowing that there are entire spheres existing in their spirit space and time, with humanity living in these spheres that have never walked planet Earth. Here, if your soul condition is good you can go to all the spirit life. You can walk through all the spheres. I reside in the Celestial Heaven. I am aware that I cannot proceed to another sphere and walk that sphere until my soul condition and spirit attributes are in that condition that permits me to do so. I have been able to walk through all the spheres to where I am now. My love of God is unsurpassed by any other image. I feel God's Divine Love strongly in my soul as I continue to explore the enormity of these places and the humanity that reside in these places knowing that a lot of these individuals have lived here a very long time.

In my spirit life, I have enjoyed conversing with individuals who were the explorers, the early explorers. As a child, I was fascinated when hearing about their explorations when seeing documentaries on TV; I liked looking at the globe. Looking at the globe of the planet Earth that I had in my bedroom took my imagination to the reaches of the planet. I would dream about going to all these places. In the Celestial Heaven, there are maps that display constructs of the known spirit worlds. I can't put into words exactly how these forms of energy are made to display geographical locations, but there are spirit maps so that we have a dimensional reference to the entire mortal spirit world with other existing spirit domains that exist beyond the Celestial Heaven. I have been informed by Luke that certain individuals who live beyond the Celestial Heaven have communicated to you before. My immediate aim is to leave the Celestial Heaven and begin my exploration of these spirit spheres. The First Parents know their way around and I am looking forward to receiving their guidance. At the centre of these spirit maps is the central recognition of the existing Soul, God. In earthly maps, the sun is at the centre of our local universe. Here, the Celestial Heaven isn't at the centre of these spirit maps. It is an extraordinary thing to see for here such spirit maps are formed from living spirit energy that makes spirit material so everything is living which is unique in itself! I wish I could explain more but I don't have the vocabulary to identify how some of these things are at their intrinsic fundamental existence. There are those who know about these things.

I never left a footprint behind in my life. I respected nature and now I am leaving behind my loving print. Thank you very much. R

34

Samuels speaks:

I am with you again. I have been present when each received communication has taken place in this collective spirit work. I am very interested in seeing how this experience transpires as I have never participated from the beginning of a spirit work you have both received. In the past experiences, I would join you and then leave, or I would stay for a while and observe the experience. I am happy with the progress and the information conveyed as it broadens the experience of soul-life.

I wish to convey the teaching about God's Divine Love being unconditional. Over the time that you have both been receiving spirit communications just about each individual is living with some capacity of soul condition by having received Divine Love. There has been a reason for this, to convey as much experience as possible about living with Divine Love so that another my draw inspiration from these shared experiences and derive confirmation and confidence in their experience as there is so little that is evident among the peoples of the Earth as so few are aware of Divine Love and the Immortal Life it brings to the soul. For those of us living in our spirit life involved with this Love, over time it becomes palpable to our spirit senses that there is no shadow at all involving our spirit life. The unconditional nature of the Father's Love is never more evident than in the fact that when residing in the spirit world you do not have to participate with this Divine Love. This is a good truth to be reminded of as it provides the example of how loving Our Father is, and that such a gift is never enforced upon us to be received that then guarantees a true life in the human afterlife. Every single individual who has shared with you their involvement living with the Divine Love has chosen to become involved, freely and independently. It is a very good confirmation to be reminded of this as it situates our individual experience as always being independent.

So much spirit truth has been conveyed to you but this must not be confused with situating the Father's Divine Love as a conditional experience and one where the individual may feel a lack of independence. The existence of Fatherly Spirit Truths is conditional because *they exist* formed with an existence that has not been mortally created or established. The truth that we have taught you about the Divine Love being non-evolving is a truth, a conditional truth but only conditional in the way that the Father has given form to this energy of Love so that It remains consistent for all Eternity and that it doesn't change Its form when entering our souls. It would be a confusing time for us to experience such soulful change from a form of energy that itself were to continuously change. So you see, there are many conditional truths that the Father has established that will never change in all Eternity but this must not be confused with the experience of living with Divine Love that results in the loss of the individual's independence.

Some individuals reside in their natural spirit life who have remained in their soul condition of natural love a long time since they passed into the spirit world. These individuals in their good condition of natural love live good harmonious happy social spirit lives without participating with Divine Love. All the individuals that you have received are living with Divine Love for they have made a choice to progress independently their soul condition and to advance through the spirit domain toward a more active, living soulful life.

You must never feel put upon by yourself or another to receive Divine Love. Receiving Divine Love should be participation in which you are involved because you like to be involved and you love what you are gradually being involved with. I could point out vast array of social human experiences where people feel put out or unfulfilled, or a life that has been wronged by one thing or another. Divine Love isn't emotional. It is a pure form of energy that is soothing for the soul. It has been conveyed to you that it is a balm for the soul. In fact, being aware of the availability of the Divine Love is a gift for the exacting reason that to have a complimentary gift that is so easily acquired is a benefit and a resource for the individual. What you see here in the spirit world are individuals from all kinds of human experiences having received the gift of Divine Love then celebrate how easily it is to receive this Love and what a benefit to their soul and spirit life. For you there and for us here, what I teach you is the same regarding the Divine Love for individuals who would like to experience participating with a little gift of Eternity.

Thank you for this loving exchange. D. Samuels

35

Luke speaks:

Some are fascinated by the reality of an existing spirit world. Some of these individuals aspire in their interest to have clarified realities involving the spirit world. We know that there are many names given to the spirit world with cultures throughout humankind identifying their relationship with the spirit world. Human civilisations in ages past have given their name to the identity of an existing spirit world. The afterlife is a common term identifying an existing life after human life. Some have come into contact with communications conveyed by individuals residing in the spirit world. There are many individuals who fear the existence of a human afterlife or existing spirit world. From our position, the widespread humanity that resides here is so true that we can see and intermingle with all that the Father has created. So is the history of humanity that has lived their life on Earth that precedes those living on the face of the Earth this day. We see and participate with the amount of humanity that God has established with love by creating and incarnating the attribute of soul into each physical human life.

It is understandable why people may live in fear of an existing afterlife, for it represents a time of change, an ending to a mortal existence that generally includes emotional love with loving relationships. Most people living today have goodness in their hearts and have formed personalised relationships that represent family that extends into deep mutual belonging. From our perspective here, there is much goodness in the world today. From your perspective, you may hear or see such acts of fear that may cause you to doubt any existing goodness in the heart of humankind, but this is not true. With each passing day as the world of people realises its worldwide humanity, natural love in its living goodness in empathetic souls is reaching other people and being felt and seen in living action with greater abundance. In the communications James Padgett received, we introduced the teaching involving soul-life as having its attribute of soul-life in natural love. Humankind has always lived in its attribute of natural love. As the human world becomes more aware of its interconnectedness the attribute of natural love is reaching toward greater visibility especially as the younger generations desire to thrive in an interconnected world community. The younger generations are aspiring toward liberty, their independence, peace and a clean world. We are not blind here in the spirit world. We know that there are places among the peoples of the world that still choose to promote fear which results in isolation and smallness of cultural worldly action. We know everything human-world today. We know because we attend to all the souls transitioning into their spirit life. The Celestial spirits are ever present attending to the integration of humanity that leaves the shore of planet Earth and begins their adaption to their life here. I realise how wonderful and good a physical life is. I know how the individual may believe how much they matter in their own life and how much one loves their life. Endings can represent the impending unknown…

The teaching of natural love conveyed by us in the messages James Padgett received is good love. You have both received further teachings that identify why this love is good love and how it forms the foundation of humankind. We have taught you where this natural love comes from, for we have taught you where the attribute of each individual soul originates from prior to its incarnation. You must understand that this natural love is not a mere shadow in the soul. The attribute of soul and the essence of this natural living love in it is an energy that has been directly formed, created and generated by the Eternal Creator, God. This natural love is robust, tactile and soulful. There have been tremendous outpourings of this natural love in times of modern-day living. There are empathetic souls all around the world today, touching another's soulfulness and assessing these individuals who may be too meek and weak within themselves to stand on their own two feet. There are so many people who aspire toward a greater human potential that can be realised among the living. Positive affirmations are circulating the planet which assist toward a certain comfort and a belief in the goodness of the worldly and universality of man.

So many individuals have arrived to begin their spirit life with the words indelibly marked in their souls, 'if only'.

Many of you will believe in the existence of goodness in the human heart. Many of you worldwide will believe in humanity for you will be participating with the incredible creations that your fellow humanity has generated toward a better quality of life. Many of you will not like fear or to be controlled or manipulated by fear. In my words here I wish to convey that there are many of you who believe in the existence of your human soul, that love rules the world, that you have empathy for your fellow friend or unknown friend, that you will believe in God or whatever a greater Creative Soul represents in name or form, and, that a human afterlife exists. Most of you will not see in full sight the nature of God's Spirit World and how we live here until you arrive here. Most of your beliefs that I have identified are beliefs without sight and delineation but you may feel such truth to exist in your beliefs. In a universal language, this is the beginning of a faith hewed out in the natural goodness of the natural love in your soul. The Divine Love compliments this goodness and reinforces with Its Grace, that feeling that love in living action *is* good. My words are to bring comfort and support toward goodness for the Light of God can never be extinguished in all Eternity.

Everlasting with Divine Love, Luke

36

Samuels speaks:

I have observed there are times when the Celestial teachers speak living Spirit of Truth that reverberates throughout the realm. I wish to add that there will never be a material Kingdom of God built or established on Earth or in the spirit world. The soul is organic, living and a beautiful life-force existing within each individual. This is never more evident than seeing how individuals progress in their soul condition here as their natural love realises its fullness by having the Divine Love compliment it. The truth of it is, why there will never be a 'kingdom' relates directly to the fact that there will never be a kingdom established by using God's Divine Love. The Celestial Heaven is not a kingdom built and established solely by Immortal spirits. It has been taught to you that the Father of the Eternal has engaged specific Spirit Laws and nutrients to establish the spheres that are the environments that humans live in that comprise the spirit world. This is true. Living here reveals to us how of the soul and spirit we are, and that there exists no kingdom within us, only the organic nature of our soul-life. I do know how difficult it is for you to perceive the actual living energy of your own soul-life when clothed in the physical being of your body. But, soul we are and will always be.

It has been taught to you that the Divine Love is specifically for your soul. I will confirm this to you again, as it can be that one can forget this and be easily mislead into thinking or believing that the Divine Love is for everything and in everything. When you reside in the spirit life what you are clearly introduced to is the living reality of how particular the Divine Love is for only soul-life.

There is no natural selection in the mortal spirit world. The organic spirit environments do not control the human residing in these environments insofar as humans on the Earth have an organic predisposition toward the energy of the sun and other planetary influences that may determine certain survival outcomes. It is quite simple. No sun = no life on planet Earth that humans can survive. Here in the spirit world the light source is Eternal and will never dim or cease to exist. It is quite incredible when you consider how extraordinary the human afterlife is, insofar as being exposed to the creation that makes up the spirit world and yet the only real way to fully participate with it, is by allowing - with love - your soul to develop by receiving this beautiful gift that is freely available for us to receive. If there is any form of selection that exists in the spirit world, it is that choice to accept that you are soul and to lovingly begin accepting the Living Divine Love into your soul. This begins your progress toward the fullness of your potential. There has been a lot of energy coming forward from Luke and other individuals present, so we will withdraw now until we meet again.

D. Samuels

37

Hello; my name is Rudolph Steiner. As I speak to you, you can hear my English word spoken with my Austrian accent. My desire is not to convey to you anything that will change the contributions that I made and established in my human life, but to confirm that I am living my soul-life, which has become fulfilled with my acceptance of the Father's Divine Love.

I am aware of how much information you have both received that involves the soul-life and the formation of the spirit world along with personal experiences conveyed by loving spirits. I will say that my participation in my spirit life with Divine Love provided that part of life that completed the fulfilment of my understanding about the nature of the human soul. In my progression toward the Celestial Heaven that happened a while ago, the reality of my soul became intrinsic so that I could identify this next part of my life brought about by receiving Divine Love. I will never reincarnate from this spirit world that I reside in for the Immortality that I live with all the time and the Spirit Laws that God has established that ensure the harmony of all the spirit world sustains life here. My spirit life is permanent. It is permanent for all of us. Like so many individuals, I arrived to begin my spirit life with my particular beliefs, some of which dissolved instantly. My belief in the existence of the human soul remained even though the reality of soul, or the life of the soul as I understood it to be in my human life, differs now.

Here, you are simply exposed to truths that have real transparency. Many individuals who are living in Divine Love are well versed with soul-life so that any misunderstanding about the nature of soul has quickly vanished. It is so much easier here!

On Earth in physical life, you can have the belief that you will reincarnate after you have died and that this process forms part of human existence. I can tell you with complete authority that no human incarnates from this spirit world back into physical human life. The truthful word here is 'incarnate'. Once you understand the true nature of the soul and spirit body and how the individual personality resides here in soul and spirit body, it is clear that the soul only ever incarnates once, which is at the inception of human life. My soul will never again incarnate so that my personality becomes part of a physical forming body again. It is so easy for me to speak like this for this is how I live. I live all the time in the progressive clarity of spirit-living truths. So many of us do. Physical human life is diversity with belief. This is social liberty and human wonderment to live with beliefs. Here, it all changes. It doesn't change due to other individuals forcing us to change to their beliefs. Life changes here due to the whole fabric of life being entirely different from what is established socially on Earth. When I spoke to you about the Immortality of my soul, this is not a belief created by myself or that I believe in another spirit's belief, it is a truth! A truth that is living due to the Divine Love that is living. When you partake of this Love it becomes part of your soulful nature. It is with absolute clarity that this Divine Love does not originate in the souls of mortals. We have clear spirit-vision about this. We know this Love to originate from the Soul of God and we - by partaking of this Love - experience how it changes our soul condition. We clearly see how our experience benefits by having this Love in our life. There is not enough that can be said about how significant this Divine Love is in the life of a spirit.

Everlasting

The truest teaching I can convey in my life as a spirit involves God. I have learnt so much about physical human life now that I have lived so much of my spirit life; I can include God in this narrative. I did not establish my connectivity with God based solely on my own research on the human condition. I was introduced to God by those already well established in their soul-life progressing in Divine Love. This brings a certain humility to one's life. This is how it is here. No spirit exceeds God and no spirit exceeds the spirit world. Everyone living with Divine Love celebrates what it is that they have come to know by another who has come to know by another, and such knowledge begins with the Father and was revealed to Jesus by the Father. It is really simple. When you know a truth and accept its form here, all the anxiety that comes from certain beliefs leaves. Because we know about the Divine Love, where It is from and how It functions in our soul-life, we, in our acceptance live without unknowing. There is so much in a physical human life that involves unknowing, which is a certain true condition of being human, that it can hardly be believed that one may ever live without unknowing! In my spirit life, there is so much knowing that I have had to grow to accommodate so much knowing. This is a reversal from my physical life. Living with the Divine Love becomes such a palpable reality with personal and intimate knowledge, that it is without question as to its existence. It would be different if there were only a handful of individuals here aware of this Love and proclaiming its existence - and you could not see in these individuals any difference between their spirit condition with your own condition - but you do! You are introduced to the proof that the Divine Love exists from those who are teaching about Its existence as you can see that these individuals differ to your own condition and are teaching their way of living with this Love that is consistent with everyone else that you see living happily in this Love. If one were to receive such spirit beliefs from only a few spirits, one could be cautious as to the whereabouts that such knowledge has come from. When you see the vast humanity living in this Love from all diverse human cultures and generations past, there is no question.

Like many individuals, I crossed over and having adapted to this change of life environments, I was introduced to the vast humanity thriving in their life here in the spirit world. A large part of this humanity living with this Divine Love forming the way of their life. I went from not knowing anything about living the Immortal soul-life into experiencing the Divine Love for myself with my soul partaking of the Divine Love that gave my soul, and consequently myself, the real Immortality. Everything was new. I had no prior experience or knowledge of the Father's Divine Love during my physical life. All of this came in my spirit life. I cannot comment on the Divine Love as experienced in my physical life, as I was unaware of this Love and how pertinent it was to my soul and the repercussions that this Love would have. Like so many individuals living their spirit life, living with Divine Love begins in their spirit life, which means that all our experience is derived from spirit-related experiences and not from physically lived experiences involving this unique Love and form of energy.

I have tried to imagine how it would have been if I had known all that I know now when living my physical life. I have concluded that it would have been a different human life because I would have lived aware of a form of energy that brought about substantial change to the condition of my soul exposing me to a greater human awareness that I alone could not have provided for myself. Some of you are living with this awareness and understanding how significant this Divine Love is and the consequences it has to your soul-life that are, to say, far-reaching!

In my spirit life, I have been far more interested understanding the nature of God as my principal interest. In physical life, God is that image, or who and what that image means to people the world over, throughout history and always present day. Never at any one given time can the collective face of humanity agree on who and what God is in the physical world of men and women. Over here, this is entirely different. There is such vast humanity living so lovingly in the Divine Love of God that we are all irrefutable in our knowing who and what God is. We know that God is Soul and we understand that we are living in our attribute of soul that God has given life to, which is the very essence of the unique individual, us. There is no selective process here as one personality being more favoured than another personality. The going here is our collective knowing the importance of our own soul-life, that receiving and accepting the non-evolving Divine Love fulfils our unique essence of natural love furthering our capacity to love the Soul, God and each other.

Living here in Divine Love changes the perspective of mortal life. There is the wonderment of the spirit world this has been identified to you by other individuals. It is incredible as there are different layers in this spirit world that one can travel through seeing the humanity that resides in these spheres. There are those places where the humanity residing is still yet to individually participate with the Divine Love having yet to make that choice. Then there are the places where I live, where humanity is thriving, individually advancing toward more of their spirit life being realised.

In my human life, the idea of personalising a relationship with God was an idea that lay beyond me. In fact, such an idea would have seemed foreign to me. I understand that a personal faith or a belief can begin the process of individualisation with personalisation of God beginning to happen. But everything changes when you know that you can receive into your soul the Divine Love that is living and is part - or forms part - of the personality of the Loving Soul-Spirit Father. The catalyst for change as I have experienced is of all things ... love. This is the outcome of my life and the knowledge that I wish to impart here. The catalyst of change for me was in part the existing spirit world that I became part of it, but the real active change came from my awareness that I could participate with this connecting form of energy that would reveal who and what God was to me.

Being the spirit I am, my soul is in perfect natural love. My life has changed. I am one among many living and celebrating in the true Immortality of my soul-life that the Divine Love brings.

Thank you for this opportunity to speak. Rudolph

38

Elias speaks:

I will confirm that you will not receive communication in any form from any individual residing in the lowest sphere who are in a depraved condition of being. I mean depraved by the individual being in that condition of soul that is the poorest condition in natural love a soul can be. There is no point for such communication to transpire between an individual in this condition with you both, as the individual will not be able to perceive the love necessary for the Father's Spirit Law of Rapport and Communication to be activated.

The truth of this Law requires love to be present; a good condition of love present in the souls communicating brings this Law to its activity. This Law can act when individuals are communicating from the spirit world and when only in their natural love without any Divine Love involved. In other words, an individual living in the soul condition of good natural love can convey experience and information to a medium who is also of service in a good condition of their natural love. The Father's Spirit Law which I am speaking of can only be activated between souls living love. There have been plenty of mediums with good natural love receiving messages from individuals residing here, who are living solely in their soul condition of natural love. This Spirit Law is not exclusive in its operation and activity between souls who are only living with the inclusion of the Divine Love. All the Father's Spirit Laws act when love is involved.

The most depraved humans living in their spirit life are unaware that any such Spirit Laws exist. Their soul condition is so poor they cannot perceive the existence of such Laws and are unable to interact with any Spirit Laws barely recognising that anything exists beyond their own isolated personality. They continue to survive even though their natural soul condition disharmonious to everything else that establishes the mortal spirit world, yet the Father's Spirit Laws exist in love, hence they sustain the survival of these spirits. I have reconfirmed this truth to you so in the future for the reader there will not be any misunderstanding about who and what is communicating from the spirit world. Only love bridges us here with you there in terms of spirit communication. If you are unable to accept this truth, then you are unable to accept the Father's Handiworks as establishing harmony between the spirit spheres in the spirit world and the earthly world.

We cannot alter how the Father's Spirit Laws work. We can't manipulate them. They are beyond mortal tampering. If you cannot accept the Spirit Laws, like the Spirit Law of Rapport and Communication from your human perspective, you are effectively nullifying the existence of such Handiworks and ultimately denying the Love of the Father. Everything that involves mortal natural love and Immortal soul condition involving the Divine Love is love. This is what we are all to learn and to live independently and individually.

I have been bold in my words to you. I have not coloured this teaching as it is of the utmost importance that the humble reader feels protected and not obscured by all the beliefs about what can communicate and the fear that can be generated in the human life when receiving from the unseen and unknown face.

Your friend and teacher, Elias

39

Hello; my name is Louise. I have been living in this life for several years now. I crossed over in my mid-twenties; it was an unfortunate accident. One moment I was thriving in my human life, the next moment through a careless action my spirit life began. It took me quite some time to adjust to this change. I felt sad for a long time, for I realised that my human life was incomplete. I held many hopes for my future, none of which happened.

I received much support at the beginning of my life here, I was never unloved. It took me quite some time to adapt. I had never really taken any time to think about what happens when your human life is over. I thought I was going to live a long life. I came from a good background, a loving family with lots of opportunities. To this day, I can always remember my intuition telling me not to step into the car with my friend who was unfit to drive due to being drunk.

I have made new friends here. I have a social life, I am busy being social and reasonably happy. I know that my friends and family are still at home in the country I lived and they miss me as I miss them. I haven't made the change that other individuals have spoken about to both of you. I have been encouraged to share, which I feel good about. I still feel young. This is a vast place. I haven't travelled too far, staying close to where I live. Socially my friends and I, that are about the same age, still speak about the things we liked doing in our physical life. We laugh about the things that we did and the times we spent with our friends. We are aware of what is happening in our social circles on Earth as we are modern and contemporary. We still feel that we don't want to miss out on anything. We all know that change has happened. It still feels a little strange being social here knowing that we have all had to die to be here. I wasn't the most intelligent person on Earth but I had a fair idea about fashion and things that a young woman would know about in the place that I called home. Home is where the heart is, as they say. I still feel that my home is with my family on Earth. I have settled here but a large part of my heart with my memories misses what is no longer. The change that has happened to those I have observed speaking to you is a bit overwhelming for me to make. I just can't at the moment embrace my living with God. I lived a free and happy life. I still feel free and happy but to embrace my living with God at this time is something that I don't want to be involved with. Most of my new friends feel the same. I think that this has got more to do with my feeling that I would be making a change, which means moving on from my connection in my heart with my loved ones on Earth. I am not judged nor am I ever put upon to make this change. I have seen those living that differ from me, they have said that there is no hurry or that I must change now.

I will stop now but before I go, I just want to say thank you and a big hug to those who have encouraged me to share a little with you. Louise

40

Hello; my name is Gregory. Many years ago, I got in trouble in the surf. I was a strong capable swimmer. I had lived by the sea all my life; I grew up swimming in the surf and open water.

One fine summer's morning I went out on my own, but for some reason I cramped in my leg which was unexpected and painful. I was in the waves and I took a few mouthfuls of water, which then started my fight for life. It was an isolated beach that I had run to as part of my fitness regime. I lived in the 1930s. Beneath the sea, I heard the waves crashing about but then came a peaceful silence. I thought that I had died. I heard a voice speak to me telling me that everything would be alright and to make one last effort toward shore. I did this eventually hauling myself into the shallows utterly exhausted. I thought about this experience over the coming days, realising that I had lived through a near-death experience. Needless to say, I continued swimming but limited the distance of my running before I swam. I thought about that voice wondering if a voice from beyond had saved my life. For the rest of my life, I never doubted the existence of things that I couldn't explain. I was a practical functional man but this experience in the sea that day shook me to my core. I always respected my capabilities with the sea from that day forward.

When my life ended from natural ageing, I came to the world that I had sensed under the sea that day. I was greeted when I awakened by that same loving voice. It was my grandmother. She had been a terrific woman in her life, a stoic individual. I always liked her and like me, she always had swum in the sea. We were lovers of the sea. I adapted to my spirit life. I am living with Divine Love. My grandmother taught me about this way of life, which I gladly accepted. I had swum all my life; in my spirit life, I could review those glorious experiences being in the ocean in all that sun, sand and surf. In my spirit life involving Divine

Love in my soul, I really could thank God for that life! Due to the experience I had, as I progressed I became interested in near-death experiences. I have met many individuals living here who had near-death experiences and had said how it had opened their human awareness up to other things. I knew what they meant. My interest related to the soul. It is one of those things that people discuss, about the timing of life and death and the fate of it. I could have so easily died in the surf that day. How is it that some die only to reawaken from death continuing to live their human life where others die and awaken in their spirit life? I have often thought about that day in the surf. What would have happened if I didn't hear my grandmother's voice encouraging me on; would I have made one last effort?

I have spoken to the more learned teachers who know about soul. I did this quite some time ago. They said to me that only God, the originator of the mortal soul, is with the Eternal Love for each mortal soul knowing the timing of such incarnation into physical life and transition into their spirit life. Humans perceive death purely from a physical circumstance, but the soul is an attribute from God. As we know, men and women appear to die for lengths of time only to be brought back to life. When is one pronounced dead? From my perspective the soul doesn't die; I am living proof of this as are all residing here. There are many permutations involving the experience of time in death and dying. The Father brings the soul across in the spirit body in only the timing the Father knows. Only the Father knows the consequence and outcome of each human life. The mystery here that I have asked my grandmother about involves her input at that time I was drowning. In her soul condition, she knew a fate about to happen. What she didn't know was if I would hear her words and that God knew my soul was to continue living my physical life. I can't really explain any more than this. For me to do so is to speak on behalf of God. I wouldn't dare dream of trying to explain the entire machinations of every single human life. All I can do is acknowledge my soul-love for the Soul of God and that I didn't die alone in the surf in the sea that day.

Thank you for receiving my experience, G

41

White Feather speaks:

The teaching that you have received about the Divine Love being non-evolving will establish a new way for men and women to interpret how the Divine Love is in their life. This will also provide a unique insight into how we experience the Love here. I am happy to see that you are continuing to receive our communications and of course, the Divine Love. I have been a companion on your journey as you have continued to work in unison with us so that more information is brought forward for the leisure of the reader. I use the phrase leisure, as individuals can take their time with their interest with existing realities that exceed the singular surface of physical life. Truth, the Father's Truths are dynamic, but it is the dynamic of the Divine Love that brings about change, that causes change in the soul. You can have the entire truths of Eternity existing as they do, but without the Divine Love becoming part of your soul, the soul will never become changed in its condition or any more than what it is in its singular natural finite attribute of love and unable to experience or participate with these existing Living Eternal Truths. This is why living with Divine Love, a soul's life is the expression of progression. The wonderful thing being aware of all that we have conveyed over the years to you both and the reader, is that so much information that is loving is freely available. Ultimately, this is what all our effort has been about. What began with James Padgett and as you now receive 100 years later, is the ongoing expression of information involving the life of the soul that is a freedom of information that no one here or where you are can individually control for their own possession. The Divine Love is non-evolving. This has been clearly taught to you. The fact that this Love doesn't evolve means that in any individual's progression, such a form of energy can never be manipulated into ownership for self-serving purposes. The physical world of men and women have never lived with a worldwide awareness of such an existing form of energy that *is* love and that brings change to the soul. If the world knew about this Love and how it relates to the soul, then everything in the human world involving the human soul and humans would change. Being aware of love would change the world. What I say to you here is not uncommon. Over here exactly what I have conveyed to you is happening in real spirit time and life. Vast populations of humanity are having their human awareness recalibrated to the expanding realities relating to the life of their soul living in their spirit life.

I will stop now. Beautiful to see you both again and to speak in the language of spirit and love.

Your friend, companion and teacher, White Feather

42

Hello; my name is Kate. I died several years ago. I was an organ donor. My passion in life was music, I loved music. I had a condition that I was born with that eventually took its toll. My life here has been happy. I lived my human life knowing that it would be inevitable that I would not live to a ripe old age. Having this condition changed my relationship with life. I knew I had a limited time, so I made the most of my relationships and my love affair with music. I had tried to play the guitar and the piano but I couldn't create; I could play other people's music. My musical interest, diverse ranging from classic to contemporary in all forms of music.

My life here, as I said, has been happy. I still have my love of music; I feel musical. I have good relationships with other people of all ages. I haven't embraced God's Divine Love; I am not ready to make this change that I have seen others make. I am enjoying myself in the relationships that I have, but I will embrace my soul-life at some time in my future. Like me, there are so many people here aware that another way of life exists. I am still quite young and I will never grow old here! I accept that much of my life will only be what I lived and not the life that other people live, living a full physical life.

Love, Kate

43

Hello; my name is Maureen. In my 40s I had a fall hitting my head which resulted in an injury which put me in a coma; I was on life support a long time. My family had to make the choice about turning off the life support system. I was a mother with two children, happily married. I will spare you the details involving how it must have been for my husband to make this choice.

In my coma, I was unaware of any cognitive activity or spirit presence. I can see this time with a clear perspective. My soul and spirit body remained present even though I was technically dead, being kept alive by artificial means. The area of death has changed so much around the world, as technology, medicine, science and knowledge increase so that individuals can be sustained in living when they can't manage this on their own. I am speaking to you out of love and compassion for those who may experience a loved one in this situation. I live here now. My soul has received Divine Love. I have progressed in my condition of soul, that has afforded me the knowing that God cares for all souls and looks at this from an Eternal perspective. People living their physical life may only perceive from a singular perspective, therefore the reality of soul-life and the spirit body remain unknown entities. I know that to your ear it may sound somewhat judgmental when you hear our perspective communicated so freely, but this is how it is. Human life doesn't begin with man and end with man on the face of the Earth. Human life begins with God who gives our soul life. This beginning continues into the spirit world. This soul-life can continue with greater perspective when Divine Love becomes involved. My perspective about human life extends from my soul condition being in a very good rapport with the Soul of God. I am happy living with God and accepting God's Divine Love into my soul. My perspective on human life covers physical human life and human life in the spirit world. I communicate here in my spirit life with individuals who haven't chosen to involve the Divine Love in their soul, and I communicate with individuals who have included Divine Love in their spirit life. I have seen how impermanent a physical life is, this impermanence only to make you recognise how gifted each human soul-life is! Learning about human life involves life here, it has to for this is where human life is destined. Try to see the afterlife as a continuation of a gift that is your own life and never feel afraid that this life is ahead of you. The soul can begin accepting Divine Love now.

I will finish by saying that I loved my husband for letting me go.

Everlasting, Maureen

44

Elias speaks:

Part of the extensive vision that involves God's Divine Love is seen in the way that people living their physical life can readily receive this non-evolving form of energy just as we here in the spirit world are able to readily receive this same form of energy. This demonstrates the reach of the Father's Love and the dynamic by which this Divine Love is not solely relegated to the spirit world.

We have taught you that certain Spirit Laws are the Handiworks of the Father that are only existent and applied to those of us residing here in the spirit world. Not all of God's Spirit Laws apply in their action to both the physical world and the spirit world. The Spirit Laws involving how the Divine Love enters the soul, how the soul integrates this Love, how the spirit body adjusts to the improved soul condition are Spirit Laws that act singularly in both worlds. The Spirit Law of Compensation is another Spirit Law that acts in this way. This Law relates to soul condition, the condition of a soul's natural love. A person living their physical life is a soul, and therefore is with condition with that soul as life experience lived determines if that natural love is living in harmony with the Father's Spirit Laws of Love. A person can, in their physical life, live perfect natural love and be receiving Divine Love without any compensation. I say, 'Spirit Law' as 'Spirit', for we here identify the Eternal Fatherly Creator as being, The Being of Eternal Soul, Spirit and Love.

As the mortal life becomes Immortal due to receiving Divine Love, soul perceptions become aligned with this Immortal condition and such perceptions about the nature of God - being Spirit and Soul - can become palpable to you; this offsets the singular physical palpable life experience. As the soul that you are becomes more familiar with the experience living with the readily available Divine Love, perceptions of spirit and soul become more visible. This happens to us living here as we move from purely our natural condition into a more wholesome and unified condition of soul brought about by the continuing influence of the Father's Love received.

Your teacher and friend, Elias

45

Saleeba speaks:

I am settled in my spirit life; I know that you both know this. I have a long history. I have lived a long life; I say this to you as all spirits have their past. When I became a spirit, as my spirit life increased I was able to view my human life, my physical life, with an entire complete perspective.

Everlasting

As I have conveyed to you, I lived a large part of my spirit life in perfect natural love. When I began receiving Divine Love, living my soul-life with my acceptance of the Soul, God, I progressed to reside in the Celestial Heaven. I was able to view my entire spirit life with a complete perspective. Living in the Celestial Heaven, I had both spirit and physical human past.

Every human residing in the spirit world has lived physical life. Most people are unaware of their soul having been formed by God and what constitutes the nature and essence of their existing soul. Therefore, most who arrive here only see their origin being their physical life. Throughout the communications that you have both received over the years, individuals have shared a little of their physical life experience with you. This gives the sense and feeling that the spirits are defining their current spirit life experience by including the past. The words such as, 'when', 'was', 'in my physical life', 'when on Earth' are true as each individual has their past. One day, the reader will experience this same perspective.

I am explaining this to you for you have seen this in the communications you have received. The truth that defines the perspective of time as being past, present and future is defined by the Divine Love as existing in its form without mortal time. The Divine Love is situated in its outcome of time relating directly to its origin, the Soul, the Eternal Father.

We have defined the Divine Love being non-evolving. Relating to this also means that there is no time evolving any experience in the Love. As the Love permeates our souls, our soul is receiving a non-evolving form of time. What is interesting here, is to identify that in the soul, there is no time. Before incarnation, the soul doesn't live with any mortal time in its essence of natural love. The Father doesn't pre-program the soul upon its creation to a model of time recognisable as past, present and future. It is only your model of time that forms an individual construct for your memory. When the soul has received consistent amounts of Divine Love over a long period of participation, receiving a timeless form of energy into a timeless form of soul, is harmony!

As the soul adapts by receiving Divine Love, the spirit attributes become more established in the individual personality.

Can this timelessness (as being The Time of the Eternal Father) be recognised? Yes. This timelessness is placed in a context to our memory as past, present and future. We are able to live in our present with the perspective of experience as time lived past; we live in the present and what is perceived to be our future, which the Divine Love in Its Immortality presents to the memory.

Humans relate their memory with past, present and future. Celestial spirits relate their memory with past, present and future; also with an additional period of measurement, the timelessness of Divine Love and individual natural love living in our soul, causing our soul-life to identify with the Eternal Energy of the Present Universal Soul, God.

I am trying to explain this measurement of experience the best possible way so that you may gain perception and perspective with your inclusion of the non-evolving form of energy, the Divine Love. My memory situated as an attribute in my spirit body can form memories of this measurement of experience relative to my finite form as I live my usual spirit life. I am not alone, as everyone in the Celestial Heaven is aware that they are living with a unique form of experience that defines our participation in normal spirit life for us.

In your physical life, your construct of memories is based on past, present and future with yourself and other individual personalities that you have formed relationships with. In our Celestial life, it is the same only that at our soul and spirit centre, we have the Father's Eternal, non-evolving form of timelessness as a real measurement of experience in our lives.

This experience of time in our spirit life serves a very important relationship that we individually share with the Father, each other and the spirit environments we reside in.

If the human world on Earth were all aware of the existing Divine Love with vast populations receiving and living with this Love, this teaching would be commonplace adding another layer to the measurement of human experience in relationship with the human, physical, and spirit universe. Some of you may have already experienced this.

I am shining my love toward you both, love Saleeba

46

Hello; my name is Timothy. My physical life ended twenty years ago. I was in my late forties. I lived on the northeast coast of Australia. I lived a life that involved the sea, I lived in a coastal town. On my walks along the beach, that I could walk to in a few minutes from my coastal home, I would think about things of spirit as I had an interest in such things. I had read a lot of books, spiritual books and books involving spirit communication. Some of these books had been widely read, such as the Seth books. I had also read the Urantia Book. I was unaware of the messages known by you all as The Padgett Messages. In essence, I found spirit reality fundamentally interesting. I liked being by the sea taking swims but I wasn't a surfer or an open water swimmer. I liked being by the sea and the freedom it symbolised. I felt, always felt, that my soul and body could breathe being by the sea.

My first impression when I awakened in the spirit world was that I was involved with spirit now! I was somewhat prepared about living in an afterlife, for I had surmised in my earthly life that the human afterlife was a concrete fact. It existed, but my perception about the form of this existence was in bits and pieces so to speak. I felt very calm after I had awakened from what appeared to be a missing period of time. There was my physical life with my condition, then when I died, missing time. I awakened in a beautiful setting comforted by individuals as calm as individuals can be! I knew I had died but I couldn't figure out how I came to be where I was. I know this now as I understand the Spirit Law of Transition established by the Father. I died in my sleep. I was administered progressive medication to ease my pain from my condition; I simply stopped breathing. I was told by one of these spirits that I died at 2 A.M. Other than the nursing staff I was alone. My immediate friends and family had left for the night planning to come back to the palliative care facility early in the morning. We all knew the inevitable fate of my life; there was a lot of love involved. I wasn't afraid, I had lived a good, full happy life; a life lived by the sea.

The process of adaptation began. I was introduced to this new way of living by those who comforted me. This comfort wasn't because I was in pain or suffering, this comfort assisted me being in a new environment all alone without any prior experience. I didn't resent being where I was or that my physical life had ended. I had lived a good full life respecting myself and other people. I was a quiet soul, thinking that one day I may become a writer. I enjoyed the presence of my own company especially on my beach walks. I never felt alone for I had my connection with the sea. I never married and never had children. Apparently, my condition could have been genetically passed on so I remained single. I had girlfriends but was not in a relationship at the time of my death.

My acceptance that a human afterlife existed made my adaption to my spirit life seamless. I didn't feel in any emotional or intellectual conflict about wanting more time on Earth so I wasn't confronted by living in two places at once in my mind. I accepted that this was the next part of my spiritual journey. I learnt about my spirit body quite quickly. I learnt how to socialise, and the basic rudiments for required living in what you know as the First Natural Sphere. This sphere is simply the arrival zone. There is no other way to say it!

There are people who experience dying, there are other people who experience death with an immediate conclusion. I had time in my process of dying to process the life I had lived. The beginning of my spirit life was the experience that involved living again. I was not influenced by my past human life, as I was complete with the life I had lived and the way I had lived it with those I had shared my life with. Life was all about living again. On one hand, I had experience and maturity from my human life but on the other hand, I was a person in the innocence of a beginning. I had all the maturity of my adult earthly life and my childlike beginning in spirit. I really enjoyed learning about my spirit body and attributes. At first, I was clumsy, most of us are. We have had no prior experience asserting our personality through the attribute of spirit body. Our personality was all about being physical. Due to the fact that I was so complete at the end of my physical life, I felt free to explore my spirit attributes. As I gained control of my faculties it dawned on me at what a marvellous creation this attribute, in its established functioning was! The truth that was so clear to me was that this spirit body was so *made* for this environment. As I gained more experience I could see how my spirit attributes came into their being. Without much time, I felt comfortable living my new life. I realised that my experience of dying afforded me the life experience evaluating my life. It had been a gift. So much about life here or there where you are, is about the way you choose to evaluate your own experiences.

As I entered the arrival zone, as leaving the comfortable place I transitioned into, I could meet other people which helped socialise my experience. I didn't meet millions of people all at once. I was instructed by those who comforted me that there was an area or a location in this sphere where I could find a comfortable place to live while I continued my adaption. My memories of the sea, where I lived on Earth, very real to me. This was a bizarre experience for me; having such living memories involving a dynamic scape that didn't exist here! I was living in a new landscape - a spirit-scape - that was truly magnificent to its form and creation. One outstanding fact that kept coming to me, as I could think quite clearly in my spirit body, that back on Earth I had thought a lot about spirit reality. I had ideas about it. Now, I was living in it!

On Earth taking my walks along the beach, I would try to conceptualise how this place was. Now I am living in it with the reality of spirit and Earth as a perspective and structural context of difference. The fact that I could think about the Earth and my life there from the place I was now living in, was a miracle to me. Try and imagine it for yourself. As I gained more spirit life experience I began to wonder how such a place might have come into existence. Imagine being forty years of age living your physical life and instantly arriving in a spirit body life that you never imagined you were living with during your entire earthly physical life! This place is already established. Humanity is living here. Some individuals have been living here a long time, so much so that they don't seem in awe of its creation. I started thinking about what I would do here. My thoughts were real to me. I could think about going for a walk through a spirit-scape just as I could think about going for a walk through the seascape. I had seen some individuals who appeared in their spirit appearance quite illumined. I had no idea what this was that generated such difference.

What you have heard as I have been speaking to you is the lack of God in my experience. On Earth, I believed in the sense of a Creator. That's about my measure of it. The sea represented 'spirit'; it had a great spirit to me. Being by the sea I felt in touch with that sense of the Creator that I had some vague idea about. In my spirit life being newly arrived, I did not meet God. My time was about adjusting to my spirit attributes and learning how to live here. In eight months, I had a conversation with one of these illumined individuals. I still had the real concept of the passing of earthly time. My spirit-mind was bringing new information from the external environment which was spirit-time. It does differ to earthly time; I believe you have received messages on this before. I never felt alone in my spirit life. So much about my human life was in such a good condition of love that I felt loved. I never felt lost. The conversation I had with the illumined individual was a loving conversation about the nature of soul. It was about the soul that brought the knowledge about the Divine Love into the conversation. There was nothing persuasive from the individual I was conversing with as this individual was outstanding in his presence. I didn't require any conversion or change of belief. It was quite the opposite. I saw that I was speaking to my future spirit life. It was clearly stated that I could remain as I was or begin exploring the rest of the spirit world and life. To do this, you had to be in the right soul condition so that your spirit attributes could perceive the reality you were experiencing. My parents and grandparents were still living their earthly life. Eventually, I met my great-grandparents. I didn't meet them until I was well underway with Divine Love. From my Celestial life I was able to see how slow and uninterrupted I was so that my period of adjustment and adaption happened in a harmonious speed and time. I began receiving Divine Love after I had listened to the illumined individual. He became my spirit guide and teacher. I would joke with him that I would read about spirit guides back on Earth and now having a real life spirit guide teaching and guiding my soul toward the Father's Soul with love and happiness. Spirit guides do exist as I have been guided by one! There is a lot to be happy about when looking at things here with the memories of your ideas about such things such as spirit guides.

As I progressed in my soul condition, I felt very comfortable. It didn't phase me at all that I was including God in my life. I could see quite clearly in my spirit guide and the other advanced individuals, that the only way to progress in the spirit life is to include God in your life. What better way to increase your involvement with your spirit attributes than by doing so with love? This suited me perfectly. The Divine Love, in my experience, is a soft, gentle love. I was taught that this Love doesn't evolve but I would change, and change I did! Much has been conveyed to you about progression through the spheres; this is a wonderful journey. The spirit-scapes differ as you learn to live more in rapport with the Father, which is reflected in your ability to understand and participate in your life in each varied spirit-scape. I met my great-grandparents on my way to the Celestial Heaven. My whole experience living my spirit life has been an experience of beginnings. To this moment, I still feel I am at a beginning. I have memories from the time I first arrived from my human life, as I have memories that are now created from my spirit life. I realise much has changed, I have never been afraid of change. This brings me back to my days and evenings walking along the beach thinking about spirit reality. Believing that there is a reality of spirit beyond a physical life symbolises change to some degree. Living here exposed me to a change of living. I still receive spirit guidance from my spirit guide, in fact there are numerous individuals I receive guidance and teachings from involving the life of my soul. I feel fortunate to have lived the life I have lived. I was as complete as I could be in my physical life living by the sea, now, complete in my spirit life living in Divine Love.

Thank you for this privilege of sharing. Timothy

47

James Reid speaks:

The Celestial teachers are pleased that you are both open to receive experiences from individuals residing here who have yet to take up their Immortal soul-life. It is important to receive these individuals who give their account, for the spirit world involves humanity living with and living without - or I should say - living with or without the inclusion of Divine Love. Hearing from individuals who are living with Divine Love, and those who are living without Divine Love will provide a more complete perspective for the reader involving living with Divine Love. Needless to say, the vast humanity living their physical life is living without the inclusion of the Divine Love, accept for a few who are aware of the availability of this Love and the true Immortality it brings to their soul.

The Immortality that has been taught by the Celestial teachers and shared by other individual experiences relates to the soul. We all know that it would be unusual to speak of an Immortality that makes a mortal physical life live forever on Earth. Understanding that there is a finite limit to physical life places the true Immortality into a truthful perspective. Receiving the Divine Love into your soul in your physical life confirms that your soul is living with the true Immortality but the physical life is subject to its mortality that will eventually end. The Divine Love that brings the soul its Immortal life is truly the everlasting Love!

Now that I have had time to adapt to my spirit life, learning about my spirit attributes and soul-life, I am with that perspective of Immortality having progressed through all the spheres that brought me to the spheres that comprise the Celestial Heaven. The depth of my spirit-vision has become substantially and progressively realised in solid form. Quite simply put, the more I was able to perceive the Divine Love in my soul and the effects that this Love along with my natural love caused in my spirit attributes, the more Immortal I became and felt compared to feeling purely mortal. It has been conveyed to you about how permanent life here is. This is true. It is permanent in Love, Spirit and Truth. This permanency I have not found to be socially overwhelming. I like the fact that I know who I am, I know where I am and I know where I am going to be. I know that the spirit environments will not alter or change my outlook within my soul. There is nothing to fear about the truth of feeling and being permanent. I say this due to the fact that in physical life, the expression 'living forever' can seem rather dwarfing. Due to the changes that have transpired in my soul and spirit attributes, my whole sense of feeling permanent is a comforting truth. I have changed from my physical life. I will continue to change but this change is not a change of direction or drama or a social life sustained in broken relationships. Change for me in my spirit life has been a process of loving liberation. There is nothing that involves any change sent by the Father that will bring about any disharmony when in your spirit life you are humming along living a beautiful life. This is another part of the change that transpires here. Living every moment in living love. In our physical life, such are the robust relationships we form with other people and with landscapes and environment. Each person may hope that tomorrow is a better day or another day just like the one lived; no one really knows what tomorrow will bring. Having lived this myself, it all makes for a socially dramatic life. It is not wrong or right, it is just the drama of human social living. Here, part of the change requires one living with Divine Love in their Celestial life to experience consistently living love. There will never be any dramatic upheaval in all my spirit future. The only drama I experienced in my spirit life was adapting to my spirit body from the habit of my living a reasonably long life in my physical body. I found the experience enlightening. As you both know, I was already aware that a spirit life existed, and that the Divine Love was real in my human life.

One other thing that speaks to me clearly here, as I meet socially with other individuals, is the sheer vastness of human existence and the existence of the spirit world. This sense of extension does become part of your soul perceptions. There is no escaping this. Meeting individuals that lived their human life long ago, meeting individuals who have just arrived to begin their spirit life, being part of this ongoing humanity and spirit world environment that exceeds your arrival is a truth that I think about quite a lot. This brings my perceptions closer toward the Father. It helps me realise how permanent the Father is! It helps me see how this loving Creator has been part of humanity ever since the first souls formed and will always be part of humanity. We are inextricably linked with our Creator. Individuals are living in their natural love who may feel this truth. Individuals are receiving Divine Love who will know this truth and live in the spirit of it.

I will not speak more at this time. This has been another good moment between us. James

48

James Reid speaks:

In physical life, a person may contemplate the existence of a true Immortality. That person may try to evaluate what Immortality might look like if one were to really see a human living in an Immortal condition. Life teaches us that our physical existence is never permanent. People have contemplated the existence of Immortality in various contexts that might define a more fundamental examination of human nature. The question is, 'Is man Immortal'? At face value, asking this question knowing that physical life has its inevitable conclusion places the identity of Immortality against an impermanent physical existence. If Immortality does exist, then what is Immortal in the nature of man?

In my spirit life, my capacity to perceive the existence of my soul increased as I received Divine Love. My soul perceptions and spirit-mind, able to perceive this living form of energy within my soulful nature. The physical attribute in all its constitution is not Immortal; it is impermanent. The soul that incarnates into this physical attribute with spirit body formed, is permanent. This permanency identified as surviving the impermanent physical body by arriving in the spirit world. Is man or woman Immortal? The physical aspect of man is not Immortal, however, the soul and spirit body that constitutes the real man or woman is permanent. This is seen in the nature of the man or woman living in the spirit world. Asking the question about Immortality relates to the full aspect of human nature. Human nature involves soul and spirit body.

Is the natural love the true Immortality? Does this essence formed by the Father before the soul's incarnation have to its essence an Immortal nature? It does, in the sense that the soul and spirit body continue to live as the real man or woman in the spirit world. I have heard individuals explain to me that when they lived in what is the Perfect Natural Sphere before the Divine Love was available, it was discussed that a certain human Immortality had been realised. Some of these individuals, having lived in this sphere a very long time, were situated in a status quo of spirit life. Some of these individuals were the great ancient philosophers who had thought their way through the realm of being human. The questions that they had asked during earthly life about defining or identifying Immortality had been partly answered by the change that had transpired to their existence when their physical life was over yet spirit life continued. They realised that the singular earthly life, as being purely physical, was not Immortal. They explained to me that by being perfect, they assumed that this perfection was a state or condition that existed in the nature of man or woman. What was interesting, was how they explained their ideas of what they thought perfection to be. They concluded in the Perfect Sphere that no other man or woman coming forward from the earthly coil into the spirit world brought anything that could advance their position in the natural spirit life of humanity. So supreme were their intellects and for so long they remained in this spirit status-quo that they reasoned they had obtained human evolutionary perfection. Oddly enough, their intellects were so highly developed in the attribute of their natural spirit mind that some of them dismissed the presence and life of the First Parents as a fabricated non-event. There was nothing in the Perfect Sphere that gave a comparison to any other spirit that defined any individual living in this sphere as being superior or different. They said that the First Parents did seem to know about an extensive universal spirit universe, but none of us could experience what they spoke of. The spirit world is so vastly different in each sphere, that these individuals concluded with their intellectual rationalisations that anyone could make anything up and believe it true!

What interested me when listening to these individuals, was that they didn't question how in fact, such a spirit life and world came into being! The individuals living in the Perfect Natural Sphere are still very mortal, even though their soul and spirit-mind permanent, seemingly Immortal.

The arrival of Jesus into the spirit world heralded change everlasting. With Jesus' arrival to the spirit world, the real teaching about the true Immortality began. This has been conveyed to you before. Only the Divine Love can bring true Immortality to form part of the permanent nature of the natural love in the soul of man and woman. The individuals that I have spoken with live in the Celestial Heaven. They changed their ideas about perfection and what is the true Immortality when they began receiving the Divine Love, that Living Energy that brings soulful realisations involving permanent Eternal Fatherly Truths. What is significant here, is our freedom to explore such truths when living with Divine Love as it brings to life measurement of structural differences that involve the nature of man and woman insofar as what love is permanent, permanently impermanent and permanently perfect and Immortal.

Love, James

49

Hello; my name is Tallis. I wish to confirm the teaching that Elias recently conveyed to you about the dynamic of the Spirit Law that assists spirit-to-human communication.

I lived a wretched human life. I won't explain what I did, but my actions led to my soul condition being that of the poorest of natural love. In my human life, I knew I was doing wrongful things to other people but this didn't stop me. When my time came, I transitioned into the First Natural Sphere. My human life was what it was, but my soul and spirit body was still intact even though I was socially and morally corrupt. Once I had adapted, I was guided to a sphere for me to live in. I was a mere silhouette of a man. The individuals guiding me were gentle with me and did not judge me. I couldn't resist, as I felt utterly powerless to do anything. I couldn't exert my personality in any way. I was unused to this!

In the environment I lived, the spirit-scape that surrounded me, I felt suffocated. It would have been impossible for me to leave this sphere on my own and direct any form of experience into the physical world. I was bright and intelligent, but a complete manipulator and taker of other people's lives. This all happened a long time ago. I had no idea about anything involving what had happened to me once I had died. I had my memories, and that was it. It was explained to me that I could change my condition, which wasn't permanent, but I was required to undo what I had done. I had to begin with myself. This was a hard thing to do as I had never loved myself. My experience of restoration, that is restoring the condition of my soul into a good condition of natural love, took time. It was a succession of admitting my arrogance. Eventually, I was able to live in the First Natural Sphere, the sphere I originally arrived at the termination of my human life. I died at the hands of others who had found out what I had been doing.

I live in the Celestial Heaven now. That life, my earthly behaviour, now has complete redemption. My respect for life is a living gift. I am fortunate that I listened to those spirit guides who pointed a few things out. I love everything about my soul-life. I would not like anyone to think that I did such horrible things to others and became a Celestial spirit in the blink of an eye. My restoration to my perfect natural love was a sight that I alone had to bear. That is not with me now. There are so many individuals living their soul-life in the Celestial Heaven who had to restore their soul condition back into the harmony living good natural love. We all have chosen to include living with Divine Love because we wanted to, which meant all our actions seen in the love of God. I know the real power of love. I have had to assess my human life and what a wasted life it was! Not only this, that I ended other people's lives who were good souls. I have had to meet these individuals as part of my redemption and restoration.

The teaching Elias conveyed is concrete. Individuals residing in the lowest platform of the spirit world cannot communicate or influence anything or anyone other than themselves.

Thank you. Much appreciated.

50

James Reid speaks:
I will take this time to reconfirm that the reality of Divine Love is synonymous with the life and involvement of soul. It is important that the reader understands this connectedness when ascertaining how we experience progression in the spirit world. This is an obvious truth to state having received information from individuals living their soul-life

involving Divine Love. This truth has been continuously reconfirmed. We feel it necessary to continue confirming this because it is real. The Divine Love exists as does our attribute of soul. When these two forms combine, progress happens. It will be clear to you that when an individual shares their experience of their spirit life without these two components being engaged, any real sense of progression through the spirit world is unrevealed in their discourse. Natural love is a dynamic component of the soul. Alone, it is unable to bring you through to the Celestial Heaven or Divine Love spheres. The natural love is a superb love. This has been illustrated to you; this love is never meant to be seen as being a mere shadow in the expanse of soul-life. The availability of Divine Love brings perspective on natural love and its place in soul-life. Remembering that the soul incarnates into its physical life, therefore, it is in natural love that incarnation and individualisation of the soul begins. Personality begins forming in the essence of natural love. With Divine Love being available, this experience of individualisation can then take another step, which is perceived as a progression of the personality involving the soul and its individualisation.

In my spirit life, I have not found the Divine Love or the Father's Truths to be disruptive in any way, shape or form. Accepting the Love into my soul has for me, been a mutable experience. In fact like individuals I have conversed with, those of us who are relatively new to our life in the spirit world, being introduced to individuals who have been living here for what would be thousands of Earth years in time, is far more relative in terms of participation. Living with Divine Love is a beautiful experience here in the spirit life. Being taught about this Love from an individual like the beautiful Saleeba, her appearance is so present and ageless, yet had lived before you on Earth for thousands of years and also for thousands of years before Jesus. Saleeba has spoken to me about living with the Divine Love as if it is all new at this moment. I have found this very interesting. Other individuals have lived before Saleeba. They are living here in the Celestial Heaven. I have conversed with some of these individuals, the ones who have learnt English, as I do not speak ancient languages. I am trying to convey to you a spectrum of a portrait of time to illustrate how central and present the Father's Divine Love is relative to the history humanity has lived. This is truly one of the wonders of spirit life.

Many perspectives involve living here; it's part of the reason why it has been necessary for you both to receive information from the diversity of individuals residing here. Each perspective contributes toward small amounts of information that establishes a sense of the grandeur in which we reside and live all the time.

Love, James

51

Luke speaks:

At times, you have both wondered why the communications that you have received differ in voice than the style James Padgett received. The Father's Truths have never changed. The experience involving living with Divine Love has been conveyed to you with accuracy and diversity. Diversity is the operative phrase to illustrate the great and vast number of souls who live with the Father's Divine Love outside of James' experience. James received messages from Jesus and those of us in Jesus' band that introduced soulful teachings involving the natural and Divine Love.

It could be asked, 'Why didn't Jesus simply teach about the natural and the Divine Love in the way that he conveyed such teachings through James' ability when he lived on Earth'? There are teachings conveyed through James by Jesus reteaching the teachings that have been attributed to Jesus' life on Earth. There is no better example than the teaching of true Immortality. It is very difficult to separate the human life of Jesus from his teachings that involve the Spirit Laws that govern the principles of natural love with the Spirit Laws that involve living with the Divine Love in a progressive experience, from the social dynamics that were implicated when the man Jesus lived, loved and taught among the people of his day. What is true and consistent for all souls is that the Divine Love that we live with here in our spirit life is consistent and true and unchanging. The distinguishing difference between natural love and Divine Love is visibly seen here in the spirit life without any social distortion. Jesus, here in the spirit world has taught all of us about the natural love and the Divine Love without any implicated social disruptions. People still living on Earth will have their reason for believing in Jesus. Here in the spirit world, we are participating in the Divine love in our soul-life, therefore, we understand the human and spirit life of Jesus - not from a purely social context - but, in his account of his life and his relationship with the Father. Living with Divine Love here in our spirit life is an example to us all, that our soul exists, that our natural love exists, that the Divine Love is the only way any individual progress is established through the spirit world that includes the perfection of our attribute of natural love. We are living with Jesus in the spirit world in our natural attribute of love with the Divine Love of God and loving social interactions without any distortion.

Much has been conveyed to you both about the experience James Padgett lived. Many readers have taken or received the information conveyed through James Padgett on face-value. Essentially, some of the truths that we revealed at that time speak to the diversity of individuals appealing to the soulful nature and the message or teaching about God's Divine Love that has resonated in the mind, soul and heart. It is very easy to receive Divine Love. To participate as the soul you are with the Soul of God is experiencing Divine Love as a simple experience. It is never meant to be complicated. Spirits understand this once they move past their beliefs so that they can participate freely in the Love as the Love brings about the necessary changes that result in freedom of movement and progression through the spirit world.

Today, with both of you actively receiving Divine Love and having so much experience, which included an extensive study of the material James received, we have been able to bring to life the most modern and detailed account of soul-life as lived here that is relevant for the modern person today who aspires to know the best of what can be realistically perceived. I, along with the individuals communicating to you both at this time, are also taking into consideration men and women of tomorrow. In 500 years time and beyond, a substantial amount of information that we have conveyed to you will survive and be relevant for the ever-progressive soul aspiring to know the soul-life, the spirit world, the full extent of the natural love and the Divine Love and the full realisation of life expressed when including the Eternal Father in their life.

If you sit back and think about your own experience happening at the moment, imagine what people will be able to know as commonplace knowledge about the soul and spirit-related themes when so much more about God and the spirit world and the human nature is absorbed into earthly life from these messages.

Your teacher and friend, eternally, Luke

52

Luke speaks:

We have identified many of the Father's Truths. The Celestial Heaven is a real place of existence. The Father's Truths provide us with the ability to understand relationship dynamics between ourselves, the spirit environments we reside in with our individuality and personalisation of our soul-life with the Eternal Soul, God. The Father's Truths that we relate with provide perspective, shape and form so that attributes of the Father's Spirit, dynamic and workings have palpable connectivity with us. Some of us are impassioned when coming into contact with a truth that becomes a cognitive experience in our spirit personality. The Celestial Heaven isn't just an adult place. People are residing here in just about all ages of their life. There are children, teenagers, young adults residing in the spheres that comprise this wonderful place. Everyone socialises freely without having any separation due to the Father's Truths. I can teach you about the true Immortality of the soul, I can reveal to you how the spirit body cannot exceed the condition of its soul nor can it act in a spirit environment beyond the condition of its soul. I can teach you that the spirit body cannot alone determine the outcome for the soul in the spirit life. There are so many individuals residing in the Celestial Heaven that are at an age in their spirit life who do not understand these living spirit truths. The Celestial Heaven is not a place where one is to become an adult and master of all knowledge before progressing into the First Celestial Sphere. I convey this to you so that you can see the movement of spirits flowing between the Divine Love Spheres where souls are adapting to their living in Divine Love.

A person who is ten years of age, relating to Earth age, and receiving Divine Love is quite capable of their movement through the Divine Love Spheres to reside in the Celestial Heaven. The natural love in the soul is an individual essence, just so long as the individual is with the cognitive capacity to decide for themselves to receive Divine Love, that individual can receive Divine Love and have their natural love perfected. This will open up your vision to the movement of spirits between spheres living with Divine Love. So much truth has been conveyed to you from adults residing in the Celestial Heaven, but the social truth is realised when humanity can reside in the Celestial Heaven with age not being a barrier in the experience of Divine Love. Whole families that have embraced their acceptance of Divine Love are staying together and moving as one to reside in the Celestial Heaven.

Many truths have been created by the Father. None of these truths excludes anyone from personal loving participation with the Father by receiving Divine Love. The fact that people from all ages can experience this Love here demonstrates how accessible this Love is; how immediate it is and being sympathetic for the soul when the other faculties of a young spirits life are not sufficiently formed to cognitively relate with the vast dynamic and workings of the Spirit Truths. It is a beautiful experience to see the beauty of the populations living their spirit life in the Celestial Heaven with the social dynamics of this humanity freely living in harmony.

Eternally, Luke

53

Luke speaks:

Was man always meant to live with the knowledge of soul-life and the availability of an individual soul-ship with Divine Love when living on Earth? We have conveyed to you much about the life of the First Parents as time has gone by; James Padgett received communications from the First Parents. Their life is not a general discussion taking place among the human population in the world today. What you do know is that they lived able to participate with the Eternal Father readily receiving Divine Love. They were teachers as well as parents. Due to the assertions of their personality, the Father ceased the activity of the Acting Spirit being able to bring the Divine Love into their souls and the souls of all men and women until the life of Jesus. The Father reengaged the activity of the Acting Spirit so that the soul, Jesus, could receive Divine Love throughout his human life. This remains to present day and well into the human and spirit future. If the First Parents had continued to thrive in their human spirit life in their harmony with the Father, the Acting Spirit would never have been disengaged by the Father.

The generations of humans after the First Parents died due to natural causes, lost the information about such a universal form of energy true and consistent for the soul forming part of the human earthly and spirit makeup. Generations of humans lived and died transitioning into their spirit life without ever knowing that the Divine

Love existed. We have conveyed to you much about the life of the First Parents living in the spirit world solely in their natural love.

Jesus did not live a long human life. In a small window of time he personalised his relationship with God living in his perfect natural love, interacting with the Acting Spirit that had been reactivated bringing the Divine Love of the Father to his soul. He has been living with this Love teaching all the generations from the First Parents to present day in the spirit world about the true Immortality that is involved in the soul-life. When you look at how many generations have lived without any knowledge of the Divine Love and what this Love represents to the human, a clear perspective is revealed demonstrating how small the amount of time is that the humans on Earth have ever been aware of this non-evolving form of energy that changes everything about knowing what it is to be human!

Right through the mortal spirit world, the choice about knowing that one can participate with the true Immortality, visible and known. Not everyone has chosen this; you have received accounts from individuals who are yet to embrace their soul-life but have stated that they are aware of the choice to make. They have seen those who differ from themselves moving freely about. Life in the spirit world by the example of those living with Divine Love and the availability of Divine Love confirms that humanity, humans, were always meant to have that visible choice to make; that living with Divine Love forms part of soul potential of human nature. If the First Parents had continued to live in harmony with the Father in their natural life when receiving Divine Love, and having never created the scenario which they did which resulted in the Father deactivating the Acting Spirit, then for the generations that came after the life of the First Parents the knowledge involving this gift from the Father would have formed part of everyday human living and knowledge. Some would have made the choice to participate with God by receiving Divine Love in the natural course of their human life. If the First Parents had lived out their human life then proceeded into their spirit life with the Divine Love being readily available for humans and human spirits to receive, the First Parents would have opened the Celestial Heaven.

If this had happened and the life of Jesus still happened in the time it did, his teachings would have revealed more truth about the soul-life involving the Immortal personalisation of the Father in one's natural love living with Divine Love. His teachings would have been progressing on from the foundation that the First Parents laid and subsequent generations have lived.

Your teacher and friend, everlasting, Luke

54

Luke speaks:

The Father's Truths are Eternal. These truths relating to our souls are not floating around waiting to be discovered in the great spirit space and time. I have never looked out into a spirit sphere searching for a glimpse of eternal truth existing somewhere waiting to be discovered, identified and named. An example of this is the truth relating to Immortality. The true Immortality that we have taught you, doesn't have its existence in the fabric of a spirit sphere. It is not floating around waiting to be recognised to then give it form and purpose in its substance. Such a truth, like Immortality, exists due to the existence of the Divine Love. You can search all your earthly and spirit life for a sign that Immortality exists, but, you will never find Immortality living and existing in your natural love.

The existence of Divine Love proves that there is an existing form of love external to the mortal soul. When this love is received with abundance, the individual living their spirit life will gradually realise that their spirit attributes slowly evolve, gradually changing far beyond any other spirit attribute that lived solely in a natural soul condition. What is evident and why we have spent time reconfirming to you the real Immortality, is so you will have that perspective about the fundamental nature of the natural love in the mortal soul - which is a particular form of energy that the Father has given life to - but a form of energy existing in the soul created without any Immortality as part of this natural love.

The Father in the creation and forming of each mortal soul has not prepared that soul with an Immortal condition as a predisposition to the soul before incarnation.

Mortal souls before incarnation are without personality or spirit body or Immortality. The soul is made by the Father to fit perfectly into a spirit body and physical body, and for the forming of personality and the commencement of individualisation. This happens to every human and Immortality is not present or forming any part of the individual personality in its incarnated form.

Why this is so important to know is that it teaches what a truth is, how it looks, the shape it is, but most importantly, that it is living! The Divine Love is a living form of energy therefore, the kind of characteristic that Immortality appears as is a living Spirit of Truth. There are many truths as we have explained to you; there are truths relating to different aspects of spirit and human life. If you would like to think of Earth's gravity as a planetary truth, this gravity is with its particular form and acts accordingly to other fields that cause such planetary movement. There exist truths which identify how the spirit body functions. The beautiful observation about truths is to see how they are in the form that they exist and why they exist. A human can say, 'It's the truth'; 'I believe in this therefore it is a truth'. In an earthly human context, beliefs are personal and subjective therefore, a truth for that individual is subjective. Gravity exists whether you believe in it or not. Planet Earth as part of its form is with a force of energy established in the form it is and acting as part of the planetary movement. This is not subjective or objective, it is a planetary fact and a universal truth. We have conveyed to you in previous teachings that there is a spirit gravity that exists throughout all the spheres and throughout all spirit space and time. It has its form and acts in its way invisible to our spirit senses and optical vision, but it does exist assisting all spirit spheres in their existence relating to the universal Eternal Soul, God.

The most intrinsic dynamic of all truths relating to mortals is what transpires when Divine Love becomes part of the mortal soul. It has been taught to you that Divine Love and soul relate to each other; I will include that Divine Love as well as the Father, is an inclusive truth. These three parts culminate in an existing truth that we live here in our Immortal spirit life.

We have explained to you that God's Divine Love is a form of energy that doesn't evolve. That as a unique form of energy, it is perfect in its form and function without it being abstract or chaotic in any way. It doesn't change. It changes us! Receiving Divine Love is a subjective, soulful experience. If you like, it does result in an individual forming a belief that God exists. The Divine Love exists whether one believes it to exist or not. The Divine Love is a living confirmation that confirms the existence of a living, loving Soul, God. The Divine Love being non-evolving and changeless in its existence is another truth. I can perceive this living truth with my soul perceptions. I have been living aware and experiencing this Love ever since my arrival into the spirit life those thousand and hundreds of years ago.

Here in the spirit life, we cannot exclude God from any discussion involving the forming of the spirit world, the life of Jesus and the existence of Divine Love. When speaking about the mortal human soul and spirit life, we cannot exclude God from this discussion. The Soul of God is the foundation of humankind. This extends over the full surface of what it is to be human. Our natural love is so good, expressive, giving, as it has been gifted to us. We implore you to embrace the very best in the gift of natural love that you have all been given recognising that you are individual and diverse. You are not just earthly people, rather universal citizens capable of living spirit, love and Immortal Truth. Try to include an inkling of awareness that Divine Love exists; that it is universal truth and a universal truth that is love-in-the-living as a form of energy sympathetic to your condition of soul irrespective of the condition of your natural love and preexisting earthly beliefs. This truth is beautiful in form and not one to live in fear of. There is nothing to fear in the God of Love; the Love that has given life to your soul and the potential to receive and become part of the true living Immortality that we express in our spirit life everlasting.

You received the essence of my teaching well. Your friend and teacher, Luke

November

55

Luke speaks:

Ever since humans conceived that a spirit world might exist, a vast array of ideas, cultural beliefs, individual beliefs, religious and spiritual teachings, imaginings, a plethora of wonderings - human wonderings - have formed part of earthly life. Humans recognised that human life, their human life, in a physical form and body, was not finitely everlasting. Religions, spiritualities, nomadic man and cultures have all created gods to assist their way of life, their ideas and allaying fears to the uncertainty of a life given survival beyond death and among the living. Present day wonderings remain ongoing. The quest to find, identify and establish the truth is a quest searched out in the years of humankind. Stone and materialism laid and founded for gods.

Everlasting

Individuals have tried to identify the nature of human existence, the existence of the human soul and what happens after you die. Information purportedly given by spirits to man outlining the vast knowledge that spirits have that may provide benefit for an earthly man aspiring toward more than ordinary life. All the while, the spirit world has existed. People have lived, died and lived transitioning into the spirit world surviving death and adapting to their spirit life. Now that the Divine Love available, all that was wondered on Earth and lay concealed, revealed in plain spirit sight and wonderings turned toward knowings. I include myself in this, for I once lived as a man trying to understand the life of my friend, Jesus, and the spirit world that he taught us about. I saw the way he lived. He was different, it was as if he knew God personally and intimately, speaking to me and to those who lived with him as if God was with us and part of Jesus' life. He taught us quite clearly that he was not God nor ever would be, that no mortal soul would ever be God. Now his life among humans is left to the world of wonderings with everything else involving the spirit world.

What no one considered in their earthly wonderings, including myself when I lived, was that the spirit world was a place so accurately formed and that its whole existence is incredibly simple! What no man or woman considered is that this spirit world is simply the next environment for a human to live in so that human life would continue not perishing away to organic matter and remaining of the Earth forever. What no man or woman considered is that God formed a spirit world so intricately simple and uniformly designed so that humans when arriving were required to do very little other than to continue to live in their individuality.

As we have taught you, the existence of the human afterlife and the attribute of mortal soul and the Divine Love are not created by man or by any other super-angelic personality. The fabrication of the spirit body - that invisible body that every human has lived in throughout their human life - is the Handiwork of the Father. As soon as you begin to see the human afterlife as the place established by God for the continuation of individuality and survival of the human soul, then you will be able to understand why God formed such a simple place vast in its dynamic, to ensure that the soul condition thrives in its life.

In my teaching today, I desired to explain this simple purpose for the existence of the human afterlife so that one may have clarity in their progressive education about the life of their soul and not to be confused with the myriad of human wonderings about such an existence and how and why it exists and the purpose for this existence.

Thank you. Your teacher and friend, Luke

56

Hello; my name is Chris. I have been living here for ten years. In those ten years, I have adapted to my life here. I have made new friends and have maintained old friendships, life goes on!

I have recently started to receive Divine Love. I thought this might be a good thing to do. I met someone who was living with this Love, a feminine individual. We got on very well, so well that I felt that I would like to be with her. She explained to me that the only way we could live together would be if I were to receive the Divine Love that she receives. I was not godly in my life, in my human life or spirit life. It feels and sounds a bit strange saying to you, "That I liked this woman". I never married in my human life as I never connected with anyone. I was an ordinary man living an ordinary life with an ordinary job in a country town in the back blocks of Australia working in a post office. I liked my job for Australia is a big country. Back in the day that I was growing up, space was vast and communication was a vastness that did take time that we tried to fill. I lived to a ripe old age. My mother raised me, my father passed away soon after WWII, in which he served. The feminine individual was sweet to me. She told me many things, that she too had lived in the same country I had lived in, but far away from me. She had been a spirit for twenty years before I joined this life. She was one of many children. She taught me how to receive this Love. Being a simple human spirit, I liked the fact that to receive this Love was simple. It feels a little odd speaking about love as this subject is one that I never spoke about in my human or spirit life. I loved my job and the country I lived in, but 'love' in an organic sense, I had never expressed. My progression to be with my new love happened quite quickly. I was as honest as the day was long. I grew up in the old day where the land was true. I can still remember the heat and the dry, which I liked. The woman, the female I live with in the Celestial Heaven, has taught me quite a few things so that I know how to live with God in this Love in my soul-life. I am not a teacher but a social participator.

Thank you, Chris

57

Hello; my name is Celia. My entrance into my spirit life was easy. I passed away quietly without any fanfare, departing dear Earth with only a handful of close friends beside me. When I awakened I was greeted by my husband, who had passed a short time before me. I felt joy in my heart seeing my husband again; I was relieved. I had no concern for where I was or how I came to be there. What mattered to me was that I was reunited with the love of my life. We are still together making slow progress in the Love. My heart is as happy as it was in those days when we were vibrant and young.

Thank you.

58

Hello; my name is Blessington. I am here to confirm that the soul-life is real as is the Divine Love and the Immortality that Luke has explained to you. I was no great philosopher in my human life, I was a man of the land. I could read the seasons in Tasmania. I lived a long time ago. I would find it difficult to relate to the world today. My memories are as clear as a bell. I really liked the eucalyptus and the rugged terrain that I lived in. I lived as a free man. I have never communicated like this before but, Zara knows of this place Blessington, having lived there. My presence is a surprise. I am so pleased that two who have come from this land are involved with Divine Love.

Well done. B

59

Hello; my name is Kingsley. I am the husband of the woman you gave a reading to yesterday. Many of your relatives, including Constance and my relatives and including one of my sons, were present. We knew that you knew this, but during the reading we advised you not to open direct communication with us to my wife. She is in her middle 80s and soon to be with us here. Zara has been looking after her on a regular basis; she is not infirmed but with a condition which requires assistance when she's out and about. This has been a fortuitous meeting as my wife originally from Tasmania knew Zara's parents, meeting her father for the first time at the 1956 Melbourne Olympics. My wife's father was involved in medicine and in WWII. He and Zara's father have met and have a lot in common. It is extraordinary how the convergence of age and time can bring connections together. As you know, Australia is still a relatively young country with established families dating back to small populations where established families knew of each other. I wish to confirm that we were with you yesterday and that you brought a lot of happiness to my wife whom I still love and adore. I will be there when her time comes to cross over. She has a wonderful spirit to her nature.

Thank you, K

60

Hello my darlings, it is I, Constance. I am here to confirm that we heard your thoughts last Wednesday when you were walking through the gardens of Como House in Melbourne. You were thinking about us, your relatives, and how I had been part of this recent work of spirit communication involving the soul-life and Divine Love. We didn't communicate with you directly as you walked the path in the sunlight, but we knew that you were aware that we were close by and that it was all about the Divine Love and that good progress made in this ... everlasting.

You have both continued receiving, which we are very happy about.

Love to you both, C

61

James Reid speaks:

I was with you both yesterday when Luke and the other individuals communicated with you. I liked the clarity that Luke imparted involving the existence of this spirit world as a factual consequence that God established for the continuation of the personality, spirit body and soul-life. Over here, as I have had time to evaluate my experience, the factual consequence of my life living as a spirit, has been my participation with God's Divine Love. As Luke explained how factual the spirit world is, part of this fact is the everlasting presence of the Divine Love. I know that we keep speaking about this Love, but you must understand that without it the whole reality of humankind would result in our existence being different. You have heard from individuals who lived their spirit life in the time before the life of Jesus. Some of these individuals were ancient, living a long time in their natural spirit life never being able to exceed the limitation of their perfect natural love.

The availability of Divine Love releases spirit life. It gives us something for us to look forward to. It generates movement. It alleviates the time construct of existing solely in the natural spheres. It provides the depraved, in their soul condition, a progressive way to redeem their natural love, restoring their soul condition to a good condition so their quality of life isn't with eternal and permanent depravity.

The Divine Love presents our attributes existing in our spirit body to reach a universal soul condition so that more life, spirit life, is available for us to individually participate with. The Divine Love provides us with the opportunity to understand what evolution is from a human landscape to a spirit landscape, and how external systems relate with us and we relate to them as we advance. It also offers us the resource of knowledge. By receiving Divine Love over a period of time, that sense of inner knowing is all-pervading. It is general knowledge here in the Celestial Heaven, that man was always meant to live with a truthful knowledge about the existence of their soul, human and spirit love, and who and what God is, as being Living Loving Soul and Spirit. We were never meant to live in separation from God for all eternity in the spirit world.

Luke has taught you about the true Immortality that the Divine Love brings to the life of our souls. For me, all that I have conveyed to you here is based on the greatest truth of all ... that the Divine Love provides each of us personal contact with the beautiful, truthful, loving soulful nature that God is. In my Celestial life, I can socialise knowing that I am aware of the life I am living in harmony with God. There are spirits who know far more than I, and I know far more than those who are beginning to receive this Love for their first time.

One attribute that I have embraced as I have matured in my spirit experience, is the attribute of my being philosophical. I have learnt so much that this inspires me to contemplate the eternal narrative that I - by living with Divine Love - find myself engaged with. I was a doctor in my earthly life but I have no need of this here. Learning about the greater spirit universe fulfils my requirements as an individual with an inquiring mind. The Celestial teachers assist the soul-life of individuals and not the spirit body. The Father completes the spirit body through the transitional phase of earthly life to spirit life. I know this as a truth for this happened to me. My spirit body was in perfect condition relative to my soul condition when I awakened after the death of my human life. It is the soul that requires attention from the get-go of spirit life. Restoring natural love to a good condition or learning about the influence of Divine Love as being part of this restoration, the Celestial teachers are the doctors of the soul.

It has been explained to you in previous communications that the natural love, being finite in its spectrum from most depraved to perfect natural love, is without any other boundary. The most depraved do not disappear and become in their depravity, non-existent. The individuals living in their perfect natural love do not mysteriously transform or relocate to some other place in the spirit world. Natural love is with a spectrum of soul condition with a finite boundary of spirit body/soul bookends. Human personality exists in this spectrum of natural love. There are only a finite number of causes to disrupt the spectrum that relates with the Spirit Laws of God involving the harmony of natural man and woman on Earth and in spirit life.

Involving Divine Love doesn't change the spectrum. It has been explained to you that once natural love is perfected, even the Divine Love cannot perfect it any more. What the Divine Love does is add or provide a whole new spectrum to the spirit attributes of the individual extending the soul bookends from the perfect natural love to the Soul of God, which is the new boundary for the perfect natural man and woman.

Before I go, which I must do soon, I would like to leave you with this thought. Of the Earth, there is nothing that has this Divine Love to it. Other than the soul of men and women, the Divine Love is not established for anything else. Living here has provided me with this thought which is common knowledge here. My appreciation for this truth is with the utmost respect. I have been able to realise how difficult it really is to place your own experience with the Father and this Love, when in all that surrounds you of the Earth, nothing can relate with what you are receiving and then sharing your expressions of your experience. I lived, as you know, aware of the existence of this Love in the later part of my life. I never really appreciated or respected what I have just conveyed to you.

My love to you, James

62

Luke speaks:

We have spoken to you about the restoration of natural love. This restoration is not a crusade through the spirit world to restore all that is imperfect in natural love to its perfection. The restoration we speak of is a personal assessment of your own physical life that may have led you to a relatively poor soul condition. There is only one thing that can restore natural love - love. This is what constitutes the energy and life of each soul. It is how each soul came into its existence from the Father's creation, and, it defines the essence of being human. For all those people who have said, "That love is the answer to all things", they are right! Restoring natural love is effectively restoring soul condition in natural love. This love can be restored by living more harmoniously to the Spirit Laws of Love that God has established as the only viable, happy way to live a fulfilled human and spirit life. It is a beautiful truth to know that God knows about love and happiness!

A spirit can restore their natural love to a better condition with the Divine Love or without the Divine Love. Forgiveness and acceptance are attributes of love as is goodness. The Spirit Laws that assist the living of love were never created by the Father to penalise a human for all eternity. They establish the status quo of the spirit world so all have an equal chance in their choice to live love, be this love in the natural or the Immortal Love.

In the Perfect Natural Sphere, there is a vast population that resides there as I speak to you now. What you see when you are there is a considerable amount of humanity living in harmony in the perfect human form in their spirit bodies, their natural love restored to its perfect condition, their souls living in harmony with God. They are very happy and content. Saleeba has explained much of this to you. I never lived any amount of time in the Perfect Natural Sphere as the perfect man, for I received Divine Love progressing through the spheres to the Celestial Heaven. Due to the diversity of human experience on Earth, other than the life of the First Parents before their fall from grace, humans have never seen the whole population living in perfect natural love on the face of the Earth; always has existed the full spectrum of natural love.

Restoration of natural love is a personal organic involvement that requires choices to live a good life respecting yourself and others irrespective of cultural and social diversity. This extends from the individual soul into all aspects of living such as respecting the environment you live in and the species you live with.

The Divine Love restores natural love but you are still required to look at any intimate memories or actions that you have lived that may have caused a complete disrespect to yourself or another or the environment or species. If you are disrespectful, which infers that one is ultimately disrespectful of God, which is in action, disrespecting love and its existence. The comparison between the Perfect Natural Sphere to the spheres that comprise the Celestial Heaven is made solely through the visibility of Divine Love, which in turn is the distinction between those who are aware of the Soul, God, with those who are unaware that God is Soul.

Luke

63

Saleeba speaks:

The year 2020 will signify 31 years that you have both been aware of the availability of Divine Love, actively participating as two individual independent souls receiving Divine Love, but also aware of the existence of Celestial spirits. Both your interests insofar as the spirit world, spirit guides and communication, God and understanding human nature, preceded the time that you found the selection of communications that James Padgett received. It is important for the reader to understand that both your genuine involvements relating to 'spirit' has been ongoing in one form or another since you were both teenagers. Never group related or invested in any religious society, it has been an individual interest culminating in an adult life's work.

We have communicated to you both an extensive array of spirit life experience. All through this time, you have both remained consistent in your receipt of Divine Love. Day by day, all these years aware of your participation with the Eternal Soul, God, and the experience that Divine Love has added as an extension to physical finite life. Your understanding of the intricate workings of the soul-life has progressed throughout your lives. Always, you have both been aware that the boundary between your physical life to our spirit life, open. Your lives, open to receiving our guidance, aware that we are never far away.

Everlasting

We are to include you both in this spirit narrative, for you are both living your soul-life aware of Divine Love and in love with the Soul, God. You acknowledge us, aware that humanity is participating here in this incredible spirit world where a vast amount of humanity is living and progressing in the same Divine Love that you are living with. There are individuals, as there will be those in the future, who also live like this thinking, contemplating, experiencing, desiring to know all that they can know about the full spectrum of human nature and what constitutes true human life in all its perspective. We have written about you both before. You have both moved yourselves completely aside from our communications, that the reader can receive spirit life experience in pure form. We must include you in this spirit narrative as the reader may only read this one book; a little history fills out the vision. If one were to read all the information that we have conveyed over the years, they will see that we have tried to remain as present as possible for that timeless feel to the narrative so that our language will relate to the reader's present today and well into the future. We have not desired all our effort to be seen and read as the language of the past.

Humanity is only going to become more diverse worldwide. The age of technology and information will become more mobile as the younger generations seek their independence roaming around the world switched on and linked in. Never before has the human social world been so revolutionised as you are socially today. People are looking to be more socially expressive, individuality being recognised and personality flourishing. The more humanity becomes expansive, the more the rigid will try to hold on but the sheer force of global information and the fact that people are colourful will bring the surface of the world toward greater inclusivity rather than greater separation and exclusivity. This will present its own problems but there has always been drama when human's social life desires to become more expressive and expansive liberating that one unique quality that every human has, individuality!

The information we have conveyed, open and transparent. The Divine Love fits perfectly into individuality. Each soul is an individual. This is seen in its' living truth throughout the spirit world. The relationship between earthly life to spirit life will go on for some individuals. They will be fascinated by the whole reality that an extension to human life exists. This is how you have both been. From our position here, living with Divine Love is a known fact of human spirit life. Today, we are seeing men and women sharing in the same known fact of human spirit life. This is a revelation. We truly foresee that more individuals will recognise their soul-life in their physical life recognising that they are participating with the Father as we are here. This is the ultimate expression of Heaven on Earth. Let us take this expression one step further, recognising Celestial Heaven on Earth by those living their individual faith in Divine Love acknowledging the Soul, God, with the ability to perceive their natural love perfected while continuing to feel covered in the Living presence of Divine Love while living social, earthly life experiences. This is not a dream nor a distant fantasy. The receivers of my communication have been living this for a long time. The continuity of the communications that they have received is consistent and transparent with the essence of each contributing spirit living love.

It has been another lovely moment shared. Always and everlasting, Saleeba

64

Luke speaks:

It is one hundred years in the making; it could be said that it is two thousand and twenty years in the making. Today, more people are finally aware of the availability of God's Divine Love than ever before in the human history of Earth. The messages and teachings that we conveyed to James those years ago are now being read worldwide with the awareness that an existing form of energy completes the soul-life. We have been able to bring forward much more information in the communications you have both received, which will assist the individual in the future human history. Daily, individuals are finding, reading, contemplating the information contained within James' experience. From the outside looking in your perspective may seem as if progress is slow; slow can sometimes be good. Slowly the Padgett Messages are finding their way into human life, which means the truth about the Divine Love and the natural love is dawning in the hearts and minds of readers. This is reflective of new information for humanity slowly being processed. Other than the short life of Jesus, very little has come to life about the true teaching of God's Divine Love; how this Love relates with the mortal soul and what - by receiving this Divine Love - a man or woman can embrace in their human life.

I would like to present this scenario to you: if the First Parents were seen on Earth when Jesus lived, humanity would have seen a different kind of human living on Earth. If Jesus and the First Parents, Amon and Aman, were living and teaching among the peoples of the world today, with these three individuals manifesting their superlative power afforded to them by the Father, dormant humanity would realise the full spirit and its existence as forming part of the physical universe. If this were happening today humanity would be forever changed, no longer being dormant to the nature of soul-life, spirit attributes and the existence of the Eternal Nature of the Living Soul, God. These three individuals would symbolise the living convergence between man and woman with God, and the spirit component that would make the spirit world transparent. Today in the spirit world these three individuals are living here, visible, transparent, and do move around all the spirit spheres so that humanity sees the living proof of what I have presented.

I will leave you now having presented this scenario for the reader to contemplate the real living wonders that exist in the present and the future. Luke

65

Hello; my name is Andrew. I have lived a Celestial life for a long time. I was nobody important in the history of mankind. I was as many are, a passenger through life then into the spirit life we go. I do feel important communicating with you, for I am contributing toward an everlasting truth and one that I know something about. I like that I am with the opportunity to speak to you about this Divine Love.

Living with Divine Love does make one feel important here in our spirit life. My reason for declaring this is due to the fact that the attribute of a soul that we are, is perfected in our natural essence of love. This is important to us, for Our Father gave life to our soul in the first place. Having received enough Divine Love those many years ago in my spirit life my natural love perfected, which meant that I became aware of the significance of my soul-life as how the life of my soul came into existence. I am important to the Father as the Father is important to me. I am glad that in my spirit life there was a way forward for me to realise my full potential as the personality I am. I lived in a time when slavery was present among certain nations, how deplorable this was! I was a slave. My potential for living a human independent life in the culture of my people was circumvented by the human trade of money. That was a long time ago. My spirit life presented freedom and independence. Strange to think that I had to be here to experience this and not in my earthly human life. I have forgiven those who trespassed against me. Over here, the tables are turned. Those who treated me with a lack of common human respect had to amend their compensation for their human transgressions. As it is here, many of those who trespassed against me over their Earth life accepted their transgressions, forgiveness found and compensation alleviated. They live in their perfect natural love having progressed through the Divine Love spheres as I did. I know many of these individuals and we are good friends and have contributed toward other individuals learning about their soul-life in the spirit world.

Everyone here is with their choice to amend for any transgressions committed in human life. Over here, there is time. There is so much time without any other ending to complete this time. The only thing an individual can do is to choose to live in the harmony of love. This is the great realisation that exists in all the spirit life.

As I said, when I left my earthly life I was an individual blunted in my human potential. In my spirit life, the opposite! I didn't have any compensation. I was a man of sound mind and heart, always forgiving those who trespassed against me. I knew that my life and other men and women like me had been violated, but my soul was always facing toward my love of God and that of my fellow man. Some slaves developed such hatred that they developed compensation themselves. There were horrible things done to us. Some slaves lived good lives due to their owners. It is incredulous to think that people can own other people in their earthly life. From my perspective, this kind of human transaction is morally untenable.

My potential fulfilled in my spirit life. Meeting Jesus with various Celestial teachers was more than I could ever have asked for. I was taught about the soul-life in relationship to the Soul, God. I embraced these teachings, receiving Divine Love, living my Immortal soul-life. I have helped many individuals residing in the Hells toward their fulfilment of a better life. Many of these individuals have progressed into the Celestial Heaven. Over here, the perspective of human life and humanity changes. As it has been conveyed to you, if you could only see how much love is living here, why love is supreme in living action, and how we are all related in the mortal gift of soul-life, then the world as people know it, the earthly world of humanity would change. I know that so many spirits living in their natural love and with Divine Love would like nothing more than for the humanity of Earth to recognise the gift of soul-life. For what is blind on Earth men and women will see the truth of it when living here. There is no hiding from the true condition of your soul condition in the spirit world. Many spirits have yet to embrace their soul-life here, some you have heard from, but they all recognise how true the gift of human life is.

Thank you, Andrew

66

Hi you two, it's your friend, Georgie. Been quite some time since we last caught up. I am really well. The time or period of my transition is well past me now, I have adapted to my permanent life here; I have accepted this. Those years of my illness well over my earthly horizon.

As you both know, that was a difficult time for me. Now I can look back on that time as a period of growth and progression. My illness was all about my physical life. I excluded anything about my soul in my earthly life, I made no effort to learn about the truth that I was a soul and that spirit existed. That is why it was a difficult time for me, dying and then awakening here. There were emotional reasons too, being a young mother with young children, a husband I loved all taken away from me.

Now my love for my soul and my life - albeit short - I have a greater love for. I know that my children will grow up without their mother, that my husband will never receive communication from me, but my life here is full. My love is strong with all my spirit attributes flowing in the form they are to. I reside in my Immortal life happy and content. It is amazing that with time, surrounded by those who care, by receiving Divine Love personal disadvantages are melted away with true love replenishing my natural love as such fear and loss dissolved. I now revere life. Through my time of dying my husband loved me so much. I was fortunate as my family loved me. I look back at my human life remembering all the good times with fond memories, even dying part of my memories, but I am living now a full spirit life.

Think of me in these terms as that is how I am. My love to you both, your friend, Georgie

67

Luke speaks:

At the centre of all our communications is the expansive experience of our living with God's Divine Love. Essentially, by reading what has been conveyed, you are introduced to spirit's life experience living in the spirit world, living with Divine Love. The vision of the spirit world is then seen in a perspective of the Divine Love available with a vast population residing in the human afterlife aware of their soul-life with a progressive experience known.

This is an obvious statement when I state that peoples of the Earth are not receiving Divine Love abundantly, having figured out how it is to live the soul-life with the Father then communicating this to us by sharing what they have learnt so that we may begin our participation in Divine Love. Virtually everything known to men and women about the life of Divine Love, the energy that it is and what it means in a universal context and the convergence with mortals, is conveyed by spirits living with Divine Love in the spirit world.

We know that men and women know that the Divine Love exists; true, palpable to the soul and physical senses and most importantly, can recognise that this Love received when sincerely open toward the Soul of God for one can feel with feeling, that this convergence of energy flows. The natural love of the human toward their love of God, the Divine Love of God from the Soul of God flowing as God's love toward the natural love of the human.

My purpose for speaking to you about this is to place the Divine Love in a context for you so that you are not reliant solely on spirit communication or your interest with the afterlife. Receiving Divine Love involves the soul. Men and women may desire to receive this Love in the abundance that it is without ever directly desiring to communicate with us or to receive communication from us, or to identify human life as lived in the spirit world. Effectively, a life living with Divine Love directly involves the Living Life that God's Soul is. This is what is important - profound - when you understand the context that the Divine Love exists for the soul, be it on Earth or in the spirit world.

The essence of my teaching is to convey that one may not know anything about the spirit world or interface directly with communication from spirits in order for the soul in an earthly life to live abundantly in their faith in Divine Love. Divine Love involves your soul with the Soul of God. This is the unbroken word of truth. I am pleased to have completed this time with you as there was a length of time in the middle of this teaching when we had to separate. Your friend and teacher, Luke

68

Hello; my name is Clarence. I am here to convey a little of my experience. My spirit life has been defined by relationship; my relationship with my wife is the most important aspect of my spirit life. My wife's name is Leslie. We lived together as husband and wife our entire adult life; we were inseparable. We lived an uncomplicated marriage through decades of change. Our love for each other was affectionate to begin with. We were born in Australia, we never travelled, content in our work which was bringing up quite a large family. We had eight children, all of them have prospered and we have a lot of grandchildren. We lived through both wars.

As life takes its course, we both entered our spirit life quite close together in terms of age and time. I went before Leslie, then Leslie from natural causes, joined me here. There was hardly any elapsed time so our relationship, our marriage, continued in this new environment. We had no fear of dying or living here, we had lived full earthly lives with good health, good family and honest life.

We adapted to this next phase with enjoyment. We were together so we learnt how to live here together. It was so much fun learning new things from relatives who had long since lived here. It was really a magical time. Our children were established. There was nothing back in our earthly life left unsaid or undone. The beginning of our spirit life was uncomplicated; a happy time. We actually joked together that this was the first time that we had travelled somewhere together! I hope you see the humour in this. Our children travelled, we loved listening to them share their stories and showing us their photos. In our spirit life, we were proud of our children and grandchildren. We were proud of the way that we had raised them to be empathetic wholesome people. We were not religious, rather open-minded. My wife, Leslie and I would go for walks through the county discussing how it is to be raising eight children. As the decades came and went during the 20th century, we recognised that we were required as parents to keep an open-mind letting our children grow in their own sunlight.

As we adapted in our spirit life, some of our relatives introduced us to a more extensive life; a life that was available to live. This involved Divine Love. Leslie and I were good people. To us, the Divine Love represented a good form of love. We had no experience of this Love, but our relatives were such beautiful examples of what this Love provides; Leslie and I decided to give it a go. There was a lot of laughter, happy, happy spirit days. We would find ourselves laughing all the time. You see, it is like this. In our human life, we watched each other grow older. In our spirit life, we watch each other grow young! Leslie and I became young again. This was an incredible experience. We were told this would happen. We had observed as we progressed through the Divine Love spheres that we were never introduced to anyone from the Celestial Heaven who looked - in their spirit appearance - old. We settled at about 30 years of age. This is difficult for me to convey to you, but we do appear as if we are around that age again. The spirit body is made of different material to the physical body. Individuals here seem to appear at around this age. We joked to each other that we might regress in age to be teenagers again, we could fall in love and become married all over again! We seemed to stop de-ageing; we didn't make this happen, the spirit body established itself in these environments to about that age. Thirty years of age in a spirit body appearance does not look like a thirty-year-old man or woman. The outer spirit body has real texture to it, is smooth but with a deep texture like skin. It is very receptive to touch and the spirit light that illuminates all these spheres. What does it say about evolution when a body here de-ages when all we are used to in our physical life is the evolving and ageing body? The teachers have been very wise speaking to you about the differences of evolution, what evolves, what doesn't evolve, how evolution happens in a physical life compared to a spirit life lived in only the spirit body. Ageing exists here but in a spectrum of both directions. Infants mature, the aged become youthful. The appearance of this ageing spectrum in the spirit life differs when Divine Love is involved. When Divine Love is involved the spirit body reflects a more intense life and colour than the spirit body when solely living around the soul in only a condition of natural love.

Leslie and I are soulmates. We have learnt about our soul-life, where the soul originates from, why it was formed, how it was formed, the purpose for its incarnation, what it is made of and how it defines everything in the life of a spirit in the spirit world. Most importantly, we understand that the Divine Love, made for the soul, brings Immortality. We like that we are soulmates. We are continuing our relationship here, which is special to us. We both love the Soul, God; grateful that so much has been provided for us but most of all, that we are alive, that human life doesn't end at death. In time, all our children will be here as will all our grandchildren. Life goes on. My relationship with Leslie is lived in the Celestial Heaven. We have a beautiful home, a lovely garden where the colours are iridescently deep. There are colours here that I have never seen before; I can hardly describe them to you as they don't exist in the earthly palate of organic nature.

For two people who never travelled while they were alive, we have travelled a long way now! We have travelled through whole spheres of spirit life experience. The bizarre thing is, we have moved spheres without requiring any suitcase or passport and everyone we met is just lovely and so helpful. We feel special but we were never special. There is nothing other than love here.

Thank you for receiving me today. Leslie is with me, and we both send our love to you and our children and grandchildren. C

69

Hello; my name is James. I lived in England a long time ago. I was born a King. History knows my life but it doesn't know my spirit life. Religion and politics are part of many people's lives; neither of these two things exists here. Human beliefs change. Part of this change is acquiring new skills to live here. In human life, intelligence can be affected by many contributing factors like education and nutrition and physical conditions. My purpose speaking to you about human life is for me not to be King but to be a soulful man.

A real eye-opener about becoming a spirit is how one may leave the Earth with their importance and place in history only to realise the kind of history that is established here. When I arrived here, I was in awe of how small my human life was compared to the kind of life humanity was living here. It made me realise what it was to be truly humble and an empathetic person. I met individuals who had ruled people in all capacity. When I embraced the living of my soul-life, as being aware that I was soul as each human is, when I began receiving Divine Love consciously, defined by my active participation toward living an Immortal life, I had to be taught about this life by very humble souls. The general public in my Earth life could not teach me how to be King for they would never be a King or Queen. Over here, the common man and woman are all with equal opportunity to participate freely in the Immortal life. The individual who symbolises the greatest amount of power in all the spirit world is Jesus. He alone knows all there is to know about mortal man and mortal man's relationship with God. He is with such power but this power is never centred with himself, placed at the centre of the spirit-verse and spirit world. He lives here as he lived as a man, with God our Heavenly Father at the centre of all life, earthly and spirit. It makes me shudder when I think about the way humans treated each other for so many thousands of years when here in the spirit life it is completely the opposite. When I first entered my spirit life adapting to these environments, I was astounded at how modern and empathetic toward each other those residing in the natural spheres were and those living their Immortal life. I often wondered what it was all about, why humans of history were so quick to send people to their deaths when there was so much love in each soul. I have learnt a lot about being human since living here. When I go to the natural spheres, the last thing I desire is to be introduced as a King. I am a teacher of the soul-life as I know that living with the Eternal Father is the most a soul can aspire toward. It brings out the real love that we are capable of living and expressing.

I will not write more at this time. James

70

Hello; my name is Tom. I grew up in Western Australia. I lived up north of Perth, I was a maintenance man fixing things in the local town where I lived. My passion in life was fishing.

I never read the Bible nor was I religiously educated; I pretty much stayed away from religion. In this country, we have Easter and Christmas. They were family reunions for me, social gatherings where one could be as religious as they liked to be, or not religious at all. In the country I lived in, during the last decades of the 20th century, no one is forced to be political or religious, a choice left up to the individual. It's one of the great freedoms of the Australian way of life that I respected. It is a great country.

Everlasting

When I transitioned into my spirit life, I died content with my physical life. Like so many Australian's, quite possibly like so many in the world, we have a vague idea that there is more to life but nearly all our physical life is dominated by our physical and social commitments.

When I was fishing I did so with a few mates, we loved it. We never talked about God, mainly sport and local community things and of course, "The one that got away" and, "The one just caught"! My spirit life was an easy experience. I had lots of fond memories, no compensation as I had lived a respectful life. I treated others with common respect, I knew what it felt like when other people treated me with disrespect. I didn't like it so I never treated other people in this manner. I even respected the sea and the fish. You learn very quickly when spending time at sea, that the sea never respects you but you have to respect it.

I am living with Divine Love. This was an easy adaption. Some of my relatives taught me about life here; I liked this. What sped my acceptance to this Love is that I knew in my mind that my physical life was over. A good life completed. It's like fixing something. Once you fix the washer, you don't have to return to fix it again or try to improve on what has already been fixed. My physical life fulfilled and complete. I found it thoroughly fascinating that as I advanced in my life experience in the spirit world, my memories of my human life were really about the sea. Living as a spirit for a length of time, other memories about my life were not important to me. I married but that didn't last; I had no children. I had a sister but she moved away to the East Coast. Where I lived it was quite isolated. Tourism hadn't found a foothold here. I lived in a place called Broome.

I found it utterly fascinating that I, immersed in the environment of a spirit sphere, was able to have vivid memory of the sea. I realised that I had retained so much about my experiences at sea, but there was no sea to be seen in any sphere. My love for saltwater - that expansive horizon - the whole texture of the sea filled my memories while my new experience happening along, happily so.

Experiencing Divine Love is very simple. I adapted to this experience with ease. I did it because I could. Over here, they relate to God as Spirit and Soul. I had no experience of spirit or soul in my human life, I met people who were different to me and I thought they had a great 'spirit' about them. I understood that when people are lost or the sea claims their lives, we know this as souls lost at sea. History had defined people disappearing at sea as lost souls. I accepted this but I never thought that I would ever be lost at sea, so I never thought about myself as soul. In my life I came close a few times, most do when spending so much time at sea. Rogue waves, engines breaking down, the turn of the weather. I died from cancer in the latter part of my life. I accepted this fate continuing to go to sea until I couldn't manage that any more. I had a liver condition. I drank a bit with the fellas and my diet was pretty poor even though I ate fish. For me, it is an unusual experience to have so much memory about the sea living in a place that is without a sea. It is a unique perspective. I was considered a chatterbox, especially when we had had a good day out cleaning the fish afterwards in the sunrise or sunset. Sometimes we would spend hours at sea at night, fishing into the dawn. My memories are crystal clear. I can feel myself still at sea, but I am not. I am not living in the past. I have been taught that the spirit-mind, which acts as the spirit-brain, is living with such a different kind of energy than the organic brain that memories are vivid and can be relived as living and are not memories functioning at the speed of the physical organic human systems. In my spirit body, my recall of memory is faster and really vivid. It's quite surreal learning to adapt to this.

I have made some good friends, we get along really well. It is very social here. I haven't met anyone who is a soul lost in the spirit world. I like the feeling that God is Spirit, Love and Soul.

Thank you for receiving my message, Tom

71

Luke speaks:

Having contributed those years ago when James Padgett received a diverse range of subject matter relating to the soul-life, we introduced a structure that formed part of our teachings. We structured the spheres in name and number giving form to the spirit world which provides the reader with a sense of comprehension insofar as understanding the perfection and limit of natural love in relationship to natural love progressing to its perfection when including the Divine Love. The natural love is a good love; a true love in the soul. We have conveyed to you how good this natural love is.

In the First natural sphere, the Second, Fourth and Sixth, individuals residing here are living their soul-life harmoniously in their natural condition with the Spirit Laws of Love that the Father has established. In the First Divine Love sphere, the Third, Fifth, Seventh and Celestial Heaven, individuals are residing in their good natural love progressing with Divine Love, living harmoniously with the Spirit Laws of Love the Father has established. As I travel through all the spheres I have mentioned, I see visibly the kind of harmony all individuals are living with. It is harmonious. My reason for stating this is to provide you with clarity involving the Spirit Law of Compensation. If all individual humans living in the spheres I mentioned are living in a good condition of natural love and harmonious with the Spirit Laws of God, then is the Spirit Law of Compensation acting in any of these souls? You have learnt that due to the condition of a soul in its natural love, that soul cannot progress to another sphere until that condition of soul is improved. This is a truth but one that doesn't involve compensation. The only spheres that involve the Spirit Law of Compensation acting with humans is in the lowest spheres, often referred to as The Hells, where the condition of the soul in its natural love is out of harmony with the Spirit Law of Love. These three spheres have been identified as The Hells or Spheres of Disharmony. The actual fabric of these spheres is not disharmonious or a real hell. They have been established by God so that those humans living outside of love have a residence in the spirit world. The Hell, or Disharmony, exists entirely within the soul of that individual and in no way reflects any part of the creation of these spheres by God. I am conveying this teaching to you so that you might better understand where disharmony exists in the spirit world and that disharmony doesn't exist through the entire mortal spirit world.

    I will state here that this teaching works entirely with the identity of natural love and Divine Love relating to individual soul-life with the Spirit Law of Compensation. In the First Divine Love sphere an individual may have certain memories that require their attention as they begin receiving Divine Love although their natural love remains harmonious with the Spirit Laws of Love. The Spirit Law of Compensation only acts in the confines of the natural soul. It cannot influence any outcome of the Divine Love as this Love is of God's Soul and exists without any disharmony. I am conveying this to you so that you may understand that most of the entire spirit world lives harmoniously with the Soul of God. This is true for those individuals living entirely in their natural love in a good condition without knowing anything at all about the Soul-Life of God or the living with the

Immortal Love. You do not have to be aware of God to be living harmoniously with God. This is evident in the spirit life where so many individuals are residing in a particular sphere living their spirit life in the attributes of their natural personality barely knowing anything at all about the true existence of their soul, yet still in good natural love they are harmonious in their spirit life with the Spirit Laws of Love.

I have never travelled to the First, Second, Fourth or Sixth natural spheres to teach individuals why they are living out of harmony. Other than being polite and nice, there is nothing I can teach them until one of these souls asks about the difference between them and me, and what this difference means. Once asked, my teaching about Immortal life begins, beginning with harmony. When I visit the three spheres where individuals are living in soulful disharmony, I can do something, which is to explain about the Law of Compensation and how love may be restored if the individual chooses to begin in their disharmony back toward harmony in love.

The perfection of the mortal spirit world will eventually reveal that there will be no individuals residing and living in their disharmony in their natural love.

I will stop now. Your friend and teacher, Luke

72

Luke speaks:

I would like to clarify the teaching of an untruth that may be perceived as truth by readers who may have read the story about the "Lucifer Rebellion".

The reality of Divine Love that brings true Immortality to the mortal life of a soul is pristine in its non-evolving form of energy. The Divine Love is an existing form of energy that is with real form, substance, depth and directness, insofar as this form of energy extends from the Father's Soul in reach of all mortal souls of the Earth and spirit world.

The life of the First Parents and the life of Jesus involves the presence of Divine Love. It has been conveyed to you that the teaching involving the mortal life of a human soul involves two loves: the natural love in the soul and the Divine Love that exists external to that soul which when acquired receives all the benefits that the Divine Love provides that mortal soul.

The story about a super-universal personality influencing human life or the life of the First Parents or the life of Jesus is erroneous. If there is to be any good taken from the fictional story involving the Lucifer Rebellion, it is that this story depicts this personality establishing itself as the centre of attention rather than the attention of this personality directed to the Soul that God personifies.

The First Parents committed their error by themselves. This error involved no influence or direct coercion from planetary princes or super-universal personalities causing the First Parents to separate from God by following these personalities to a better universal plan for humans to live by. The only individuals who circumvented the Divine Love from being available continuously after the life of the First Parents were the First Parents. As we know, that fall from God that the First Parents committed was restored in the natural spirit world where the First Parents lived once they had died. It was with Jesus that the Divine Love available again.

The story of life involves the Creator who is the originator of the mortal soul in all its dynamic. No mortal human on Earth or in the spirit world has any influence over the existing form of energy that the Divine Love is. The Divine Love, whilst having been formed for mortal souls, can never be determined to its function or outcome by mortal souls. The Lucifer Rebellion as a concept is flawed as it does not illustrate the true relationship that exists between the mortal soul with the Soul of God that involves the two distinct loves. The human world was isolated from God after the life of the First Parents, but only isolated insofar as the Divine Love being unavailable as a resource of energy for mortal souls by the Universal Acting Spirit deactivated by its originator, the Eternal Soul, God. As we know, the Universal Acting Spirit was reengaged by the Father when Jesus lived his life on the Earth. Not even Jesus had the power to reactivate the Universal Acting Spirit. The First Parents and Jesus are without any control to determine any outcome involving God's Divine Love.

There are super-universal personalities that exist. These individuals require no evolution to obtain perfection in their personality with the Eternal Father and cannot disrupt the evolving planetary worlds in any way, shape or form. This is due to the fact that the existing Divine Love forms part of the entire universal matrix of existing evolutionary worlds and universes where mortal personality acquires soul at the commencement of incarnation, individualising personality through physical experience, then subsequently living in the spirit life once that physical life is complete. Planet Earth with its humans is not the only existing planet with human mortal souls. There are other forms of physical life living with souls individualising through their human experience. These souls being formed and originated by the Father just like humans of the Earth.

In any physical life, there will always exist the conundrum between the personality of mortal man or woman asserting its dominance when the real existential truth is formed by God being part of God's Personality, Supreme. Here in the spirit life, when you have had time to adapt and acquire Divine Love interfacing with definitive, true, existing spirit realities that involve living as the personality you are in the Immortal life and living the soul-life you were destined to live, then the reality of the Eternal personality becomes transparent and identified in its true context to mortal personality.

My purpose speaking to you about this today is to clarify that the Divine Love is the true connectivity with universal life and not a personality. Even Jesus teaches this as he alone is a compelling individual personality. But with all his power of personality, he never distorts or interferes with another personality which could distort that soul from living in love and in their Immortal life with the Father.

Fortunately, the Lucifer Rebellion is a fictional story that has no weight to it here in the spirit world, therefore, it has absolutely no causal effect in the outcome of human life relating to past consequences.

We have taught you a lot about the life of the First Parents. They are unique individuals, different from all other humans as Jesus' life was and still remains. But these three individuals for all the life they personify, are souls living within the boundary of two existing loves: the natural love and the Divine Love that provides the real Immortal life of the soul.

I know that not all readers will find this subject interesting, nor will they find many teachings that we have provided involving the Fatherly Truths pertinent to their human life. It can be a spiritually sobering thought when one realises that personality will never usurp what is already established and created by the Father for the life of the mortal soul. Today, any mortal soul can make a beginning. Divine Love available, Universal Acting Spirit engaged equals a fact everlasting.

Your friend and teacher, Luke

73

Luke speaks:

Recently, I spoke to you about the Spirit Law of Compensation, the harmony that exists in the spirit world and relative soul condition. I would like to speak a little more about this.

When Jesus began his teaching with James Padgett about the natural love and the Divine Love that defines a full soul-life, The Golden Rule was laid out in plain sight and plain word, "Do unto others as you would have others do unto you". This is the principle teaching that defines soul condition that relates to natural love. Never more evident is this principal teaching with its effects seen than when people cross over to begin their spirit life. I conveyed to you how harmony exists among the peoples of the spirit world. The Spirit Law of Compensation interacts with The Golden Rule. In order for you to understand what soul condition is as it relates to natural love, it will be necessary to locate where the real convergence transpires between The Golden Rule and the Spirit Law of Compensation.

If you think about the harmony of natural love as being a good love living in a soulful rapport with the Spirit Laws of Love established by God, then the relationship between The Golden Rule with the Spirit Law of Compensation can also be thought of as harmonious and seamless without one recognising that the Spirit Law of Compensation having to act upon your soul. If you understand harmony as lived by people in the spirit world, then you will be able to see what is disharmony by the relationship of The Golden Rule and whether or not the Spirit Law of Compensation is required to be applied.

Every single action of man or woman in physical life is weighed toward love or away from love. We know this is true, for we have the vision in the spirit life of seeing how people are in their soul condition when they arrive at their spirit life.

The Golden Rule defines all Spirit Laws relating to the soul condition in natural love.

Over here, we are able to see people in the First Natural Sphere having arrived and being attracted as they adapt to the environment that best suits the condition of their soul. If an individual is taken to the lowest spheres where the poorest of condition live, we know that The Golden Rule was breached during their physical life. With the Spirit Law of Compensation coming into effect and applied to the soul in that breached condition of soul disharmony. Compare this to a person coming into their spirit life with their soul condition having not breached The Golden Rule. As they adapt to their spirit life the Spirit Law of Compensation remains inactive and non-applied. You have heard from individuals who have arrived here after their physical life without ever experiencing the effect of the Spirit Law of Compensation acting upon them for they did not breach the workings of The Golden Rule. Human history is a history fraught by the breaching of "Do unto others as you would have others do unto you".

Thank goodness the Father formed a Spirit Law that acts upon the soul with clean precision otherwise what transpires on Earth would continue here and quite possibly throughout all the spirit spheres. Since the population of people in the spirit world constitutes every individual having ever lived on Earth, disharmony with harmony would remain a human drama in the spirit world without any outcome or purpose.

You have heard that some individuals upon their arrival here have proceeded to the lowest spheres due to their soul condition, then over time have restored their soul condition to a good natural love. As their condition improves the easing of the workings of the Spirit Law of Compensation takes place until they are living without any interaction with this Spirit Law. They are free; they are living within the golden rule.

I spoke to you about the Lucifer Rebellion and what this fictional story symbolises. Due to the fact that the Divine Love exists, I will now speak about control.

The narrative about the Lucifer Rebellion symbolises control. Super-universal personalities controlling mortal outcomes by utilising their inherent spirit power to manipulate mere mortal outcomes. Greek mythology speaks of the same narrative; this narrative has been portrayed throughout human cultures ever since humans have lived. The First Parents have conveyed their experience about this in some of their spirit communications, with the presence of control forming part of their narrative when providing a reason for their choice of separation from God. They assumed control, but not influenced from a super-universal spirit existing in the spirit universe. They assumed control in seeing to their equal standing with God. When the Divine Love ceased to be available to them, they lived as mere mortals in their natural love now subject to the evolution of natural love and realised what little control they had. They eventually died of old age and passed into their spirit life. Jesus never controlled the people he lived with. I never felt that I was being manipulated or controlled by my friend. All of us who lived with Jesus were encouraged by Jesus to establish our own individual life with God and among our fellow man. He taught us about The Golden Rule, pointing out that these laws were fundamental, true and consistent for every single human and that he was not the creator or enforcer of these laws. He also taught us not to fear God but to live in the love of God. He said that any man or woman seeking control of another man or woman would try to sit themselves at the seat of all power, which meant that ultimately one would live in fear of God for such is the human nature when competing for supremacy and control. No human can control God or the outcome of any of God's Handiworks, including the Divine Love. The only thing that people can really control is other people.

Over here, the perception of control fades away. Humans have no experience living in their spirit body on Earth. So much about a person's life beginning in the spirit world is all about a complete loss of control. Living with Divine Love is not a controlled life. The Father has not formed the Divine Love to gain control over our soul independence. So many of you are receiving Divine Love today, but you are all doing whatever it is you like. Living with Divine Love makes an individual here feel more independent than ever! We are able to live in the control of our own independence as there requires individual responsibility but no spirit feels that they are being controlled by any other personality or law, and especially not by God.

As time goes by there are now numerous books involved with spirit communication that individuals read with the literature comprising these books appears related to Celestial spirit communication. Many have found the Judas of Kerioth messages an inspiring read. It is not for me to critique all books associated with supposed spirit communications, as inspiration can come from anywhere that may teach the individual more about life. What I will say, which is quite significant that in the Life and Teachings of Jesus chapter that forms part of the Urantia Book, everything in that narrative derived to the past. There is nothing living in the present. For instance, Jesus is living and teaching the way of the true Immortal life in the spirit world today. The Divine Love of God is the true Immortal **cause** that defines the difference of all things involving life in the spirit world. As time goes by the reader needs to keep an ear open to the present for this is where the living is and where the experience of Divine Love teaches the individual about their soul-life and the Soul-Life of God.

It has been a pleasure to be with you again. Your friend and teacher, Luke

74

Luke speaks:

I realise how difficult it might be for you to gain real soul-perspective on the full dynamic that the Divine Love is and what this energy involves insofar as assisting those of us living here to progress into the soul condition that we live in in our Immortal spirit life. I am aware that one may be reading these words their first time without having any prior knowledge pertaining to the existence of the Divine Love, what this Love brings to the soul, how this Love came into existence and the difference that living with this Love establishes in the spirit world. I am aware as I speak to you that most men and women are with limited experience insofar as understanding how this spirit world is comprised, formed and originated into existence by God. We have conveyed so much information, practical spirit life experience and teachings involving the full gamut of soul-life all in the knowing - our collective knowing - that men and women in their physical life are with such a clear lack of visibility to the palpable realities of the Soul, God and the Handiworks God has established that define human life.

I am aware that there will be a lot of information that we have conveyed, that when read, the individual may have absolutely no idea what they have just read and the meaning of it. How is it when one is suddenly introduced to the reality involving two individuals that are personified as the First Parents? What will it mean to the reader when we state that here in the Divine Love spheres and Celestial Heaven Jesus, moves about teaching about the Immortal soul-life that involves the individual with God, with none of these teachings referring at all to any religious belief, structure or context?

What will it mean when we have conveyed so much information about the attribute of the spirit body that is so visible, transparent, real to us in our spirit life when you cannot see it all? How does it sound when we communicate our voice that speaks about the Divine Love with such palpability when in your experience, the palpability of this Love is hardly felt in your physical senses? What kind of image are you seeing when you do not see the humanity you live with shining in a soulful life and aware of the gift of Divine Love when we have revealed to you that a vast population of humanity celebrates their soulful life completely aware of the Divine Love?

All these questions and all their answers is the wonderment in a life everlasting. The spectrum of human life is a dynamic convergence between physical life and the existence of spirit and soul, which is suddenly revealed when a person transitions into the spirit world into their spirit life. As these communications continue from our collective voice over the years, a surface of spirit and love is shining toward you in the essence of our communications which mirrors the surface of your physical life and world. Only once before has such a surface been mirrored. It was mirrored when Jesus walked the Earth, as in him, his soul was activated in perfect natural love covered in the Divine Love of God.

When individuals begin receiving the Divine Love here in their spirit life the veil that has concealed God begins to disappear. Living a physical life or spirit life involving the Divine Love personifies the inner soul you are, radiantly opening out toward transparency of love and spirit. I am aware that a person reading spirit life experience their first time and introduced to the availability of Divine Love, that this experience true, as the teachings we have conveyed will read like a breath of fresh air to the soul, in spirit and everlasting love.

Your friend and teacher, Luke

75

James Reid speaks:

I am living my soul-life. This expression is with real meaning here in the spirit world. I am living my soul-life and I am living my spirit life. I am living the life of my soul in my spirit life. I do not desire at all to sound complicated mixing phrases together. But some expressions are substantial in their meaning especially when such expressions culminate together, like living the soul-life; living the spirit life. My spirit life involves my soul as my soul has become active in my spirit attributes. I am aware of my soul due to my receiving Divine Love which has had Its causal effect within me by perfecting my natural love, developing my spirit attributes and defining my individuality.

Everlasting

Socially, I do not lay bare my soul to every individual I meet and converse with. I live here much as people do on Earth, socially being involved with people without laying bare their soul. Most people live like this, as do most spirits. Life in the Celestial Heaven is a different life than all the other spheres. What we know is that by receiving Divine Love consistently, our natural love is perfected and our spirit attributes are advanced with the life of our soul living with all its energy active within our spirit body. We know that we are soul, that our unique attribute defines our individuality. In effect, what I am saying here that each time you meet another individual in a Celestial sphere, you are effectively seeing the end result of the inner soul-life personified through the spirit attributes and personality of each individual. In this convergence of social rapport, we are the full expression of our soul-life expressing love through our spirit-personality attributes. There is no need for us to lay bare our soul. What we are seeing is this attribute actively living through our spirit-personality.

At the beginning of our adaption to our living here from our physical life, we receive a lot of assistance so we are not overwhelmed by the changes required for living here. As it has been illustrated to you, life in a spirit body is very different from life in a physical body. When progressing through the spirit spheres receiving Divine Love, if the individual has a propensity toward finding things out, one can learn all there is to learn about the functioning of their spirit body. Lots of people I have met aren't interested in the internal dynamic of their functioning spirit attributes. Even in the Celestial Spheres, individuals like to be social like they were on Earth. A lot of people don't even want to have their soul defined to them. They know that by receiving Divine Love change has been brought about. They have acknowledged that by simply living a social life, the changes are part of this new life. No spirit has any jurisdiction over the life of another soul. The soul-life is between the individual and with God. We have conveyed over time a lot of information that relates to the life of the soul, but this is information, that is all. There is a boundary that exists between individuals involved in their living with Divine Love. We can introduce the availability of Divine Love but we cannot entitle ourselves or assume responsibility for another soul as an outcome of their experience with Divine Love. We can guide the form of sharing our experiences which involves extensive themes, but the individual is to their own soul. Not even Jesus assumes responsibility for saving other souls. What he does do is introduce individuals to a more loving way of life which involves the soul. Jesus never introduces another to the Divine Love teaching that he himself is the source of this Eternal energy of Love. If he did, or if any of us did assume responsibility for another soul in their experience of Divine Love, then this could potentially establish a relationship whereby the individual in a less substantial condition begins their experience receiving Divine Love and progressing through the spheres then entering the Celestial life without ever assuming any responsibility for their soul-ship with the Father. This gives room for that individual - if this were to happen - to reject their soul-ship which would cause disharmony between the individual teaching them about the Divine Love and with themselves. This does not happen. When I began receiving Divine Love in earnest, I was taught about the responsibility that I was undertaking. My choice, my voluntary choice for this soulful way of life was my own.

You may have seen this in your own physical lives. There are quite a number of you aware of the Divine Love, aware of Its continuing availability, aware that you are soul and aware of the spirit teachings that have been presented that have contributed toward you being aware!

Experiencing the Divine Love is the foundation of this experience. How you choose or select the way for you to receive this Love and the duration of time spent being with the Soul, God is determined by your own feeling for participation. As soon as another person tries to organise or take or assume responsibility for your experience, things can become abstract. The boundary of the soul is an individual experience. This fits perfectly with the soul-life involved with the experience receiving Divine Love. Jesus has taught humankind about The Golden Rule and he has revealed many truths relating the soul-life with the Soul God, but he has never taught that he is singularly responsible for your soul. The onus is on yourself to voluntarily involve your soul-life with the Eternal Soul, God. Understanding this represents individuality, which is seen living here throughout the Celestial Heaven. Speaking about individuality can sound a little overwhelming. How much individuality can one person have? Here in the spirit life in the Celestial Heaven, all the 'individual' your soul is manifest through your spirit attributes and personality living in love and celebrated. No individual here exceeds another individual for we are all living the fullness of our individuality. I personally found it comforting in my experience receiving Divine Love in my spirit life, knowing that individuals way more advanced in their knowledge that involves living with the Father were so respectful of my own individuality. My own experience awakening into my full soul-life was a personal experience that was never bound to the confines of another's beliefs or expectations. I was free to pursue my own relationship with my soul discovering the Father's Soul. You might find this comforting too.

This is all I have to say at this time. It has been lovely to share with you again. James

76

Hello; my name is Justin. I have been living my spirit life for the equivalent of five years of Earth time. I was a modern man, up-to-date and up-to-speed with worldly affairs, had travelled with my employment in the world of technology which was with an international and global vision. I was not a founder of a global giant technology business, I was a technician able to work with code, software, programs involving mobile phones and computer hardware. I liked my life. I liked being at the leading edge of innovation, creative ideas but most of all involved in a worldly global movement.

I awakened shocked that I was where I was, for I had never given this potential any thought. Being involved with technology meant I connected with social information. Writing code and software created a sense of connective power. This code shaped the technology users life toward a new horizon and future involving technology. I was not alone in my being like this. Many people see themselves at the centre of the human world involved with technology and establishing new frontiers of collective human progressive awareness. And the truth of it was, I and others felt that we were changing the surface of the world.

I think that it is a wonderful gift that there are people who are truly modern in their approach to a future horizon, that humans are capable of understanding the dynamics and convergence of technology with the organic human life form. In my time here, I have been shaped by the change of perspective. My perspective is with greater vision. This has confirmed to me how modern humans can become in their thinking about connecting a singular human horizon through information, technology which makes a human global vision for humankind acting with more efficiency and world awareness. I have seen in my short time here the difference between the earthly humanity to the spirit humanity.

Everlasting

The earthly humanity is diverse with cultural beliefs; here the spirit humanity has their beliefs rationalised as everything is offset to the existing Spirit Laws of Love created by God. As I have seen and quickly ascertained, the diversity of human beliefs is rationalised in the entire spirit world to the Spirit Laws of God acting upon the soul. We don't see this with visual clarity in our physical life.

I have been introduced to the Divine Love. This was explained to me by a Celestial teacher. I grasped the essence of the teaching quickly. It didn't take a long time for me to understand why to receive this Love, where It would lead me, and how to receive It. Having such a worldly vision was an attribute to my having worldly spirit-vision. As soon as I was taught about the vision of Divine Love being the form of energy available to every soul, I understood this with ease; receiving the Divine Love was effortless. My main relationship with life on Earth and of the spirit, is vision. As I progressed through the various spheres I was in my own experience adapting to more spirit-vision. I found this to be sympathetic to the inner dynamic of my personality. I never required a Celestial teacher to speak to me about a truth for a long time. I had had a lot of human life experience thinking globally at a micro and macro level. I am happy, I am feeling the Love. I like the whole vision about God being Soul and the originator of all the things that I am being exposed to. I never thought about God in my human life. I thought about people, people were my immediate purpose. The truth of it is, there are more people here than there are living on the Earth at this time and there will be far more people in the future living here as the earthly population increases and the generations slip into their spirit life.

In my discourse to you I haven't mentioned death. I never thought about death or dying, I just died one day. Before I knew it I was living again. My transition was a pause, not a deletion. They are very aware of the changing nature of the human world here in the Celestial Heaven. Extraordinary individuals are living here as you might well imagine. These individuals were visionaries in their day in their life. I am fascinated by the fact that I can converse with individuals who are so humanly evolved that they are on the leading edge of creation and how God has established these Handiworks of creation to be! I am not in a relationship in my spirit life. My relationship at present is my connectedness with those who are on the cutting edge, so to speak, of spirit life. I believe individuals are residing in spheres beyond the Celestial Heaven. I will get into the soul condition so I can go there. The whole idea of conversing with these humans and the First Parents fascinates me.

I will leave you with this departing gift. For those of you who believe in love and goodness, strive toward a connective human vision so that this platform of soulful life may be extended hand by hand, mind by mind, heart by heart around earthly citizenship. In time you will be able to look back like I have and be grateful that you have served life toward these attributes and not served yourself. There is a lot of colour in all the universes. Pick one, let it shine. Thank you, Justin

77

Luke speaks:

We have taught you that the Divine Love exists as Its own form of energy accessible for mortal souls all around the earthly world and throughout the spirit world. The individuals that live in the spheres beyond the Celestial Heaven are just as able to continue receiving Divine Love as you are in your physical life.

The earthly landscape in contrast to the spirit sphere landscapes differ in the diversity of their organic life and energy, but the Divine Love remains unchanged, constant and true for all souls. You can be where you are in your physical life receiving Divine Love just as I am here in my spirit life living in the Celestial Heaven receiving Divine Love as are spirit-humans residing in the spheres beyond the Celestial Heaven receiving Divine Love. Let us say you are the person 'A', I am person 'B' and the person residing in the spheres beyond the Celestial Heaven is person 'C'. Our environments differ but we are each experiencing the same Divine Love. What this means is that our relationship with the Source of this Love involves the same Immortal Truths that we are living. This also shows our souls, which were made by the same Source of Love, are equal in their ability to receive the same Divine Love at the same time regardless of the environment. This establishes the fact that the physical life and earthly world is not greater or less than the environments of the spirit world. Once people of the Earth understand the significance of this non-evolving form of energy that we participate with, Divine Love, a new perspective about the nature of God becomes visible. Never before in the history of humankind has man understood the nature of God, as being a Soul and Originator of a form of non-evolving energy specific for the soul - the Divine Love - that individuals can readily experience, physically feel, palpable to the senses and individualised in faith. This brings a new human awareness about God and how men and women can involve love, spirit and truth in the living of a soulful life in physical form.

God is love. This is true. We have explained to you that God's love is expressed in God's Handiworks, such as the forming of the mortal spirit world and the forming of all mortal souls. God has also formed the Divine Love, which is part of God's love but a distinct, unique form of love specific for mortal souls. There is God's love and God's Divine Love. One day, in the human fabric of earthly life, it may be known that one lives in faith and belief consciously in God's Divine Love. It may be said and heard around the world "That I believe in the God of Divine Love". If such a word heard, this will be consistent with mortal spirits in the Divine Love, Celestial Heaven and Universal Spheres. The people of the world will see and hear this as a new revelation about God. We here living in our spirit life do not see this as new but a fact of soul-life, which is true. Human history has had moments of illumination where God has been re-identified which has evolved god-awareness in humans. Receiving Divine Love requires nothing more than awareness and participation, love and an openness toward the generosity of spirit. What a progressive and immediate revelation of God this is! Some of you are aware of the Divine Love and consequently, you have a different awareness about who and what God is.

I will leave you with this thought. Your friend and teacher, Luke

78

Hello; my name is Troy. I see my spirit life as a matter-of-fact. The consequence of a reckless action on my behalf that ended my life, now I am here. When I awakened, I was in a room that had real texture. I couldn't relate to my environment, had no idea how I came to be here, was confused and afraid. I was alone when I died. I was at high speed on a country road when I lost control of my motorcycle. I hit my head and was instantly killed. When I awakened I had the memory of my accident. I could still remember that moment losing control and the split second before hitting the tree. There were people with me when I awakened. I had never been in a hospital, but I can only liken to what a recovery ward might be like. Time to recover after something serious had happened. It took me three months to overcome my trauma. I lived a fast life on my bike, never thinking this fate would come to me. As time passed I missed my family, friendships and relationships. This happened quite some years ago; I am well and truly in my spirit life living with Divine Love. I know that other individuals have shared their experience of transition but each individual is important - you learn this over here. On Earth, there can be an apparent lack of respect for human life, that changes over here! Living your life involved with speed increases the risk of arriving here. I am content with my physical life.

My experience has taught me how important family and relationships are. All the people here begin as I did, in a family, even people who are isolated or abandoned or whatever the circumstances. Over here, family comes into perspective. The human life is so important as there is no procreation here. What begins in a physical life binds us to our parents for forever. These relationships are everlasting. Even if there is disharmony and if family members are in the poorest of soul condition, there is always the chance and choice for change to restore love back into these relationships. It would be impossible for one single spirit to convey to you the history of all human generations and how these relationships are in the spirit life. Also it would be impossible to convey to you the history of factual human events in the past. You have noticed what has not been conveyed to you, such as the day-to-day human life of Jesus. He himself has not conveyed to you a chronological, factual account of his human life. Nor his personal relationships, what he felt, thought and how he perceived his whole relationship with humankind, the spirit world and with God through his incremental physical experience.

As being human, we have that construct of memory involving past, present and future. Humans can think about the past and they can think about the future. So much of planet Earth in its organic existence relates with the sun and its energy of light and so on and so forth. The species of the planet are not experiencing any anxiety or vision for their survival by thinking about the next move or the future. The Blue Whale of the sea is not swimming around worried about how it will be or where it will be in ten years. Another species is not worried about the fact that its near extinction and that it may not exist in five years. Humans think about the future. It can cause anxiety but it also defines one of the many wonders about being human. Our ability to have the past, present and future existing as its own narrative when the rest of the planet in its organic form acts entirely to the energetic presence of light, draws interesting comparisons between our species with all other species.

Over here, we are in touch with past, present and future. The spirit spheres exist entirely in their energetic spirit-present. I am aware of my future and that it will involve living with Divine Love, which means my soul-life will always remain consistent and have God in my life.

Keep an open mind as our words that we speak travel across the page. We are desiring to bring as much information as possible toward your experience. Thank you. Troy

December

79

Luke speaks:

There are inhabited worlds throughout the Father's space and time that form the Spirit-Verse. It is a little difficult for me to explain to you how these inhabited worlds are. Each world is much like planet Earth, which is a planet immersed in its own universal dynamic of energy, space and time with a sun and moon and with universal fabric extending in all directions way beyond what man can see.

We have explained to you that the Earth travels around the sun, souls incarnate, souls transition into the spirit world. The planet Earth travels the orbit it does but souls are can always incarnate. Souls are brought by the Father's Spirit Laws of Transition safely into the First Natural Sphere. The First Natural Sphere is the first shore which you will arrive and stand upon after your physical life. On this shore, as you adapt gaining traction and awareness that you have survived death, you can see yourself standing in this new spirit landscape having come from the physical landscape of your human life and the dynamic of the planet in its place of energetic universe. Other inhabited worlds are established in the same way as planet Earth, orbiting its sun with other planets forming a solar system. There are no planets where souls reside that have their form established in the Spirit-Verse prior to incarnation. No soul incarnates directly into the spirit world. For any individual to become a spirit in mortal form, they first have to be in physical form to individualise their incarnated soul. Individualisation defined by incarnated soul, physical attribute, forming personality and formed spirit body.

Everlasting

In the Celestial Heaven, there is a general awareness that other inhabited worlds exist. We live in the fabric of spirit, therefore, we are unrestricted in our ability to travel spirit-space and time once we are in the right soul condition with the Father that enables such movement through the spheres toward other locations situated in the spirit universe. There are many individuals who once lived on planet Earth, have received the Divine Love in their spirit life since the life of Jesus, have progressed to the Celestial Heaven then to the spheres beyond the Celestial Heaven and out into the spirit-space and time to see such inhabited worlds and to meet these individuals living in their spirit life. It works the other way around too. We have had individuals travel to meet us here in the Celestial Heaven. Only under very unusual circumstances do such individuals travel into the natural spheres. It has happened, as you both know, as you once received communication from an individual from another planet. There is a vast population of people residing in the natural spheres still wondering if God exists or is there other forms of life in the universe? In the Celestial Heaven and the Universal Spheres, people are interacting with other soulful forms of life on a known basis.

Every inhabited world begins the same way just as it was on Earth. Two individuals that personify the First Parents - the First Teachers - begin human proceedings. On all the inhabited worlds that I know about, and there are a number of them, the First Parents fulfilled their origin with the ensuing populations and their generations evolving in a common spirit-social-human scape. The memory and teachings of their First Parents remain part of their culture. The Divine Love formed part of the structure in which the First Parents commenced their life, and their teaching about this energy remained consistent through the generations. What this means is that the population on such an inhabited world evolves without its humanity ever experiencing with separation from the Soul, God. Also, the spirit world is known and revered as part of everyday life for the inhabitants of such worlds have been taught about the nature of soul as being formed by God, so as an attribute this gift is revered in their physical life. The soul incarnates in its natural form of love just as souls do all over planet Earth. The choice to receive Divine Love is seen as a *choice of entrance* into physical spirit life. The gift of soul, the gift of natural love, the gift of Divine Love, the gift of Immortality, the gift of the spirit life in the spirit world is revered in the population of these inhabited worlds. Planet Earth is an isolated experience. The population circulates generation after generation largely unaware of all these gifts and a choice of entrance.

On these inhabited worlds their spirit world is structured much the same as ours. Their Immortal life and soulful progression begin in their physical life. By the time the individual enters their spirit life, they are living perfected in their natural love, aware of the Universal Father and in Celestial soul condition. From planet Earth, the population largely begins receiving the Divine Love in their spirit life. On these inhabited worlds a teacher like Jesus incarnates, physically evolves providing more information about the soul-life and the Universal Father. When you see a world function with its humanity perfected, the gap between exclusion and inclusion disappears. Such populations understand that their personality is a gift established by God, which then situates their humanity as not being the principle self-determining force, nature and outcome of life. They do not see themselves as the centre of their existence. The Soul, God, is at the centre of these inhabited worlds, therefore, these populations are advanced in their human attributes toward living with one another living in The Golden Rule is perfection, aware that their physical life is situated with their future spirit life due to these inhabitants understanding the quintessential truth about soul condition. There is a lot of communication between those living their spirit life with relatives still living their physical life. These populations that accept such communication exists as it happens all the time. It is difficult to explain how different these worlds are when you may have had a brief encounter with another who is residing in their spirit life. What is one percent for your worldly population understanding all these gifts, is a hundred percent in the populations of these inhabited worlds.

On some of these worlds, some of the populations live purely in their natural love so the relationship between those living with Divine Love is varied. It is why the Father creates their mortal spirit world - like ours - to facilitate those only in their natural love in their soul condition with those living their Immortal life having accepted the Father by receiving the Divine Love.

Everything that we have communicated to you that involves the soul-life, the populations on these inhabited worlds live with as general knowledge. They see their life on their planet and their planet's life in its universe forming part of the Spirit-Verse without any separation. To convey to you some idea of the Eternity of the Father, some of these inhabited worlds have existed way before our humanity on planet Earth.

There are currently other planets that are ripening in their universal evolution toward receiving their humanity beginning. I am speaking of great spirit-verse distances as the Soul-life of the Father is elliptical in its own spacial space and time. The inhabited worlds surround the Father with their physical universe. I am unable to convey to you exact measurements for there is nothing that exists in earthly humanity to draw any context or comparisons with, to, or from. The Divine Love is the common denominator. It is how we have all come to know why we are the way we are, where we are in relationship to where we can go and how we can live.

You have received my word well on this subject of the universality of humanity and Divine Love. Your friend and teacher, Luke

80

Luke speaks:

The idea that there are inhabited worlds other than planet Earth may sing to your imagination. The reality of the Spirit-Verse is greater than what any fictional writer could conceive. So vast is the Spirit-Verse that if I were to travel from my point of origin here, to circumnavigate around the Father's Spirit-Verse to arrive back here at my starting point, it would take many more years than I have lived in my spirit life! I have not travelled around the Father. If you can imagine the Father being elliptical living within God's Soul-spirit-sphere with its gravity, this is the best description of form that I can provide. I have not visited all the inhabited worlds that exist in the Eternal time and space of the Father. I have been to a few, but not many. Much of my time is taken up with my service to our humanity assisting my friend, Jesus, as those of us who introduce the availability of Divine Love. When I travelled to these inhabited worlds, I went with Jesus. He can speak universal languages which I cannot. He would act as translator. Jesus has a lot of aspects to his personality that everyday humans remain unaware of. He is known wherever he goes for his unique earthly experience. The worlds we visited never experienced the separation that I described to you yesterday.

The inhabitants of these worlds I met in their spirit-spheres which were the equivalent of our Celestial Heaven. We didn't materialise on the face of their planet intermingling socially. These citizens identified themselves as universal citizens, they had another word for being human and another word that described what the Divine Love is. On their planets, if an individual were born without any capacity for future physical cognitive capability, they were mercifully euthanised so that the individual could continue to progress in their spirit world into their maturity with cognitive capabilities without having to endure a long, arduous physical life. In their spirit world, they had spheres like our spheres for the poorest soul condition to reside, but there were never any souls residing in these spheres. As we know, there is always the chance for The Golden Rule to be breached so the Father establishes all the necessary outcomes for life in the spirit world. These worlds have lived with an entirely different agenda than our collective experience on Earth. The populations of the inhabited worlds I visited lived without any belief systems that were in error to the actual factual evidence of God's Spirit Laws existing. They understood themselves as soul, though a different word to our 'soul'. They understood the necessity of their spirit body having had visibility of it in their mortal physical life. The spirit world wasn't foreign to them. When a loved one transitioned, only a small amount of time would pass before communication was open again between loved ones. They understood their connectedness with the Energy Source of Creation. They related their physical life through their soul and spirit body, celebrating what we know as the Living Divine Love. They also shared in the one true Soul Life of God. They had a different name for God, but in their physical world, God's Divine Love is known and celebrated equally among all. Each inhabited world was populated with two sexes. They utilised the organic nature of their planets to construct communities and cities, homes and activities harmonious with their interface of the spirit component that they knew existed. In essence, an inhabited world as I have described functions harmoniously for the population doesn't see personality as the only viable living life-force that begins with the planet and ends with the planet. These populations know that their life begins with God for they are soul, then continues in their physical form and on into their spirit life, and out into the universal space, time and Spirit-Verse.

The quintessential teaching here that I wish to convey to you is that the inhabitants of these planets do not see that their life begins with spirit and soul when they are in the spirit world after the death of their physical life. How they experience life is revered for they experience living 'with' spirit in convergence with their soul-life concurrently while living their physical life. These inhabited worlds have never progressed in their evolution through conflict and separation. Every human from our world living in their spirit life understands the conditions that our humanity experienced. Over here, the visibility of that 'spirit' component that can complete a life is only revealed by living a spirit life and that is why so many embrace the Divine Love here and begin their progressive experience toward becoming a universal citizen.

Your friend and teacher, Luke

81

Luke speaks:

It is a difficult thing to convey to you real spirit vision that is situated with real dynamic, space and time into a narrative of incremental experience. It is easy for me to state that the Father is Eternal. This Eternity, or rather the existence of this Living Soul being Eternal, brings such vision. But how is this Eternity then situated in our participation with our soul attributes experiencing incrementally what this Eternal appearance looks like!

My statement relates to Divine Love. I, and other spirits have conveyed that the Divine Love is available for all mortal souls. This is a big vision. Having a resource of energy formed by God that every single soul can participate with conveys the grandeur of the energy that the Divine Love personifies as existing with real vision. Contrast this vision by our incremental experience receiving Divine Love defines the relationship between the incremental experience with the grandeur of vision.

Speaking to you about other inhabited worlds and how their populations evolved fully cognitive of the Divine Love in their lives and aware of their spirit world and the Eternal Father is the grandeur of planetary and human vision. The fact that these populations are living 'spirit' on their planet relates a vision to you that we are not seeing on our planet Earth. It has been necessary for me to bring this across to extend the life beyond our Celestial Heaven. We have conveyed a lot of information that involves living with Divine Love, perfecting your natural love, and how we progress through the spheres into the Celestial Heaven. If the Celestial Heaven existed as the final place for progression to reach its finality, this would infer that our progression is finite to a conclusion which is defined by living in the Celestial Heaven. If there were no spheres beyond our Celestial Heaven, then living with Divine

Love would provide us with our Immortality but an Immortality that is only offset by not solely living in your natural love in the natural part of our spirit world. The real Immortality of our soul condition brought about with the inclusion of Divine Love provides us with a soul condition which is visible in our spirit body to proceed beyond our Celestial Heaven venturing forth into the universal spheres that relate with space and time of Spirit-Verse. Knowing this gives the Celestial resident that sense of occasion, which is progressing into a spirit-human eternal universal citizen that can travel the Spirit-Verse of space and time interacting with other inhabitants from other worlds that celebrate the same Eternal Soul living as we are living in the same Immortality of the non-evolving energy that we call the Divine Love.

Our First Parents, though they committed their personal transgression which has been identified to you, are nonetheless extraordinary individuals. Some of their offspring are just as extraordinary for they were created by the mating practices of the First Parents so their constitution is genetically pure. The First Parents and their immediate offspring reside in the First Universal Sphere. We have conveyed to you before that the First Parents are the First Teachers and that they reside in the First Universal Sphere assisting those who venture forth from the Celestial Heaven out into the Universal landscape of spirit space and time. The First Parents are universal teachers. They have, like Jesus, an extraordinary knowledge that is innate within them about the universal consequence of space and time with the Father at the centre of all. They understand the nature of planetary evolution, mortal soul-life and existential spirit creations of the Father such as the Energy of Divine Love and what It does. They also understand soul-ship with the Father and how the human being is formed in all its definable nature. They understand the existing Spirit Laws that work to establish the running of spirit worlds and the realisation of interfacing between finite personality with Fatherly personality.

Every inhabited world begins with their First Parents. The reason for this is to lay the groundwork for the generations to populate and to perceive their existence first and foremost as finite soul. Then, it is to teach about being a soul in a relationship with the Spirit-Verse and the Eternal Soul, God. On all inhabited worlds the human population doesn't begin through the sheer evolutionary forces of species evolving out of one species adapting into another species. As has been taught, each human is first and foremost soul. That soul that you are has never originated through the planetary evolution of its non-souled species. This truth about the human soul defines the difference of what it is to be mortal with what it is to be an evolving planetary species without the inclusion of the attribute of a soul that is capable of receiving Divine Love and living 'spirit' on Earth and in the Universal Spirit-Verse.

I have been taught by the First Parents in the First Universal Spirit Sphere, that there are inhabited worlds that surround the Father, that their populations have completed their duration of life on their planets with their entire population residing in the spirit world. I have not travelled to such a world, but I do know they exist.

I will stop now. You have received my words well. Your friend and teacher, Luke

82

Luke speaks:

There have been five principal teachers in my spirit life. The first teacher, my human friend and then spirit friend, Jesus. Secondly, the First Parents. Thirdly, my earthly and spirit life experience. Fourthly, other Celestial social interactions. Lastly and most completely which culminates in everything, my intimate knowledge of the Father. I have conveyed a lot of information to you which I had to learn from other individuals. The First Parents truly are super-universal beings. I cannot compare them to any other human being. They resumed living in the Divine Love upon Jesus' arrival to begin his teaching here in the spirit world.

When we speak of other inhabited worlds, we must include other inhabited spirit worlds. There are obvious differences between both existing worlds. One is a planet while the other environments are comprised of spheres that relate to one another with existing populations that reside in each sphere. A planet is a singular surface where the population lives on that singular surface. Here in the spirit world, there is a singular surface, but this surface extends through many spheres. From what I have seen, each Celestial Heaven is contained to a relative position to the local planet, but the Universal Spirit Spheres extend between the Celestial Heavens. It is through these spheres that the Celestial Heavens are connected. Beyond the Universal Spirit Spheres heading in toward the Father, other spheres circumnavigate the Father's Sphere where The Soul who is God resides at the centre. On planet Earth, most humans still see their planet - our planet and the universe it is situated in - as a singular force of universal nature comprising of energy that works toward sustaining the importance of its own determination. In the Celestial Heaven and the Universal Spheres, we know that the physical universe that all inhabited worlds exist in is purely the creation of the Central Soul acting with energy in a different form than the energy that constructs and forms all spirit worlds. We see the physical universe as an extension of the Father's Handiworks and as inclusive to the Central Soul as any spirit creation.

Having lived on Earth myself, it is a hard thing to imagine where space, as an actual identity, came from and how it was originated so that there can be a physical universe in it. People like to play around with all kinds of time scenarios, but time is such a different thing than the construct of time that the human mind organises as memory. As it has been conveyed to you nature that the planet Earth has doesn't think about its future as a real living construct of survival and experience. Only humans are capable of being cognitive and self-aware of how one might be or where one would like to be, or is anxious about themselves in the future. The physical universe that planet Earth is part of, is without any capacity to decide for itself any outcome toward its future. The physical universe is without the cognitive capacity for self universal realisation. The energy that makes a physical universe act according to specific energetic laws that factor in the characteristic of that identity, is such as the sun acts according to the physical laws that govern its characteristics.

The Spirit-Verse is the same. It does not act independently of the Spirit Laws that govern its entire existence. When we break this down as we have taught you, when the soul-life resides in the spirit world the spirit body cannot voluntarily act independently of the attribute of soul living within it. Each and every soul from any inhabited world adheres to the Spirit Laws that define its progression through the spheres. That is why having a form of energy like the Divine Love, is the structure that provides universal movement for all spirits from all inhabited worlds. If everything surrounding the Central Source - and I mean everything - was a clock of moving parts, then the timekeeper and originator of this clock in all its parts, is God.

Apparently, from what I have been taught by the First Parents, planets are being formed for future human life. Planets are evolving toward facilitating life. Some planets have ended with all their population residing in the spirit world. There are planets like Earth concurrent with souls incarnating. What has never happened to any inhabited world, is an extinction event that has wiped out a population on a planet in a single moment so the entire population transitions instantaneously into the spirit world. There was a planet where the First Parents and the individual who personifies the teaching quality and relationship with the Father, like Jesus, and all three failed. So, that population lived its entire history solely in natural love. All future relevance to the True Immortality was taught in the spirit world.

As I have said, there are individuals created by the Central Source, that will never incarnate to acquire soul-like individuality. There are millions of these individuals in fact. I don't know how many there are, spread wide throughout all the Universal Spirit Spheres that surround the Father's Sphere. These individuals have specific universal functions and collectively understand how the Spirit-Verse is comprised by the Father. They help with the creation and forming of the Spirit-Verse in their devotion to the Central Source and the inhabited worlds of space and time.

When speaking about eternal spirit themes, it can become very generalised. The vision of the Spirit-Verse is extensive as you can well imagine, but my purpose here is to place extended human reach beyond but inclusive of the vision of soul-life living in perfect natural love and receiving Divine Love in harmony with the Father. What begins on planet Earth from a human concern about whether it is going to rain today or not, can ultimately extend to travelling through the Universal Spirit Sphere and meeting another population of individuals aware that they too are living with the Universal Source of Divine Love in harmony and good natural love.

I will stop here. Your friend and teacher, Luke

83

Luke speaks:

We are making good progress speaking about things that are far away, things that have no direct consequences involving planet Earth or the spirit world, but involving living Spirit Truths that are close and personal, such as soul condition, natural love and the Divine Love. It is important to convey to you that human life, soul-life, doesn't complete its progression in the Celestial Heaven or Universal Spirit Spheres. That there is a greater realm for the individual to define their soulfulness with the Father in. Individuality in the spirit world is not a conclusive isolated fundamental self-determining place. Mortal personality in its spirit life is not supreme in its perfection. Jesus and the First Parents are living personifications that personality in a finite mortal life is not the source of its creation. The existence of Divine Love causes us to realise the existence of the Soul, God. That we belong independently to this Soul, that we are no longer separated in our soul-ship with this Soul, that we have our independent nature freely moving through spirit space and time in Our Father's Spirit and Love. It is important to recognise just how far perfect natural love can sustain us in Divine Love. We can meet with other populations in the Universal Spirit Spheres who also live in their perfect natural love in the Divine Love of the Father.

In the last sphere of the Celestial Heaven and the First Universal Sphere, there exists vast amounts of visual information depicting the Universal Spheres that circumnavigate the Father's Sphere. This depicts inhabited worlds, uninhabited worlds that are still evolving. There are other worlds both inhabited and uninhabited in the Father's Sphere. Planet Earth and our spirit world form part of this Eternal Universal Map. Some narratives define the nature of these populated worlds so that travellers know where they are going and who they are going to meet. The visual display of information involving the demographics of the Spirit-Verse is comprehensively depicted. We do not live in the Celestial Heaven isolated, alone, absorbed and separated into our population groups. It is far easier for us to travel vast distances through a sphere like a Universal Spirit Sphere than it is to travel in any material form of transport.

The thing that speaks clearly here in the vastness of spirit space and time, is the economy of the Father. The Father has not established a chaotic Spirit-Verse or anything random. Everything has its place and spirit timing in that place. Everyone - and I mean everyone - living in the Universal Spheres or their planetary Celestial Heaven lives their soul condition that is pure harmony in accord to the economy of the Father. I will not travel a vast distance only to realise that I have ended up in some unknown place that I become lost in. When I travel at vast speed through a Universal Sphere, I know exactly where I am going and how long it will take me to arrive. Part of my soul condition provides my spirit body with the ability to move with intent at a fast speed. My spirit body in its design is capable of moving like this. Each individual can move like this when they learn how to as part of their education about the spirit-biodynamics and spirit-aerodynamics of their spirit body. If I moved slowly all the time, we would never be able to communicate together with such frequency. The Celestial Heaven is some distance away from where you are sitting. If I were slow in my travels, we would communicate around twice a week. Because I can move quickly I can leave the Celestial Heaven, travel to be by your side, communicate with you, then return to the Celestial Heaven all in the time of several hours. There is real skill involving such movement; this is so for the sheer fact of not colliding into another spirit! Any spirit residing in the Celestial Heaven can learn how to move like this. This is not a selective design or attribute of selected spirit personalities. Movement between the spheres and through the spheres is very important, otherwise we would remain located only to our spirit world with its immediate spheres which would defy the wonderment that the Eternal Father has established as the Spirit-Verse.

There is universal knowledge of an inhabited world that had seen its population complete. The population of that world lives entirely in its spirit world. The First Parents and primary teacher had fulfilled their purpose teaching about the Immortality of Divine Love and greater spirit realities. A vast majority of that population accepted their living the Immortal soul-life progressing to their Celestial Heaven. A certain amount of that population remained solely in their natural love with individuals choosing to remain in very poor soul condition. It was that their time came when the Divine Love no longer remained available to them. The individuals chose their personality over an inclusion with the Divine Love of the Father, effectively choosing to remain as they were without participating with the Divine Love. As time passed it became evident to these individuals that their exclusion remained permanent. The fate of those individuals was to become as if they never were. The Father dematerialised their existence as only the Father can by utilising a Spirit Law that acts upon the soul to dematerialise what was once material as soul and spirit body. From your perspective, this may sound unloving. From an eternal perspective, to live solely in your natural love in a sphere for all eternity and know that there is no more mortal life living on that planet and to live for all eternity in that condition of isolation, stagnation, and poor soul condition is eternal damnation for the personality. It is merciful to cease what would otherwise eternally stagnate.

Everlasting

It may seem to you that living with Divine Love in physical life is a very immediate personal experience. From a teaching perspective the energy that the Divine Love is has real consequences that are immediate and eternal. The Divine Love originates from the Central Source, continuing to be available. But as the history of this planet Earth and its population reveals, the story involving the First Parents and the life of Jesus confirms these consequences involving the availability of Divine Love. The mortal natural souls are established only by the Father, which are very real and have their economy and time.

In the teachings that we conveyed to James Padgett it was taught, "That a river flows no higher than its source". What the spirits realised when living in the natural spheres between the time of the First Parents and the advent of Jesus, was that without the availability of Divine Love mortal man and woman living in the natural spheres were personality resourced, meaning the individual was the head of their own river. As Saleeba has conveyed to you, living in the Perfect Natural Sphere was the full expression of personality in natural love living in the spirit world. No spirit could travel anywhere throughout the Spirit-Verse other than the natural spheres. This limited all mortal movement throughout the entire Spirit-Verse. With the availability of Divine Love, with Jesus living in the spirit world after his human physical life, souls began receiving Divine Love. A phenomena began happening in the spirit world! There was movement and exploration with the Divine Love and Celestial Spheres open. Individuals were able to receive Divine Love, be in their perfect natural love, progress in the Divine Love to the Celestial Heaven, then venture forth into the Universal Spheres. Travel was potential. To travel such vast distances, part of the enjoyment to do this was to learn how the spirit body could travel according to the soul condition and intent of the individual.

It was also conveyed in the teachings of James Padgett that one day the Divine Love would be withdrawn. When speaking about the consequences of inhabited worlds we are to look at incremental progression measured in contrast with eternal universal realities. What is very important here is for me to state to you that in this period of time with the Divine Love being available for the souls of Earth and its spirit world, every soul who has ever lived and individualised will have the time to decide if one chooses to participate with the Immortal way of life. If anyone misses out, it will be because that individual will decide to remain 'the head of their river' and unfortunately miss out on travelling the far-flung realms of the Spirit-Verse.

I will stop now. Your friend and teacher, Luke

84

Luke speaks:

Speaking about life, mortal life living on other worlds and how they relate with the Universal Soul, God, and how they reside in their spirit world is a fascinating subject. It is real and it does exist. Living in the Celestial spheres this kind of information about other inhabited worlds and spirit worlds is openly discussed which adds another whole realm to our existence and what we know about our human mortal life. It also teaches us that the central Soul, God, is not a god with existence creating our humanity as a humanitarian stand-alone. God has not created humans that have lived on the planet Earth as a singular mortal event. Understanding this, as we do in the Celestial Heaven and Universal Spirit Spheres, provides a continuity of creation that our mortal life is not the centre of God's created Spirit-Verse. We learn that the available Divine Love is not just for our souls, but is a universal consequence that other mortals participate with providing us all with an Immortal spirit life and with spirit-vision that exceeds our immediate individuality. It is fair to say that a great portion of Celestial spirits are worldly. Not all Celestial spirits have travelled to other inhabited worlds, although many have. It is an individual opportunity. No one prevents another from this experience, it is entirely about soul condition and a desire to meet other mortals and travel the Universal Spheres of spirit space and time. We are fascinated by the existence of other inhabited worlds and their spirit worlds, but these mortals are as fascinated meeting us and listening to our description experience and life that we have lived on our world and in our spirit world. We all contribute toward a more extended vision about our relationship with the Universal Source of life and the kind of God that is loving and that has initiated such varied mortal life.

I am happy that you both, along with some friends, celebrated Divine Love Day. It is a day to acknowledge the availability of Divine Love, that some people of the Earth are aware of this Love, that many people in the spirit life are living with this Love, and that even more are coming to know about It. As you know, there are billions of people around the world and as we have told you, in the future in the spirit world we will see the many billions all being introduced to what they don't know. Here in our inhabited spirit world, there is still much to do as the vast population continues to transition into the First Natural Sphere to begin their permanent life here. Thank you for recognising us on Divine Love Day.

I, with several other Celestial teachers and with some of your relatives and some of the authors in this time of spirit communication, were listening to your conversation about the future involving a world awareness of Divine Love. You were wondering through your discussions if any kind of religion could be established that involved the Living Divine Love in human life. We have conveyed a lot of information to you, but never have we told you how to live your life, or a fundamental way to live, pray and be with the Father. We have never provided you with anything fundamental about involving the way you are to live your life with the Divine Love or about the Divine Love itself other than the experience of receiving and living with this Love and Its workings in the soul and spirit body. The First Parents when they lived on Earth never established a formal religion or spirituality for another to follow or adhere to. In the short life of Jesus, he never established an organised religion with his teachings as the system of belief to follow. As you have seen in the world there does not exist 'The Gospel according to Jesus' written by Jesus which has then become an organised faith and religion. Here in our spirit life since the arrival of Jesus those thousands of years ago, he has not organised any religious or spiritual structure that *must* be fundamentally followed to live with God. No one ever has, nor will this ever happen. The question remains, can we provide you with a structure that others may believe in that retains its individuality and independence, yet provides a structure that physical men and women can believe in while being aware of Divine Love to a greater or lesser degree and experiencing this Love for themselves?

In the messages James Padgett received a hundred years ago, there was an outline to a gospel but nothing in those teachings organised an actual system of belief that could be interpreted as an organised religion or spirituality for men and women to follow and believe in with a fundamental adherence. Personal and individual faith within the soul brought about by the experience of Divine Love and how to obtain this Love in the first place was introduced. The teaching involving the New Birth of the soul was introduced, but it was without the clarity of the natural love being involved which is what is perfected when receiving Divine Love and ultimately achieving the "New Birth". I could bring expressions toward you such as 'The Gospel of Divine Love', or, a 'Gospel of God', but ultimately all can be said as the Gospel of Love. Everything that we have conveyed to you about the soul-life involves love. Everything about God as the Living Soul, God is, involves love. Everything about the spirit world with the humanity residing here is ultimately about love. Living natural love or living natural love with the inclusion of Divine Love. Everything about the soul-life involves love. Love is at the seat of human existence and all spirit life and God. The ultimate gospel is for the individual to believe: that they are soul, that they are a living soul in natural love, that God exists and is a Living Soul, that a spirit world exists as does the spirit body and that the Divine Love exists. These are broad statements that are factual. It is a fact that the individual may be introduced to the existence of Divine Love and may experience this Love for many years without ever really understanding the nature of this Love or the full effect this Love causes in the soul and spirit attributes. There are individuals, millions of individuals, who have received the Divine Love their first time in their spirit life and then progressed through the Divine Love spheres to the Celestial Heaven and reside in this Heaven in their perfect natural love feeling the Divine Love, accepting the Soul, God, without fully understanding the nature of the Divine Love or of God, or for that matter the function of their soul and spirit body in its completeness. What these individuals do know is that change has happened with a sensitivity that is gentle, loving and kind, and that God has given the Divine Love without imposing any condition or fear to nullify the independence of that personality. Many people on Earth who are experiencing the Divine Love today know very little about the nature of their experience or the Love they are involved with. This is where belief comes into it. People believe in this Love without understanding It. What is really important here is that men and women believe that they can receive this Love, that this Love exists, and that It is true. A person may feel the existence of their soul to be true, or simply believe that their soul is real. One may receive Divine Love for several years without ever thinking about the nature of their spirit body. One may also believe in the existence of the afterlife without ever seeing any real evidence of this or receiving a direct communication to confirm that we exist here, but people do believe it wholeheartedly.

Everlasting

In a physical life, there are going to be experiences involved with this - which is the soul-life - that will be formed from beliefs rather than the factual visible evidence that we live with here in the spirit life. The Gospel of Love works here. It includes the human belief in love. Beginning here initiates the realisation of your natural love growing toward its full potential. By including the Divine Love, the Gospel of Love is with a broader perspective of love and belief which can extend toward the Soul, God. How far one decides to extend their belief in love is the adventure of your understanding the nature of soul-life which includes all that we have conveyed to you. I am living the Gospel of Love as all Celestial and Divine Love Sphere spirits are. There are many individuals in the natural spheres living their natural love, who are loving individuals yet to embrace their soul-life by including God's Divine Love but yet are living within the Gospel of Love.

When the individual transitions into their spirit life everything about life changes. The individual is introduced to a way of life previously unknown. This is how it will be for billions of people. On Earth, the population in its generations does not know openly about the Soul-Life of God. If human evolution is to be advanced by a new interpretation of God, then it is included in this statement: The availability of Divine Love brings the true Immortality to the individual soul and begins perfecting the natural love which creates change in the soul, this change expressed in its fullest are the teachings of the "New Birth". Involving the natural love and the Divine Love results in a whole new identity to the individual about who and what God is and how the soul relates with its originator. This is what happens in the spirit world. Other than Jesus and the First Parents, every single human that lives in the spirit world that has embraced their living with Divine Love has realised a new identity about who and what God is. The Gospel of Love involves identifying existing truths and realities that define human existence both earthly and of the spirit that have remained true and constant since their inception.

Human history has identified an attribute of Spirit calling it the "Holy Spirit". In the messages James Padgett received, we taught you what the Holy Spirit is and what It does. We have since conveyed to you a new identity of this Spirit called the "Acting Spirit" to refer to this attribute of God's Spirit in a more universal context as the Divine Love is universal. In the Gospel of Love, I can refine this now by identifying this attribute of Spirit that conveys the Divine Love of God into your soul as the Loving Spirit. In your prayers to the Soul of God, as you ask for the inflowing of Divine Love, let your soul send your natural love, your finite natural feeling, to the Soul of God for the Divine Love and asking to be covered in the Loving Spirit.

The Gospel of Love is a universal and individual truth established in the faith and belief of your love and in God's Divine Love, and that Jesus is the teacher, friend and companion living along with you in this Gospel of Love as are the First Parents and all of us who partake of Divine Love.

In the spirit life, spirits begin with belief as they receive Divine Love. As their soul condition changes such feeling for the Love confirms to their soul that God is living. Here in the Divine Love spheres and Celestial Heaven, there are spirit structures that assist the spirit body as it progresses toward fulfilment of its attributes relating to its soul condition. In your physical life, you may receive Divine Love a length of time without realising your spirit attributes, soul condition, or spirit body with no earthly structure fit for your soul to draw any comparison with. This explains why in a human life physical beliefs are established in the minds of mortals and why this provides the structure that people find comfort in. The beliefs I have given you involving love you may find comfort in - for they are truths - living truths of love consistent with our living love here in our Immortal spirit life.

The essence of my teaching is not to organise religious or spiritual belief, but to provide a sense of physical belief involving a non-evolving form of energy that many men and women will come to participate with. These beliefs will be collectively known but individually lived such as the nature of love as it involves universal themes involving true soul nature experienced in the domain of the individual. Never before has humanity ever known such a Gospel to have existed. The Gospel of Love is an individual experience that embraces universal spirit realities. This brings vision and comfort.

Your friend and teacher, Luke

85

Luke speaks:

It is very reasonable for a person having been introduced to the availability of Divine Love to acknowledge that they don't know anything about this experience or what follows. The individual in a physical life will feel that a new horizon is before them. This can lead to questions, some of which when asked may not be significantly answered that will satisfy their desire to know. One question the receivers of my spoken word have heard asked by many people is, 'Why do I need to ask for Divine Love'? Other questions that they have heard asked by a diverse range of people when introducing the awareness of Divine Love are: What is Divine Love?, When did God begin?, Who created God?, What will happen when I receive Divine Love?, Can I reach Celestial soul condition on Earth?, Do I have to keep asking for It?, and Do I already have It? There are so many questions that people can ask involving this experience that it would be impossible for me to answer them all. We have answered many questions in the communications that we have conveyed to you throughout the years. There are even more questions asked about the spirit world and spirit life. From your perspective, part of the independence being physically human is the wonder to ask. So much human history has been forged from a question asked. From your perspective you can look toward new horizons such as the soul-life, the spirit life, and God as all being ahead of you. Here in the spirit life the perspective changes. One doesn't have to ask, if there life after death, if a spirit world exists, if I will ever see my loved ones again, if I will reincarnate, and if the First Parents really exist. All these asking's answered in the spirit life. Individuals residing here ask many more questions, but they are answered comprehensively through the soul condition improving and progressing via the continual receipt of Divine Love. In your physical life, as you may be hindered by your limited ability to see and to feel, questions can continuously be asked without ever arriving at a definitive answer. And so the wheel turns. The more you ask, the more you realise there is to ask!

The best advice I can give you is to experience the Love without expectation. Be loving and free, trusting in the Soul, God, and responding to your heartfelt prayers for Love. The Loving Spirit, which brings the Divine Love into your soul, responds to love - your natural love - when your soulful heart, is sincere as it engages in faith for Divine Love.

We have taught you much about the Divine Love and the soul-life from our spirit experiences living with this Love and aware of our soul-life. In a physical life, feeling and belief may help you to begin as this experience in all its information is new and not preexisting in your earthly life. You will not read another man or woman's account of their living with Divine Love written from experience involving the Immortal Life in any history book. The history that will be written will be by your own individual experience. This living truth is what sets this soulful experience apart from everything else, for it is individually everlasting and there are not many things in a physical life that you can begin then continue when you eventually live here with the same consistency and vision.

You have both done very well receiving my word. These have been compelling moments, a true convergence of love and spirit. Your friend and teacher, Luke

86

Jude speaks:

It has been quite some time since I last spoke to you in this form of communication. A vast amount of information has been conveyed, much like a palate of spirit information relating to soul-life that expands what natural love is as an expression of soul-life, and what Divine Love is as God's Soul-Life is to mortal man. Luke has spent this time with you conveying information that is more expansive involving other inhabited worlds and their spirit worlds, and how they compare with our earthly and spirit worlds.

Expansive is my theme. It is a true expansive revealing to place the Holy, Acting Spirit into a structural context of love. It is an attribute of spirit extending from the Soul of God, so it has its purpose, function and relationship with God and with us. As long as we continue to live in the Divine Love of God, this Loving attribute of Spirit covers our spirit bodies and soul all the time. This Loving Spirit is unable to act independently to its creative determination. This Loving Spirit acts in accord with the very Spirit Law formed into existence by God to facilitate the action of the Divine Love engaging the mortal soul. When we receive Divine Love, we are effectively partaking of God's Eternal Love but we see this as not becoming eternal gods ourselves, but rather, Immortal. We are eternal in the sense that our soul participates with that non-evolving form of energy that comes from the Eternal Source, but the 'Eternal' in the Divine Love does not transform us into eternal gods ourselves. The Eternal in the Divine Love does not transform our natural love out of existence into being a soul living only in Divine Love. The Eternal in Divine Love does not transform our natural love into being eternal natural love. I know that this may sound like semantics but it is important to qualify the differences between the non-evolving form of energy that is from an Eternal Source to the finite form of energy that our natural love is and that at essence, is also formed from an Eternal Source.

The Loving Spirit that covers our spirit body engages our soul so that the Divine Love can infuse the soul never changes or acts differently. It is as constant as the Divine Love is. This Loving Spirit in all its existence has its solid form, but a form that exists outside of any form of energy that a spirit environment comprises of. The Loving Spirit, like the Divine Love, is not subject to any environmental condition, organic system, nor is it subject to any form of evolution. It is the only attribute of Spirit formed into existence that works in unison with the Father's Divine Love. We don't identify this Loving Spirit as being capable of bestowing us any Immortality; only the Divine Love we receive can do this. I will reconfirm to you at this time that so much about our experience involving the Father's Handiworks involves what already exists. When I speak to you about the way the Loving attribute of Spirit works as It brings about the Divine Love into the soul, this is not what I 'believe' to happen or surmise to happen involving these spirit realities. I am describing what is. I am describing what the Father has established for us all. The Father in the forming of Divine Love also formed the attribute of Spirit forming a relationship, or if you like, a partnership between these two Spirit-Verse realities. Citizens that reside in other inhabited spirit worlds, or on their planetary worlds that are experiencing Divine Love, are also served by this same combination of Divine Love being conveyed by the Loving Spirit directly from the Soul of God.

When you meet individuals who have lived on other worlds and have transitioned into their spirit world living in the Immortality of the Divine Love and covered in the Loving Spirit, whilst they do have their language to identify these attributes, we all share in the same universal common knowledge. There is a universal spirit language that we learn as we travel through the universal spirit spheres so there is a continuity of diversity but likeness in the images and substance of the Living Eternal Handiworks that the Father has created. I have met planetary inhabitants who have lived their physical mortal life among vast populations that have never known what religion or spirituality is. Due to the fact that their population was sustained from the outset of the success of their

First Parents and then the advent of a Super-Universal teacher like our Jesus is, the citizens of this world lived in a reality of universal experience with the attributes of the Father's Handiworks situated to their physical life. Their entire history is in unison with their spirit world, the Loving Spirit, and the non-evolving form of energy that the Divine Love is. Like our planet, they understood that each respective soul was formed in its essence without any living Immortality within it. They lived with the knowledge that their individualisation was underway in their natural essence before they made their choice individually to receive the Loving Spirit and Divine Love. They did say that some individuals waited a long time before receiving Divine Love, but everyone transitioned into their spirit life well underway in their soul-ship and spirit life aware of the Eternal Father.

The diversity of other planetary worlds is vast. The Divine Love and Loving Spirit serves this diversity but is not diverse itself. A truth that defines our planetary spirit world is diversity. What makes our planetary experience unique and interesting to other universal citizens is the lack of visibility and transparency involving Universal and Eternal realities interconnected with our physical way of life. They are also interested in our plethora of beliefs and are quite astounded that individuals do not even believe in the existence of an afterlife or that God exists! They are also interested in the fact that our spirit world is being utilised to its full resource. By this I mean that all our spheres have humanity inhabiting them. When you think about this, this is a phenomenon itself. The entire spectrum of the spirit world that God has formed for us all to reside in with all its structural spheres is being utilised to its maximum resource by those residing in their natural love and its varied conditions, as well as those residing in Divine Love and its varied soul conditions. Being aware of the Divine Love and the Loving Spirit is an expansive experience. Yes, it is for the individual to experience and it is far-reaching insofar as the Divine Love and the Loving attribute of Spirit extends from the Father to all inhabited worlds and their spirit worlds past, present and future. One is very capable of receiving the Divine Love and Loving Spirit as they travel through the Universal Spirit Spheres.

This has been a dynamic interface between you and me this morning. Thank you, Jude

87

Jude speaks:

Over the years, portions of humanity have believed in the existence of the Holy Spirit. What this means is that people have lived - or have the living belief - that there exists an attribute of Spirit that comes from God and performs a function that serves a purpose and is somehow related with the life of Jesus. There are differing beliefs about what this Spirit does, why it exists and who it serves. We have identified this Spirit in a more universal language calling it the 'Acting Spirit' to remove the religiosity from it so that the universal vision of this attribute and its universal function is aligned with the universality of the purpose it serves. The Divine Love is universal, therefore the attribute of Spirit that brings this Love into the soul adheres to this universality. The Divine Love and Acting Spirit exist outside a singular human cultural belief system. The fact that people understand that such a Spirit exists is a significant truth. It does exist. The fact that people in the physical world do not understand why it exists and the purpose for its existence is now beginning to be understood in context to its relationship with God's Divine Love. We understand how important it is that the individual can identify with Divine Love as a living form of energy and that you can feel this Love when experiencing it. This is why we felt it necessary to bring the Acting Spirit into a more loving context with potential for the individual to personalise this convergence of mortal soul, natural love, Divine Love and the Loving Spirit. The inhabitants of other worlds identify their experience with this same attribute of Spirit involved in their personalisation of their soul-life with the Father. I wish to add here that other populations identify these attributes with different names accordingly to their language. What is consistent is that we all recognise the Eternal Soul and the Primary Source of all life. We recognise the Eternal as that which differs than our mortal, finite soul-life. Other inhabited worlds, as far as we understand, have never referred to God as being 'The Father'. This identity of God is the identity personalised by our principal teacher, Jesus. Had our First Parents continued in accord with their mission, the humanity of the world would have come to have known God as The Universal Creator and Eternal Source of all life. The fact that they failed meant that when Jesus was born, there was no continuity of identity for who and what

Everlasting

God is. It was up to Jesus to personalise and identify God through his unique attribute and relationship with The Eternal One.

I will leave you now. Thank you, Jude

88

Hello; my name is Chris. I have participated by listening as Luke and Jude conveyed information to you both. I have been fascinated by the width, depth and breadth of vision that they have condensed into a finite narrative that appears on your page. I am living with Divine Love. I have been living in this Love quite some time, but I don't share the same capacity of vision that these two individuals live with. I was as much an ear to their communication as you both were. I can communicate about my personal experience living my soul-life but nothing of this involves what spirit life is like beyond the Celestial Heaven. I have only recently moved into the Celestial Heaven. I lived in the Fourth Natural Sphere for a long length of time. I had seen those that visually looked different to me in their spirit appearance. I was still defined by particular relationship with another individual which I refused to give up. That individual had no aspiration at all to inquire about the difference. The difference between those living aware of their soul-life with those who are unaware of their soul is as clear as night and day. I was curious about this difference but my partner wasn't. I struggled with this for quite some time but eventually I realised that I slowly became a spirit of discontent. I loved my partner as we had been in a long relationship in our human life, but we both succumbed to the AIDS virus as many did. The bonds of relationship that are established in our physical lives can remain as true, binding and emotional in our spirit life as they were on Earth. My partner departed his life before me. We lived a long relationship long before gay couples could legally marry as it is in some parts of the world today. We would have been married legally; we held a commitment ceremony with our friends. It was a dynamic time, the 1980's. My partner and I really loved each other. We had been promiscuous before we met which is how we contracted the virus. Though I died of a disease, all my social interactions were by my consent and an expression of love. This involved lots of consensual sex. In my spirit life, though I died from a disease that was passed on by another, due to my voluntary participation, I was without any compensation. I was an intelligent man, a writer. As time passed and I adapted to my spirit life living with my partner, who happened to be in the quiet room that I transitioned into after my heart stopped beating, I was so happy to see him. Neither of us ever discussed life after death, but we did joke that we would be forever in heaven together. Let me tell you, the heaven we remarked about is nothing like the reality of our life here! It is more extraordinary!

As I said, after a time I felt another force in my life compelling me to speak to an individual who was brighter than me. I accepted the introduction to Divine Love. I don't have the words to put into words what that inner feeling looks like as an image, but it became stronger than I could resist. It actually took more energy to deny than to accept. The hardest thing I have ever done was to leave my partner. We had to finally accept that our relationship was over. It was explained to me that if we both received Divine Love eventually our souls would separate as no Celestial spirit can engage in same-sex relationships as the truth about soulmates exists. There is so much that I have experienced which has been non-judgemental and non-opinionated by any other spirit that I look back on my life with the love my life deserved.

I will stop now as I feel quite overwhelmed. Love and bright kisses, Chris

89

Luke speaks:

The incredible human truth that exists on our planet involves the fact that most of the population live unaware of the Immortal Truth involving God's Divine Love. Humanity has lived this way for much of its existence. This presents tremendous freedom. People in their physical life exercise their personality through their physical attributes day-in and day-out to their liking or disliking of their relationships or life experience. The population of the world largely exists without having to include a choice to include the Divine Love.

I have used the word 'incredible' as this describes how some people have felt when finding out about the availability of the Divine Love having never heard of any such existence before. People in their physical life may find it incredible that such a form of energy exists for their soul that can be so readily received. The word incredible describes the feeling that a person experiences when they have found what they may have been looking or searching for much of their life. It is a true form of energy particular to their soulful need. It is also incredible that this form of energy exists and that one learns that a vast population of humanity is living in their spirit life knowing and participating with this Love and are well advanced in their personalisation with the Soul and Origin of this Love, God.

What is incredible, is that the humanity of Earth has lived for so long without ever realising the potential that this Love provides to their individual soul. The river flows no higher than its source, and the human eye can only see so far. If the world were always to remain unaware of this form of energy, men and women of the Earth would miss the choice for such potential to exceed the human head of the river and may never be realised until their spirit life. You have heard from a vast majority of individuals who never learned about the existence of the Divine Love during their earthly life. Nearly every human residing in the spirit world has learnt about this resource when living their spirit life. The humanity of Earth lives without ever seeing any evidence in another mortal physical life that the Divine Love exists. Half the world's population today could be receiving the Divine Love quietly in their own private and personal space and no one would be any wiser or see any visible difference to confirm that the Divine Love is true and was received into an earthly soul. This is the incredible freedom that humanity lives within their physical life. No one sees any visible change in the physical form, soul or spirit body. Men and women do not see each day as a visible choice to include and participate in the truest and most loving relationship of all time, yet this is the freedom that lives within the peoples of the world.

In the spirit world from the First Natural Sphere, this freedom that people lived within their life on Earth yet without ever being aware that a choice exists, suddenly reveals the visible evidence of this choice. This visible evidence is living in the souls and lives of those who have made their choice to participate in the greatest and truest relationship of all. The residents that reside in all the natural spheres no longer live as they did on Earth. They live constantly among the presence of those living their Immortal life as these individuals come from the Divine Love and Celestial spheres to help maintain the natural spheres. The choice is seen everywhere. There are so many individuals living in their perfect natural love infused with the Loving Spirit as It conveys Divine Love into their soul and moving about with their spirit bodies shining with spirit illumination that represents that choice made.

Everlasting

The humanity of Earth understands that their life is finite and not permanent. Change will come. One will no longer be living their physical life. Throughout their physical life in natural love, most live in the comfort of never knowing that a whole other life exists. Firstly, a spirit life and secondly, an Immortal life. Here in the spirit life, the individual quickly learns that their physical life did end but that life continues in another form which involves their individual personality and soul living in their spirit body. After one adapts, the individual understands that their Earth life wasn't permanent but they also realise that living in the natural spheres isn't permanent as well. They learn this by seeing those of us who have made our choice to live with a form of energy that *is permanent*. Individuals realise that though they have survived death, the course of their natural spirit life is presented with a visible choice that was invisible as it is on Earth never having seen that a permanent form of energy exists. For many spirits living solely in their natural love, seeing so many individuals who have lived through their soulful transformation unsettles that sense of perceived freedom and permanency. In the natural spirit spheres, the humanity that resides in only their natural love never again live with that same sense of freedom that they did when living on Earth.

My objective here is not to sound judgemental on the nature of freedom and existing belief systems. You must remember that my perspective about life is drawn from myself having lived an earthly and spirit life, a life that is multifaceted in my understandings about the nature of love. It is true, the humanity that lives on Earth lives largely unaware of any evidence that a non-evolving form of energy exists for their soul. Some men and women are aware. As their awareness becomes more established and as one learns about living with Divine Love in their physical life, it becomes apparent how much freedom is available in earthly life. The fact that another whole life exists, an Immortal soul-life, offsets the entire natural spirit world. No one is forced to make their personal choice to participate in their Immortal life, but, never again is the individual living the course of their natural spirit life living without seeing the spirit evidence of the choice having been made by others.

I will leave it here. I have conveyed significant vision that involves the entire spectrum of natural love. Your friend and teacher, Luke

90

Hello; my name is Rupert. I have lived in the spirit world a considerable length of time. Long have I known about my soul-life living with Divine Love and all the spheres that comprise our spirit world. I lived in the Celestial Heaven a long time; it is an extraordinary place filled with the most beautiful things that have been made by individuals utilising the various Spirit Laws that enable the fabric of spirit to be constructed into a solid form. This is a fact of life here. Individuals learn how to work with the resources that exist in each sphere to create beautiful things. Everything created is harmonious with the spirit-scape. In the Celestial Heaven, due to our soul condition, nothing is created that is wasteful or surplus. This experience of creating utilising spirit resources is a whole new experience that people here enjoy learning about. There is a large part of the spheres already created, but we have contributed toward establishing things in solid form for us to enjoy. It is almost impossible for me to describe to you what these resources are for they don't exist on planetary Earth or in human consciousness. Like everything else that involves our spirit life, you are quite literally introduced to a whole new experience!

I have travelled through the Universal Spirit Spheres. These spheres are vast in their expansiveness; and they have a solid form with a particular spirit gravity. This gravity field is established by a form of energy that acts in accord with a unifying Spirit Law that is controlled independently by the Supreme Creator, God. No mortal or super-universal personality can create such a unified field of energy that circumnavigates the entire Soul-Sphere of the Father.

Part of being a universal citizen is the awareness that there are existing spirit attributes that exceed our finite capabilities. It is much like the Loving Spirit and the Divine Love. These two resources extend to all inhabited worlds and in potential, to all created souls. The field of spirit gravity is the same throughout the mortal spirit world and so is the light source. It is an obvious thing to say, but we have to see here in the spirit world so there needs to be a light source that is sympathetic to the optical vision and senses of our spirit body. The Eternal Father is the creator of all extraordinary things! This Soul has originated a light source throughout our mortal spirit world that is not to simply light the spheres, but a form of illumination that the spirit optical senses can perceive forming such imagery into a coherent visible form. I can see another spirit because my optical senses function with absolute clarity with this spirit light source. What is even more extraordinary is that my optical vision situated in my spirit-mind can construct memories so that I can recall these memories, seeing my memories formed in spirit light.

I have travelled to other inhabited worlds. It takes some time to travel, but I can travel quickly and I know where I am going. The individuals from other inhabited worlds and in their Celestial Heaven that I conversed with were much taller than our population that live on Earth. They are super-personifications of their physical attributes due to the presence of Divine Love that each generation received which did have a genetic influence over them. I know that this may sound like science fiction, but we are not isolated to our own Celestial Heaven. There is so much more to see beyond our Celestial Heaven!

My experience being in the Universal Spirit Spheres has braced my understanding of the nature of my life into its full context. I can see why the Divine Love is available. To begin with, when I entered my spirit life I knew nothing about the Divine Love and I had no idea about this Love during my physical life. I made my choice here as I was able to see those beautiful individuals already established in their Immortal life. I hardly felt the Divine Love the first time I was with the intent to receive It. I was not emotional when I began receiving this Love. I was taught that the Acting, Loving Spirit that brings this Divine Love into my soul acts within a Spirit Law to Its requirement. I was cool, calm and collected to put it into a modern expression. As I progressed there was a lot of teaching that I was exposed to about my natural love, my soul, how my spirit body would change, and the spheres I would progress to eventfully arriving in the Celestial Heaven. I evaluated my human life as my soul condition changed, eventually having my natural love perfected with my Immortal life and having more visibility as I changed. In the Celestial Heaven I learnt about the spheres beyond the Celestial spheres. As I speak to you, I am one who can communicate from a perspective of all that I have experienced involving my progression to the Celestial Heaven with complete objectivity. I don't spend any time thinking about my life as I progressed to the Celestial Heaven. My life is all about venturing forth into the universe, the Spirit-Verse that I, as a soul, am at liberty to explore. Many of us who enjoy this experience travel together and learning as much as we can.

I will finish now. This has been a wonderful moment to make contact in this way as I very rarely come to this surface which interfaces between the earthly and spirit world. Other than communicating with you, I do not need to be here. Thank you, Rupert

91

Hello; my name is Instinia. I am an individual who has travelled from my spirit world to your spirit world through a Universal Spirit Sphere. I have done this numerous times. I have taken individuals from your Celestial Heaven through the Universal Spirit Sphere to meet individuals that form our spirit population that reside in our Celestial Heaven. I have learnt some of the language that you speak so I can speak to you in a limited way.

The reality of spirit I have known all my existence. As a little girl living on the planet Constella, I grew up always aware of an existing spirit world and attributes of spirit extending from the Original One. I am aware that you are aware of the things that I am aware of, but that you are living among peoples that are largely unaware of these same things. I never knew anything different. I never lived with my spirit unknown to me, or the energy that in your language you call Divine Love. The population of my planet was around 11 billion souls. There are still individuals living their physical life on Constella. I have travelled in the opposite direction visiting other individuals residing in their Celestial Heaven.

I think the word is fantasy, this can sound like a fantasy but for me spirit is complete as I have known of nothing else. On our planet, we are aware of the different forces that we study such as the evolving and non-evolving. I have been informed by some of your Celestial teachers that you have recently made real connection with these teachers as they have expanded this teaching about the Divine Love being a non-evolving form of energy. I can receive this energy in the Universal Spirit Sphere. I am receiving this energy as I communicate to you from the Eternal Source like I did in my Celestial Heaven and as I did when I lived as a woman in my physical life. On my planet, our relationship with life and death is entirely different from yours. It is different because we don't have death in our life experience. We are so attuned with our soul-life and spirit body in our physical life that the concept of 'death' doesn't exist for we interface with our spirit world all the time. We see our physical life as an attribute of spirit energy that simply matures our personality. When it is time for our physical body to cease existing, the energy of our soul and spirit body simply transitions so that when we awaken in the First Sphere of our spirit world, we never awaken unaware of where we are, who we are, and why we are where we are. All the Truths about the individualisation of the soul and the advent of the spirit body were taught to us by our First Parents and our subsequent Universal Teacher. I have met your First Parents and Jesus.

On our planet, we experience our physical attributes as an extension of our soul-life. We are conceived as you are conceived, our difference being that as we mature we are doing so being cognitively aware that our parents are participating with another form of energy that we too can participate with. As we mature we are free to make this decision for our participation with the Divine Love.

The planet Consella is like your planet, having landmass and seas. If you were to meet us you would recognise our physical form as being quite like yours only much taller. There are certain places around our planet where we can meet Celestial spirits as they regularly appear to us in their Celestial form. We don't call the spheres where we live our Immortal life the 'Celestial Heaven.' We have a more profound understanding in our physical life about the progressive life that living with Divine Love involves so there is no distinction in name or number for our spheres. They are all the next progressive universal experience. We even include our physical life in the progressive experience of our life.

As I have said, I have spent a lot of time socialising with people from your world. This has only been able to happen since the Divine Love became available again for your mortal experience. Before that, had I travelled to your world, your spirit world, I would have seen your Celestial Heaven without an entrance from the Universal Spirit Spheres. I would not have been able to enter and I most certainly would not have been able to visit your natural spheres to meet your First Parents or any inhabitants. It is only when travelling through the First Universal Spirit Sphere to meet the First Parents of a planet that we know that their Celestial Heaven is open with its citizens able to travel and interact with other planetary citizens. I have had to learn the language that you understand which involves the Creator's Eternal Energy that brings everlasting life to the soul. I have had to spend time being close to you as you have received communications so I could learn how this experience transpires to convey my experience to you. On my planet, what we are doing here and now, we do not need to do. This experience is entirely new to me. I am interested in your environment as I look around but I can see that your immediate population is living unaware of its potential universal citizenship. This too is new for me to see as I have only known a world and population living aware of its universal citizenship! I have been to one other planet on my travels. That planet is the same as our planet. The citizens from that planet are with a vast knowledge of the Creator and other inhabited worlds and I have learnt much from those I interacted with. There is constant communication between our worlds as we share our experiences of the Creator.

On our planet, we don't live with any longing in our soul. We live fulfilled in our physical potential due to our soul-life being in touch with the Living Energy that brings all answers to light and life. We recognise that the Creator has created all that is creation; we love and accept this. Some of our most advanced teachers have held open discussions about the nature of the Creator. Always it is known that the Creator has given life to the way we are and we accept and love this for what it is, for why it is and how we have come to know it to be. The other planet is more advanced in its teachings than my planet. They still have not answered the question, "Who created the Creator"? What we do know is that we are living. We also know that our ability to be aware is a gift of life. The other planet understands the Immortality of the Divine Love. They have studied this Love in Its form and like the population of our planet, they recognise that the basis of all mortal progression is derived from the causal effect that this non-evolving form of energy has in our perfect natural love, which you call soul-love or 'natural love'.

The Spirit-Verse is an extensive place! It extends the entire way around the Sphere of the Creator. It interfaces with all the surface of the Creator's Sphere. There are layers within layers of the Spirit-Verse. The kind of energy required to create, generate and sustain such existence that we abide in is unsurmountable for anything else to attempt to establish and sustain such spirit life. The spirit gravity in your Celestial Heaven is the same as ours and the other planets that I have visited. The light that illuminates all spirit spheres is consistent in all planetary worlds. According to the other individuals I have met from the other planet, the gravity and light are consistent to all the spirit worlds that they have been to. What does differ are the physical universes and planetary landscapes that support their bio-physical life. From what I have deduced about the nature of the mortal soul, we are all the same as far as how our soul is before incarnation, the attribute it is, how it incarnates and our spirit body forms. It would seem that the Creator has established Spirit Laws that are finite in number that serve and act with same outcome but to a multitude of inhabited worlds. The non-evolving form of energy that the Divine Love is remains consistent for one and all souls.

It has been a pleasure meeting you and spending time with you as you know about the Immortal Love and you are universal in your approach. Instinia

92

Rupert speaks:

I am here again to share more information with you. I enjoyed my recent visit to speak. I haven't spoken in such a mortal way in a long time as I spend all of my time in the Universal Spirit Spheres. I am like a deep-sea diver who spends all their time in the depths compared to a beach dweller dwelling in the shallows. I have never lost my contact with my physical origin and I still have the memories of my physical life. Initially, at the beginning of my spirit life, I was as most are, innocent and being taught about life all over again. I recognised that the Divine Love was an advancement to my evolution and is a form of energy that I never knew to have existed in the way that it does when I lived my earthly life.

I have an expansive love in my natural love for my fellow humanity. Why? Because I have seen what love can be realised in the soul of a human. My soul-life is the living confirmation of this. I have had many conversations with Luke, Jesus, the First Parents and a vast array of other ancient individuals who have all taught me so much about living here.

To convey to you how I perceive my life since living with Divine Love is a retrospective experience. Having travelled the vast distances that I have through the various spheres, my evolution has been one of moving through the spheres toward the Infinite Spheres progressing as I did and feeling closer to a living physical presence of the reality that God is with solid form. And from my Earth life to the First Natural Sphere and still with very much the personality of my humanity, from the First Divine Love Sphere to the Celestial Heaven and with more of my spirit personality developed in my humanity. As I moved through the spheres of the Celestial Heaven my spirit personality dominated my experience and human life. I was living more spirit-personality than earthly physical memory and physical human personality. As I moved through the Celestial spheres my soul condition provided me with the palpable contact of God being in solid form. From the First Natural Sphere to the last sphere in the Celestial Heaven I was always learning about my involvement with attributes and Handiworks. I was learning about my attributes functioning in my spirit life interfacing with God's Handiworks and attributes but I could not perceive God in solid form. I was told by more advance individuals than myself that God lives in solid form although my experience was all in attributes and Handiworks. I was receiving Divine Love and could identify with this Love as a form of energy, but I could not perceive its origins as with solid form. In the Universal Spirit Spheres or the Infinite Spheres as they are sometimes called, things changed! As I spent time moving about in these spheres I began to sense the palpable reality that God existed in solid form. I felt closer to the Soul, God, more than in any previous sphere that I had progressed through. I can tell you this for as I have come from a Universal Spirit Sphere to be with you. I can see the spirit-material each sphere is as I draw closer to the Earth. As I stand by your side I can see humans who are observing this experience, who are living their spirit life solely in their natural love. These individuals are loving, curious and interested, but each word I speak to you about my experience they have never heard spoken before. I can tell you this by the astonished look on their spirit faces. They are hearing about the Universal Spirit Sphere and an experience like mine for their first time. Some of these individuals have only recently transitioned into their spirit life. As I speak to you, Jesus, Luke, Saleeba, some of your relatives and most who have already communicated to you are present. Some of these individuals are fascinated by my life in the Universal Spirit Spheres. As it has been taught to you, a great number of spirits remain in the Celestial Heaven yet to venture forth into the infinite realm of our Creator.

    I have travelled to Instinia's spirit world. Instinia acted as my tour guide through the sphere. I travelled with several other spirit humans from our spirit world and an ancient spirit called Elias. He acted as a translator when necessary as Instinia had learned quite a lot of the languages we used. I am comfortable mixing with individuals that have lived on other planets. It shouldn't surprise you that I am an interplanetary traveller. Many humans are fascinated by the physical fabric of space and time. The search for the existence of other life has captivated human imaginations ever since humans looked to the stars and wondered if they were alone.

The truth that speaks to me with such evidence is how expansive and how many 'spirit' environments have been made and brought into existence. On planet Earth, a single planet with a population increasing day-by-day, is singular in its definition by being the only inhabited planet local to itself. Where I reside, spheres upon spheres relate to an extensive spirit-scape that circumnavigate the Creator. I have thought to travel around the Sphere of God. To do this I would need to pick up a travel guide, leap-frogging from one planet's spirit world to the next. I have no idea how long this would take me, but as Luke said to you, it is a very long time…but time is something I have. Our First Parents have taught me that it is possible to circumnavigate the Eternal One by being in the right soul condition, which I am, and knowing that if I happen upon a planet that is not living with the Immortal Love that I am not to interfere and introduce myself.

I will stop now. I have sprinkled some spirit-star light before you. Our natural love living with Divine Love can take us around the Spirit and Soul of the Father, and that is wonderful!

My love and universal friendship to you all, Rupert

93

Luke speaks:

Rupert touched on a very good point in his discourse to you. He succinctly outlined his passage from Earth to the last sphere in the Celestial Heaven as involving attributes and Handiworks. This is true for us all. Throughout our communications with you, we have identified a vast array of these attributes and Handiworks forming a complex image, a detailed outline that involves an individual convergence with what is mortal to what is God's domain. As Rupert concisely said, his progression involved learning about this convergence of attributes and Handiworks without ever seeing God in solid form.

As you experience Divine Love in your physical life, it is in faith that you believe God exists in solid form. You may feel the Divine Love and the presence of the Loving Spirit, but to see the solid form of God is beyond your physical horizon. This is largely true here in the spirit life. Nearly all the Celestial spirits have experienced the convergence between attributes and Handiworks as they have received the Divine Love without ever seeing with their spirit-eyes the Spirit-Soul of God in solid form.

What was not conveyed to James Padgett by Jesus or by any other spirit is that no spirit in the Celestial Heaven had ever seen God in solid form. It was taught that soul perceptions provided more clarity revealing that God is in solid form and not in abstract form. The truth of it is, Jesus has travelled through the Infinite Spheres to the Soul-Spirit Sphere and has seen God in solid form. Our First Parents have too. And along with a large number of spirits who have lived in the Divine Love since Jesus began living here in his spirit life. This truth has never before been revealed to earthly humanity.

It has been necessary for Jesus to see the Spirit-Soul of God to establish that love and connectivity between attribute and Handiwork with the origin and solid form. If we never saw God in solid form, then our Eternal existence living in Divine Love would always remain in the convergence of attribute and Handiwork.

The Divine Love as we have taught you, exists in solid form but it remains only a form of energy and is not the solid form of God. The attributes and Handiworks that we have learnt to live with required anchoring so that we didn't live in a perpetual eternity in the middle distance between two origins, Earth and God. It is every individual's right and universal passage to visit God and experience God in solid form in this personalisation of soul-life. You have to be in the right soul condition to see the Father in solid form, for it confirms the entirety of a soul-life lived. When you face the surface of the Eternal Father you know that there is nothing above, beneath, in the middle, back or beyond the individual you are loving. This in itself confirms the evolution you have lived and the evolution you have progressed through as a personality interacting with the attributes and Handiworks of the Father as living confirmation. This meeting solidifies the convergence of attribute with Handiwork as your soul condition changes at this point of meeting, for you are the created soul that God created meeting your Creator who *is* Soul. The process when beginning to receive Divine Love your first time eventually leads you to meet the Eternal Soul, God. Your Immortal soul meeting the Eternal Soul completes the individualisation of all that is Immortal and finite with all that is Eternal and Infinite. Your soul condition changes after this meeting for the Origin has been revealed to you which defines the very process of your progression as you have lived for so long in the attributes and Handiworks receiving Divine Love.

When I met the Father, the Father did not speak an actual word to me. All I could do was love the Soul in the acknowledgement of my life with all the gifts I have lived. I prayed to the Father and received Divine Love through the action of the Holy, Acting, Loving Spirit as I, in my natural love was loving the Father. I tried to gain as much perception as possible while I was there. I knew the Father was there for I reached a boundary where I knew I could not go into. I could not see into the Father's Soul or gain a measurement on the actual size of the Father but this was a vast presence!

The reality that we can meet the solid form of our Creator is paramount to a sojourn throughout the spirit life. If we were never to experience this, our spirit life would remain substantial but without the solid form of the Origin being substantiated to us, which over eternity in our spirit life, could erode our confidence as to the very nature of the Soul whom we have been receiving Divine Love from. Imagine yourself walking along a line that began long before your first step, that ends in the same place where it began but you continue taking steps never arriving and all the while receiving a substance which is changing your very essence that is non-evolving as you evolve along this line.

This has been a moment of expansive vision. I will stop now. Your friend and teacher, Luke

94

Luke speaks:

It is only with Jesus that we can meet our Creator in solid form. He is the closest to our Eternal Creator in his soul condition. He knows how to guide individuals through the Universal Infinite Spheres to arrive at the boundary that is established as the boundary of all created realms with the Spirit Soul Sphere of the Eternal One. If an individual from the Celestial Heaven travelled into the Universal Spirit Sphere then went to see the Father who is solid form, they would not know how to proceed there as it requires a new spacial awareness when arriving at this boundary.

There are spirit realities that exist that earthly humans know nothing about. I am not arrogant in saying this, nor am I judging the earthly human as being generally lacking any spirit sight. It is simply a fact and one that most residents of Earth will accept. A reason why I have conveyed to you about meeting our Creator in solid form is because it is a spirit fact that this does happen. Also, to illustrate to you that a spirit life is not a life eternally living between places and only ever receiving and experiencing Divine Love without ever being able to meet the origin of this non-evolving form of energy and source of the greatest, truest love a mortal soul can experience.

We have taught you that you are soul first and foremost. This is never more evident than life in the spirit world. We have taught you about soul condition and why this forms the basis of all movement throughout the spirit world. We have illustrated how relevant soul-life is in the spirit life and that all mortal soul-life originates from the Source of soul-life, God. Everything we have shared with you has its relevance with soul-life and the Soul-Life of God. We are personality with attributes of soul and spirit body, therefore, in the experience of being personality it is only fitting that we can meet the Origin of our beginnings. If we were never in all eternity to meet the Soul, soul-to-Soul, but to forever live in Divine Love in an Immortal life interacting with other personalities we would miss the experience of becoming cognitively aware of the most asked questions of all human time: Who is God?, Where is God?, What is God?, Does God exist?, and can we ever meet God face-to-face? In a real way, by receiving Divine Love these questions are beginning to be answered. This begins in faith. As our soul condition becomes more substantial, faith turns into knowing. Such knowing becomes irrefutable by the time the individual progresses to their Celestial life and these questions are well underway to being answered. For many, their personality needs to meet the ultimate personality ever created. I still cannot tell you the answer to the greatest question of all, Where did God come from? But I can say that when you meet God in solid form all these questions are answered in a soulful knowing that *everything* is at eternal peace and love in God.

I will not speak more. My love to you both, Luke

95

Hello; I am here, it is your friend Elias. I have met Our Father. I travelled with Jesus to meet the Eternal One who resides with solid form in the Spirit-Soul-Sphere that is a sphere unto itself. I went to a place where I could not travel beyond as had I reached the boundary of spirit world. I could not see with my spirit-soul perceptions the attribute of the Loving Spirit or the substance of Divine Love. Being as close to the Father as we were did not influence any visual outcome that made the Loving Spirit and the Divine Love any more visible. There are a vast array of attributes and Handiworks set in motion by the Father that I could not see as existing in their solid form. I could sense a complete creative power but I was never overawed by any form of energy being emitted from the Ultimate Creative Generator that the Father is. It was silent, calm and peaceful. I definitely had the feeling that I was facing the face of creation. It is a power beyond my comprehension that such a force of universal nature exists.

Like you both and other men and women experiencing Divine Love, we were introduced to this Love and its availability by our friend and teacher, Jesus. We all began our experience with this Love without knowing anything about It other than a sprinkling of truths that we can personalise. You both have been receiving the Divine Love for 30 years. I have been receiving Divine Love for several thousand years. We have both learned that this Love originates - as our finite souls do - from the Original Source of life, and the life we live flows from the Source. When you were introduced to the availability of Divine Love it was not common knowledge that eventually you could meet the solid form of God. Now that it has been revealed to you it situates a beginning with Divine Love with a clear outcome which begins with your natural faith. There are a great many souls that have met the Creator in solid form. You recently received a communication from a beautiful individual from another inhabited world. Many individuals from that world have travelled to meet the Creator in solid form. Once you move beyond the spheres of the Celestial Heaven and you engage your spirit life in the Universal Spirit Spheres, everything you know about spirit life changes! These created infinite spheres reveal to you the super-expansive nature of what has been created relative to the First Natural Sphere which is closest to humans living their mortal human life.

It is not a conditional requirement for each Celestial spirit to live in the Universal Infinite Spirit Sphere or to travel with Jesus to meet Our Father in solid form. This is an independent and individual soulful calling, but having experienced this myself, it does complete the life of the mortal soul.

The problem we have here is for us to bring a visual narrative to life so that what we convey to you has form and continuity. Above all, communicating an identifiable context that you can relate to without having ever experienced all that this meeting entails. I do not want to sound vague when such a compelling convergence transpires between the Eternal with the Immortal. My best expression can be summed up by saying that meeting Our Eternal Father in solid form provides you with the complete image and substance of your soul. It completes ones' understanding about why the Divine Love exists, and it reveals how extraordinary our spirit body and Immortal personality and soul is. It also confirms to us the existence of all attributes and Handiworks that we have come into contact with. Lastly, it confirms why life is a gift and how significant it is to be physical and then to reside in the spirit world and thank god for sending a soul like Jesus to teach us about living with the Soul, God!

Your friend in everlasting peace and love, Elias

96

Hello; my name is Martha. I have been following your experience as you have been receiving these communications. My experience has benefitted by listening to this teaching exchange. I have lived in the First natural sphere for some time. I have been happy here but having heard what has been exchanged, has struck a chord deep within me to change. I am in the process of learning how to acquire Divine Love, what It is, and how I can make myself more available to the Soul, God.

Thank you, love Martha

97

Hello; my name is Bob. I have never in all my spirit life heard an exchange like the ones you have received these recent days. I never knew that a language like this existed. I am curious now to begin my experience acquiring this non-evolving form of Love. I say non-evolving as I have heard this described to you, but I have no idea what this means yet I am eager to find out. The choice to move on from where I live feels very appealing. The individuals speaking to you are impressive. I have seen such individuals before, but I have never conversed with them. I think I was a little nervous as they are so impressive and different, but I can see now what they are speaking about is true.

I feel excited about my future and that there is the possibility for change here.

My respect to you both, Bob

98

Hello; my name is Jennifer. I have come from a very dark condition of soul. I was helped by a brighter spirit. I live in a good condition now. It is a real treat for me to feel my love again as it has been a long time since I have been able to feel what love in its expression feels like. You can live without love and being loving for so long that it becomes habit-forming and a way of spirit life. All I will say about my physical life that brought me to being unloving is that I lived an unhappy life brought about by being unloved to begin with. That is behind me now. I am going to press on and receive Divine Love. I never learnt to read or write in my life. I remained uneducated and I wasn't with any degree of any real intelligence or common sense. Feeling love again has put me in contact with my sense of true feeling and self which was unknown to me for such a long time! A horizon closes and a new horizon dawns, and one I am to embrace and travel in Divine Love.

Thank you, Jennifer

99

Hello; it is I, your friend Elias. I would like to confirm that here in the spirit life, the spirit body cannot progress of its own accord separate from the soul. The spirit body is an attribute of the Father's design and function but this does not entitle it in its forming to act independently of the soul that resides within it. Although the force and nature of personality form part of the spirit body, the personality cannot manipulate the spirit body to its will. Personality is unable to act in the spirit body manipulating the spirit body without the soul being involved. Here in the spirit life, personality cannot manipulate soul condition. Soul comes first, all else that is of the individual follows. The good thing about the spirit body is that it acts in a normal manner in its spirit existence. This means that by personality alone the spirit body can never become abnormal in its design, form and function. Once you can see this truth about the spirit body, it brings into context the purity of God's Divine Love as being the only form of energy that can bring about real change in the soul that is then experienced as normal change in the spirit body culminating in the progression of the attributes of individual personality.

There is another who will speak with you now. Your friend and teacher, Elias

100

Hello; it is your friend James Padgett. There are many spirits present as we speak to you today. There is a mixture of those living with Divine Love and those who are yet to establish themselves in their Immortal life.

This is quite a day! It is the end of a decade and the beginning of another decade. Everlasting is about the present and the future, the individual who desires to learn about living with Divine Love comprehensively. The recent teachings you have received had to happen. There needed to be an outcome and there needed to be two individuals to bring this about. You have successfully received these important messages conveyed by Luke and the other spirits who have broadened the teachings of the soulful life as well as the teachings of the surface of the Father existing in solid form. A full perspective of information is available now. From the day I first began receiving to the beginning of 2020, what a remarkable century it has been involving the teachings of Immortality!

Well done from us all here. James

101

Well my darlings, we have arrived at the end of a decade. You followed my guidance and now there is a vast array of information that the thirsty soul can drink up in the quest to learn more about the soul-life. What hadn't previously existed in the written form now exists in solid form. What was intangible is now tangible and the Soul of the Father has been met!

We are delighted that another convergence transpired and that such valuable information is available for the individual. We don't expect the world's population to drop what they are doing and to soak up these truths with immediacy, but like yourselves, there will be that one individual that our words find their way to that will mean the world and the spirit world to them. It is important to know that such truths are existing in their solid form and that the experience of Our Father's Truths are conveyed from our experiences here in our spirit life so that a physical life can be lived with more definition, resolve and a gentle eradication of fear due to unknowing. It has also been important to bring such spirit information forward for the individual who accepts the Father, receives Divine Love and wants to know more. I will take this moment to send all our love and gratitude to Cleo for her contribution.

Stay tuned, Constance

January 2020

102

Amon speaks:

I am pleased to be with you both again. The insight that Luke has brought to you about meeting the Eternal One in solid form is true. Aman and I have travelled to be with Our Father and to see Our Father in solid form. As you know, we reside in the First Universal Spirit Sphere, commonly referred to as an Infinite Sphere as it circumnavigates the solid form of the Eternal One. There are several Infinite Spheres and we have conveyed to you images that illustrate these unique spirit environments. The wonderful thing about these Infinite Spheres is that they are accessible to us and are not closed to our participation. They extend beyond all the Celestial Heavens which are formed and relate to the spirit spheres that initiate planetary mortal life in natural love and then learning to live in the Immortal Love. Aman and I have taken individuals from our Celestial Heaven to meet the Eternal One in solid form. As it has been revealed to you, Jesus provides this service as well.

Living with Divine Love in our Immortal life is very free. There is nothing random or chaotic that interferes with our life. There is such a majestic overview of created spirit templates formed into existence by the Father that are harmonious in their existence with each other. We are part of this harmony and in the right soul condition to participate fully in this Spirit-Verse adventure.

If I sound relaxed in the sheer expansiveness of vision that is being conveyed to you, I am relaxed for what we experience here is commonplace and common spirit life to us. From your perspective, from your physical life, such spirit vision that is ahead of you may sound unbelievable. To us who live in this reality all the time, this expansive vision is normal. It is abnormal to believe that earthly humans are the sole creation and participators with the Father. There is a vast number of inhabited worlds with their spirit worlds and with their inhabitants living their Immortal life or solely in their natural love. The Loving Spirit and Divine Love also form part of every single population that exists on their planets.

There are numerous created personality formed by the Father which will never incarnate into mortal life which requires the attributes of soul to incarnate thus acquiring a spirit body and personality to confirm the individualisation of that soulful personality in physical form. Each mortal personality is formed with the attribute of soul and spirit body forming part of this mortal personality. There are created personalities that do not require evolution involving a physical life on an organic planet, and then there are personalities that to produce such personality, requires a physical life.

As it has been conveyed to you, the soul and spirit body that you are doesn't require the forces of evolution to be originated or created. The Divine Love and Loving Spirit do not require any evolutionary nature to come into existence or operation.

I am pleased that this expansive Spirit Truth that involves the Father's Divine Love and its energy that is non-evolving, will bring clarity of vision so that the individual may see how it is that we live with this Love here in our spirit life. To see the Loving Spirit, Divine Love, spirit body and the soul as existing without being originated by planetary evolution or spirit world environment brings real context into the dynamic shape and form that physical life is. Never will you feel more organic than in your physical life. Life in the spirit body without a physical attribute is an entirely different human experience. It represents how versatile the construct of the mortal personality is as it can form in the physical environment that involves the earthly body that it is capable of interacting with non-evolving forms of energy such as the Divine Love and Loving Spirit and its spirit body and soul. And then in the spirit world the personality is quite capable of acting solely in the environment of the spirit body and its attributes.

The spheres do have a lot of solid forms existing in them. As spirits, we don't live in a pure spirit spacial energy as ethereal beings floating through our existence. On the contrary, we see vast spirit horizons.

The Divine Love and the Loving Spirit will never be ceased in their living presence in the Divine Love Spheres and Celestial Heaven and the Infinite Spheres. The Loving Spirit will not be de-activated until all created souls have been incarnated, physically individualised and given the opportunity when transitioned into their spirit life to partake of the Divine Love. What was recommenced with the life of Jesus now forms part of mortal life and will continue until there is no more mortal life living on planet Earth. Much has been conveyed to you both about this and our answers never change.

I will stop now. I have loved our moment together today and will see you again. Amon

103

Hello; my name is MaryBeth. It is a pleasure to meet you both. I have been living and receiving Divine Love for the equivalent of 25 years. I lived a happy and uncomplicated life. I experienced motherhood then being a grandmother and a great-grandmother all in a life spanning 103 years of age. My husband and I live in the Celestial Heaven. To you the Celestial Heaven could sound like I live in the rainbow or at the end of a rainbow. We must always remember that a rainbow has two beginnings and two endings - it just depends upon your perspective!

The Celestial Heaven is a real place. A place unimaginable to the human mind. How can you imagine such a place when you may not be aware that the Divine Love exists? We have conveyed a portrait of our lives living here in the Celestial Heaven but this still fails to convey how beautiful these spheres are! It all happens due to the involvement with the Divine Love that brings about this true living Immortality.

In my earthly life I believed in God and I was a good person. I lived through the decades when men went to war and I saw how men did atrocious things to each other. I lived unwavering in my belief that wholeheartedly people were good. There is so much that happens among the social actions of men and women that can test your resolve, but I chose my life as an example of goodness. I read the Old and New Testament from time to time and I had the belief that Jesus died for our sins. In my spirit life I learnt that this couldn't be further from the truth! It does change everything when you begin your life here. Everything you thought you knew about human existence is reformed into a new perspective. And so it should since one realises that they have survived

Everlasting

their human life only to still have their beliefs which mostly are impermanent when facing a life everlasting in the spirit world.

My study of my soul and spirit attributes is a passion of mine. I love the Father's Love. Everything that I believed to be good about people was confirmed as I advanced in my soul condition meeting and seeing the vast population accepting Divine Love from all different social cultures from the earthly life.

It is readily discussed among those of us who study our relationship of soul with the Divine Love, that the attribute of soul and spirit body are engineered by Our Creator with a dynamic template of energy that is responsive to the energy of Divine Love. What I have experienced and what I have seen is how so many receive this Love and how consistently each individual soul and spirit body responds in a progressive way that never becomes abnormal. What does not happen when we experience Divine Love is our attribute of soul and spirit body, having been infused with the Divine Love, do not become infused with this energy only to then spiral toward their evolution. The dynamic between soul with the energy the Divine Love is perfect symmetry. This is reflected in the individual characteristics of each personality individualised through their spirit body. It is really important to know that receiving Divine Love is a consistent experience. It could be very confronting beginning to receive Divine Love if the great unknown were present ... this unknown being that the soul and spirit body might move into abstract form. In your human experience I have observed that quite a number of people are aware and receiving Divine Love. This is a new social experience and social dynamic. Each individual appears to have such a varied account of their experience which is not consistent with everyone else's experience. I have observed that involving a human perspective, it seems that by receiving Divine Love lots of different things happen unique to the characteristics of the individual. It would seem that the experience involving Divine Love in the diversity of human individuality is a colourful experience. In my short time learning about living with this Love in my spirit life there is not any confusion to the normality that transpires when individuals from all walks of a once lived human life engage their soul-life with the Father's Divine Love.

I have a strong propensity toward teaching. I spent much of my human life studying, learning and imparting knowledge and I continue to do the same thing here. Only this involves a different kind of knowledge, a knowledge that was not readily available for me to study, learn and teach. Having said this, I don't know if in my physical life had I come into contact with the knowledge that has been forthcoming from Jesus and James Padgett's band, if I would have accepted it as it originated in such an unconventional manner. In my spirit experience, it is all conventual and visually proved beyond mortal belief that this is true and real and perfect for my soul and progressive experience. I can see how this form of communication could be so easily judged by a person due to the unconventional nature that bears such knowledge. This is a shame as an opportunity to learn about living with Divine Love may in fact be what their soul is seeking and longing to know.

I live with my husband, he is my soulmate. We are both happy that this is our way of spirit life living together in this most beautiful Love. Having spent all my life with my husband, as we went to the same school together where we became sweethearts and eventually married early in life, and to be together here is the continuation of our love story that spans a long time with happy memories. I have met other spirits living in the Celestial Heaven whose soulmate refuses to take up receipt of Divine Love and engage their Immortal life. From what I have seen, having a soulmate doesn't confirm that you will live happily ever after in the Celestial Heaven if only one of the individuals is living their Immortal soul-life. It requires an independent choice to begin receiving this Love and no amount of our natural love can persuade another to take up their Immortal life derived from true feelings of mortal love for the other individual. The other thing I have learnt is that in the forming of souls, the Father hasn't specified that all soulmates are to live together in the Celestial Heaven. There is no Spirit Law that exists that bends the freewill of a soul to begin receiving Divine Love due to the experience of another, and especially their soulmate, who is living with the Divine Love. This is a sad moment I feel, for relationships define us. It is quite different to see individuals abundantly happy in this Love yet their counterpart remains fixed to their natural personality and determination refusing to let their soul grow.

I have really enjoyed our time together. I have observed many of these recent experiences and am very interested in sharing the love I have as I participate with, and receive the Love of Our Father. In love, Marybeth

104

Hello; I am here to share a little more of my experience with you. I am aware that I have not been living my spirit life for as long as some of those who have conveyed information to you. Over here, one is not entitled by their spirit history. We are taught this when we embark upon our receipt of the Love. Each individual has unique abilities that contribute toward an overall experience of humanity living with Divine Love. In the First Divine Love Sphere, there is much excitement involved with beginnings. This is where our beginning with Divine Love transpires. Some individuals that I met in this sphere had only been receiving this Love a short length of time, but the grasp of their experience and the vision that they would live was astounding. Other individuals would apply their intellect with such veracity that they seemed on a steep learning curve embracing all the input about life that they had never intellectualised before during their earthly life. You can imagine how a scientist may be experiencing the science of their spirit body when meeting this body in the spirit world!

The Celestial teachers are advanced. They are superlative in their understanding about what it is to be human and they can hold a conversation with any individual. This is an extraordinary ability. There is so much to explain as individuals have many questions to ask. The Celestial teachers are patient and kind. I liked how they lived with such weight of knowledge with an effortlessness that made you feel at ease around them. These teachers never separated their knowledge from other mortals. There is no elitism of knowledge here.

Part of my observation as I progressed toward my Celestial life is that it appears that the soul and spirit body are formed for the purpose of ultimately being infused with the energy of Divine Love. This energy activates the soul and spirit body concisely to their requirements. I have never heard or seen another individual receiving this energy that resulted in making that individual feel uncomfortable. The Love is concisely infused. We never feel overwhelmed or splintered so that an experience happens that is so spiritually gifted that too much experience happens all at once which requires a long healing process through the spheres to pick up all the broken pieces. This is important to know. When you receive Divine Love, you will only receive the perfect amount harmonious to your soul condition so that you will never be overwhelmed or so adorned with Divine Love and cognitive awareness as not to be able to function in your daily life.

Everlasting

I know that you have both received a lot of information involving the soul-life living with Divine Love. I am taking this time to teach you that at an individual scale, experiencing this Love is always harmonious to your soul and spirit body. I say this because there may be people who form the idea that so much must be done in a particular way to cause or bring about one's capacity and ability to receive this Love. The best individual who can accommodate the amount of Divine Love that you can receive whenever you choose to receive It is the Source of this Love.

I know that this has been revealed to you before, but I would like to make mention of this as it is so extraordinary. As I speak to you now I am radiantly beautiful. As I received Divine Love my appearance changed as my spirit body developed from the Love I became younger in appearance. What is so fascinating about this is that I still have memories of how I was as an aged great-grandmother! It takes time to adjust to this experience involving our human memory with spirit life. Toward the end of my physical life I had the memories of how I was when I was younger. I had memories of my children and grandchildren and great-grandchildren. I was old but I had young memories. In my spirit life as I progressed to the Celestial Heaven, I experienced that incredible gift of de-ageing in appearance. As a spirit, I appear relatively young in my spirit appearance but I am still with the memories of how it was when I had aged. The interplay of memory is a significant attribute for some of us, for those of us who have lived long earthly lives. I have conversed with individuals here who lived barely any physical life at all, and for them they have no recollection of a memory formed in a physical life. Why memory is so significant is that it is an attribute that relates to the organic brain and other physical attributes that survive our physical death. The spirit-mind forming in our spirit body is with memory and the capacity to continue forming memories while at the same time retaining the information of our memories formed during our earthly sojourn. There are physical attributes that disappear once a physical life is over such as the reproductive drive and system. Our homeostasis systems such as core temperatures, immune, digestive and nervous systems have no function in the spirit body or spirit life. The attribute of memory, which does relate to the organic brain, retains its survival in the spirit-mind of the spirit body. This shows how much of personality we are and assists with our individuality and ability to equate change, which is necessary when one is reestablished after their death with their life resuming here in this new environment. I know that death is involved, and defines the living of the physical and then the living in the spirit but I wish to say that my perspective is all about life! My ability to communicate to you demonstrates life in an expansive and broader spectrum of experience.

I will stop now. Love, Marybeth

105

Luke speaks:

The idea that a spirit world exists presents an extraordinary palate for the human mind to wonder and conceptualise. The fact that in a physical life this is an unseen reality allows for more conjecture. What might be an idea for you is a reality for me. I live in this spirit world knowing all parts that comprise the mortal spirit world that relate to soul-life involving humans from the Earth. We have conveyed a surmountable amount of information that involves living with Divine Love in the spirit communications that you have both received.

I will outline here that you haven't received a direct experience from me involving the time I lived my human life with Jesus. You have not heard from me how it was that I lived with the other apostles or how I personally lived through the time, the days and nights that Jesus was on trial or his final days. You have received very little to do with events that transpired those long years ago. As was illustrated to you, you have not received a first-hand account from Jesus that details his earthly life, how he felt toward his end or how it was in the time of his transition. Also, what you have not heard are direct accounts from spirits who have taken other people's lives or from spirits who did horrible things to other people. You have not heard from individuals who were attacked and eaten alive by Great White sharks nor have you heard from individuals whose physical lives disintegrated in the flames of terrorism or blown apart in the ravages of war. You have not heard from the men who discovered the source of the Nile or disappeared at sea on ill-fated journeys. You have not heard from individuals who built structures by utilising extraordinary architectural design. What you have heard are loving experiences delivered from a cross-section of individuals representing humanity who are living their soul-life in their natural love and involving their receipt of Divine Love.

The circumstances that individuals transition into the spirit world to begin their spirit life can be quite physically traumatic. We have not found it necessary for you to receive experiences from spirits who outline every minute detail that resulted in their eventual death. This is not really necessary, for the outcome of fate is conclusive even if the individual were to outline in explicit detail their experience, still nothing would change what did transpire. The only outcome would be a graphic human life experience which is not the purpose of our work with you both. We are not seeking to redefine human history or to right the wrongs of the world or to persecute the actions of the unjust as we know from our long life in the spirit world and seeing the outcomes of all human soul condition in natural love.

When I have communicated to you both there have been a lot of curious individuals living solely in their natural condition who are fascinated by this convergence of our communication. I have asked if some of them would like to share a comment but it may surprise you when I say that they are embarrassed or reply that they don't have anything interesting to say. Not everyone desires to share their personal experience or life history. There have been many spirits living with Divine Love who would like to confirm to you all how true this Divine Love is but we have decided that to receive so many confirmations would take up too much of your physical energy and resources.

When a person living in their spirit life progresses into the Celestial Heaven, part of their natural love progression toward its perfection is to learn about empathy. Every single individual residing in the Celestial Heaven experiences empathy. This empathy is a form of giving love and is an action of humility in living action. If you are without empathy, your natural love will remain unperfected and you will not gain entrance to live your spirit life in the Celestial Heaven.

I will confirm to you again that our singular purpose has been to convey to you as much information as possible relating to the soul-life that involves living with Divine Love. There simply isn't vast amounts of information pertinent to identifying what the Divine Love is and how It acts in the soul written by men and women in all the world's cultural and social history. When you think about all the people throughout human life who have studied the planets, the sciences, the arts, the humanities, origins, religions, spiritualities and the afterlife, the study of the soul with Divine Love is missing. When you look at all the people who have come into contact with mediumship throughout the generations of humankind, how is it that present-day humanity still lives predominantly unaware of the existence of their human soul, their spirit body and a form of energy that when engaging the soul brings about the true Immortality? Why isn't this common knowledge among the peoples of the Earth? That is why our communications involve today going forward into tomorrow because such informative teachings that identify the soul-life in all its spectrum you will not find in the far distant past. If these teachings about the soul-life and the true Immortality were with such clarity and visibility, after so many generations it would be common knowledge now and our world Earth, human social awareness would have changed.

This knowledge exists as common spirit knowledge in the mortal spirit world.

I will stop now. Your friend and teacher, Luke

106

Luke speaks:

It could be said that every communication you have both received from us is one long confirmation confirming the availability, existence and immediacy that the Divine Love Is. The existence of the Divine Love defines life here in the spirit world. There are those living with It and those yet to live with It. That is it. For you still living your physical life to perceive the reality of the spirit world is to understand the availability, existence and continued immediacy of this Divine Love for the soul living with this Love and the potential for the soul to begin receiving this Love.

So little exposure and transparency involving the peoples of the Earth actively participating aware of this Divine Love explains why vast amounts of information purported to have been received from spirits excludes the dynamic teachings that involve soul-life as lived here in the spirit life with Divine Love. The question could be asked, "If throughout humankind today and generations past individuals were receiving messages from spirits, why then were the teachings involving the Immortal soul-life excluded"? Asking this question places the communications James Padgett received with his ability to receive by hand into unique originality.

In an earlier message that I conveyed to you I spoke about the influences of my teachers. I would like to include here that all of us in our Celestial capacity are learning how men and women around the social human world are currently socialising their experiences involving a

Everlasting

degree of awareness about including the Father in their lives. We have illustrated to you earlier that never before have so many around the world been actively participating in their receipt of God's Divine Love. And never before have so many been actively participating aware of what they are participating with. This leads to how this experience unfolds and that this experience relates with us here experiencing the same Love with the same workings causing the same results only we are living in our spirit bodies. When Jesus lived on Earth he taught about many things. But the human world was small in population - the world was nothing like the world today - yet, the intrinsic dynamic of the nature of man, the nature of God, the workings of Divine Love remains the same.

I know that the experience of Divine Love is a new involvement for you all. Each experience that is revealed to you is original. Padgett's experience involved receiving messages that contained information that is being read and studied today. We guided James to receive Divine Love to assist his soul condition so that the established rapport would make the channel open. Another person may experience Divine Love purely as a comforter knowing that this true resource of energy comforts their soul through their life experiences and another may simply like they know the Soul, God. This brings me to share with you a little more about life in the Seventh Sphere.

Yesterday I spoke to you about empathy. Empathy is a soulfulness. It is an attribute of natural love. The fact that humans are with the capacity to be empathetic draws out other qualities of love in the natural love that are positive and advance the soul condition toward living perfection. In physical life, a man or woman can be empathetic without ever knowing or experiencing Divine Love. The attribute of empathy is a terrific boon for the individual. The lack of empathy extends the reach of a personality acting in self-centredness or being self-serving. The absence of empathy explains a lot about the balance of the world with those who are serving souls and those who are not and only serving themselves. For the human world to achieve world peace, it has to be a world of empathy.

As individuals progress their soul condition through the spheres toward the Celestial Heaven, empathy becomes a living extension in their natural love. In the Seventh Sphere, individuals have sufficiently progressed so that any individual nature of the self-serving, self-centred personality dissolves away from that individual. The individual learns enough to know that living with Divine Love will remain an everlasting soul-life experience. This means that to proceed into the Celestial Heaven the individual has accepted that they will be living with the Father, Eternal for all Eternity. At this stage in the soul condition, the individual can accommodate their understanding that living with God is for all time and that their soul needs to be in the presence of this Love and the Father. We have explained to you how independent we are living our Immortal spirit life. Part of this independence recognises that it is not that the Father desires us to be with this Love as conditional participation, but rather we as individuals in our independence voluntarily want to be involved because It is so involving! We have a comparison between what is stagnate in the Perfect Natural Sphere to what is progressive and living and able to go beyond the centre of our own human mortal experience.

Love and peace to you both, your friend and teacher, Luke

107

Luke speaks:

I will ask a particular question pertinent to human involvement with Divine Love, "Does anything actually change in a physical life when receiving Divine Love"?

When I lived with Jesus, the man Jesus, the social dynamic presented change at all social levels. It's not every day that you get to spend every day and night under the earthly sky walking alongside the man ascending in the world of humanity at that time to such demonstrations of love in living soul-physical-spirit life! Among men and women of our day, here was a young man living closest to the Soul, God, than ever had a mortal man. Here was a man whose very life reflected many surfaces, a life with the truest surface ever to have lived. As we walked and talked sharing conversations about different life experiences all those living with Jesus, including myself, were unaware at how significant the re-bestowal of the Divine Love, by the Father re-activating the Loving Spirit, actually was. As I walked by his side I was living with a convergence whose dynamic involved: the real nature of man, the true life of the soul, an activated spirit body, an awareness of God in Living reality and an understanding about the humanity residing in the spirit world. A world that he alone understood when in his human life. What a teacher he was and yet how many of that day never experienced his teachings! He came and went in the drama of a blink of an eye. The materialism of our day was minimal as most simply went about surviving. Jesus offered something different. He stood out. He spoke to all the hearts that couldn't speak out for themselves. He had a dislike for those in power who never changed but had all the opinion and judgement on others lives. He saw this as a gross error directly violating the very principles by which he lived. The Spirit Laws of God's Love that, as the end of his life displayed, succumbed to this error committed by other men causing the end of his life. Many people have entered their spirit life at similar hands.

In spirit life, some of us have lived here for a long time. We have seen the same end working toward the same results that we were subject to. The fundamental nature of humans remains the same. It is soul first and foremost living in its condition of natural love. This condition of soul individualises through relationships being expressed through attributes of personality. Jesus was no different to this human movement of the soul incarnating and individualising and experiencing life through natural love with attributes of his personality demonstrating this love in living action. I must state here that in his adult life, Jesus lived in his perfect natural love infused in the Divine Love received by his personalisation of the Father. I must also state that how Jesus lives today in the spirit world is from this foundation established in his earthly life, although he is considerably advanced now. We have taught you that the spirit body without a physical attribute progresses from its soul condition. The soul condition progresses with tremendous capacity here in the spirit life when infused with the Father's Divine Love.

Today, you are much to yourself in your exploration about the Love you have found. Much of the world is with its materialism, as with the advent of technology social materialism is evolving at a rapid pace. The world has never been more materialistic than at this moment in time providing new surfaces that converge with belonging, separation and isolation, togetherness, world-wide awareness, information and opinion. A brand new human social evolution is materialising in a global mobile surface. James Padgett received our teachings in the day that he lived. In a short space of time wars brought the globe into a social world-wide convergence. Today people are finding out about the availability of Divine Love quickly. People's capacity to digest vast amounts of information has increased. People want to experience with speed, they want to be able to establish the identity of a new thing with immediacy.

This is the significant change happening today involving a global awareness of Divine Love. Change happens now as individuals receive the Divine Love and find this pure involvement a personal sanctuary. How the individual expects more change to happen, or how much they are willing to learn remains to the study of information or misinformation relating to the consequences from interpretations about 'spirit'.

My observation that has involved living and working with Jesus while on Earth, then working and living with Jesus in the spirit world, and also involving for a short time bringing teachings to life through James Padgett and now through you both, is that for all the experience involved with men and women receiving Divine Love in today's age, it is the interest in the spirit life and the spirit world that attracts people's attention. The Divine Love is the most significant form of energy known to humankind but still, in physical life, it is discussed the least among people who are 'open to spirit'. My comment here is derived from observation. The fact that people have been introduced to the Divine Love and are aware of Its existence and having experienced a little of It, is an incredible change in the surface of humanity.

Change is about perspective and relationship, especially relationship. When the individual recognises the existence of Divine Love, this begins the change of relationship with everything that defines what it is to be alive.

You have received my message well. Your friend and teacher, Luke

108

Hello; it is your mother Rose. I am here with our friend Kath. As we all know, Kath has been to her spirit life just over a year now. She was 75 when she died. She has spent much of the past year with her mother and father. Kath is very happy feeling free from the physical condition that deprived her of doing so much in later life. I am with our relatives and there are a lot of us present. Zara has a few of her relatives present as well. I am speaking to you as it is my birthday. I know that you have had me on your mind much today. I haven't spoken often through the experience of your receiving information about the Divine Love, but I am present much of the time when you are both receiving. I observe, never organising anything from my end here. I leave the organising to that wonderful person who has been guiding this adventure, Luke. I speak to him quite often and we have a good laugh together. He is very pleased that you have both carried on dutifully receiving. I sound rather formal, but I really want to just say that I love you and I am proud to see you happening in your life.

Love, Rose

109

Hello; I am present with you. I am Zara's grandfather, Ronald. I have never shared in social exchange with my granddaughter as I am communicating now. You will be pleased to know that I live in the Celestial Heaven with my wife, as we are soulmates. We keep in touch regularly with Fairlie, and she is here and sends her love. It was that she passed into spirit a long time ago but had left her desk for you Zara, to write at. Well, that was a sight that she had! You have written your books and received spirit communication involving the most important truth ever a man or woman will know. I know that there have been a few difficulties involving past family relationships, but all families have their social relationships bound up in the daily dramas of earthly affairs. I have always desired to tell you what a wonderful and beautiful woman you have become. As it has been conveyed to you, family becomes important over here in the spirit life. It has to due to the dramas and loves that transpire in the beginnings of physical life that can lead to all spectrums of experience resulting in soul condition. In order to progress over here, your soul condition has to be improved in its natural love, which means that all personal relationships have to be resolved so that the perfection of the individual is free to be realised in the living of one's natural love. There is no possible way you can receive Divine Love, progress into the Celestial Heaven whilst all your personal relationships are in disarray, unresolved, unloving or fragmented. In the Celestial Heaven, you are not specifically required to socialise with the whole history of your relatives, but you are required to be independently free of any compensation caused by any breach of The Golden Rule.

I am pleased that you are assisting your mother, my daughter, at this time in her ageing life. At times this has not been easy but you are sustained in Divine Love and ageing is not always a graceful experience as you know!

I lived a long time ago. I lived in the day of the old country when there were so much time and space to live in. I was listening to your conversation before I engaged with you, you are quite right in your summarisation that the Divine Love is an entirely original form of energy. Also, for the person beginning with this Love, that person is engaging with pure and perfect originality from the outset, which is a completely unique and foreign experience for the greater population.

At this moment, I desire to express along with Meryl, Zara's grandmother, our love. You looked after my wife when she was in her 90's and now you are attending to the needs of my daughter who is in her 80's. I cannot thank you enough for giving so much. I remember the days when you sat on my lap laughing and shining. Look at you now and the wonderful contribution you have made involving all of us here toward the Immortal Love.

Respectfully, Ron

110

Luke speaks:

Much to your pleasure, you have both received personal messages from loved ones. When this happens, as you have experienced over your years of receiving messages, receiving personal contact feels different from when I am communicating to you. You both know me as a figure of human history in a far distant past. Prior to your commencement of receiving messages of love and support and teachings from me, you never knew me personally or had any contact with me whatsoever. You were both aware that I was a participant and a contributor conveying teachings through James Padgett. When you both were introduced to a selection of Padgett's messages back in the winter of December 1989 in Los Angeles, and you read a teaching conveyed by me, and as the weeks, months and years passed by, it never entered your minds that one day you would both receive what you have now realised with us. It has been through your direct experience living with Divine Love that I have come into contact with you. Our convergence has transpired by the compelling interest you both have identifying as much as you can that involves the Divine Love, and this of course involves living with the Father personally.

I have introduced a vast amount of humanity residing in their natural spirit life to the way of soul-life. I can spend amounts of time with you as I have no relationship with anything of the Earth other than to enlighten about the soul-life and increase the vision that involves participating in natural love with the Divine Love. When you receive a personal message such as you recently have, your mother and grandfather are recent to your experience in relative terms of time and relationship. They have conveyed to you that they are living with Divine Love, but you also feel your family heritage, your physical origins, which creates intimate feelings. I am aware that Zara is currently studying the field of genealogy with the help of a genealogist whom she knows personally and herself is open toward spirit. The genealogist is fascinated and inquisitive that all generations are living here in the spirit life in various soul conditions and that she can trace their physical life history and how certain intersections of life have or have not resulted in generational outcomes.

I have always conveyed to you teachings about Divine Love. I have a mother and father and a whole family history as well, as does Jesus and as do all residing here. No one is a singular life force without connection to other people and is a single generational member. I know that today in a country like yours, same-sex people can marry, individuals can change their sex with medical assistance, and eggs and sperm can be frozen. The whole gamut of mortal personality is being extended into personal interests that people feel compelled to follow. I and other Celestial teachers are aware of the ever colourful images of earthly humankind, but we never let the image distract from the finite workings of the soul in its natural love. This is apparent here in the spirit life where visible boundaries and workings relating with soul condition form the basis of all imagery in mortal spirit life.

James Padgett received communication from his wife, Helen, living her spirit life at the beginning of his time communicating with spirits. Family members contributed which formed a large voice through the entire time he received communications. Your interest to begin with, was formed from your experience of receiving Divine Love with your effort generated toward introducing the Divine Love and creating a human awareness of the availability of this Love. You both didn't begin receiving communications derived solely in your desire to receive contact from your relatives.

I can stay with you for a long time as I communicate with you as I am not emotionally attached to anything of your material or social environment. Other than the two of you today, I have no personal contact with any other in the human world. I take an interest at how the social dynamic involving men and women and Divine Love is being acted out, but I have not conveyed specific teachings about the Father or Divine Love to another who is aware of Divine Love. I have been present when groups of individuals have socialised together in various parts of the world, as Jesus has and other Celestial spirits. These experiences generate a lot of activity as Padgett's Messages are the contact by which diverse individuals have begun their involvement with their receipt of the Divine Love. This will continue to happen well into the future.

This brings me to my teaching today.

When involved with other individuals or if you are alone, when you announce to the Soul of God that you would like to receive the Divine Love, try and be calm in this stillness of energy that the Divine Love is. Try to let yourself be physically embraced by the presence of the Loving Spirit. In real terms, there is very little for you to do other than to be receptive to love! Here in the spirit life people are confused and often dismayed. They are in actual disbelief that there is so little to do, especially when so many have come from an earthly belief system that has required one to do so much. I will liken receiving Divine Love as a normal circumstance of breathing. Most people never think about breathing, they just do unless one is with a condition. When receiving Divine Love the Loving Spirit will bring the Divine Love into the soul and the soul will automatically accept this Love. It was taught in a Padgett Message that a particular Spirit Law acts as the go-between of the mortal soul and the Loving Spirit with God's Divine Love. I will once again mention how significant this is, for it means that if you were to roll a ball or simply let a ball go downhill, gravity will take it irrespective of the force generated behind it. If you 'long' with all your longing, or if you repeat a mantra with all your repetition, no matter your physical intent, nothing will distort the space and time that the particular Spirit Law acts with relating to your soul and the Father's Soul. So enjoy your timing in this wonderful space of experiencing the Love! So many have arrived at the illumined doorstep of the Celestial Heaven amazed at how little one had to do in order to receive the perfect amount of Divine Love into their soul that brought about the perfection of their natural love including the lessening of any compensation. The Father in such wisdom created a unique form of energy to exist that was never going to be impossible to receive and experience.

With the Divine Love take comfort not with fear, but with the ease of which you learn how the Eternal Creator comforts you.

What a joy today has been! Your friend and teacher, Luke

111

Saleeba speaks:

People need all the encouragement they can receive as they embark upon their involvement in Divine Love. Spend some time, when in the loving care of God, to utilise the Divine Love as a regenerative and restorative form of energy. If you persist over time receiving this Love, a feeling of being regenerated from this energy may cause you to feel an activation of spirit energy in your daily life. The soul that you are has within its life and love an attribute of spirit that is particular and unique to your soul. This is the energy that your soul is within this attribute of spirit and love. In spirit life in the Celestial Heaven, the vibrancy of the spirit body is visibly seen due to the Divine Love acting within the soul of the individual. In the Celestial Heaven you see the end result of the natural love having been perfected the soul that you are fully functioning and as its energy interacts with the interior of the spirit body. The spirit body is a living, vibrant, vital body of systems relating to the soul. In your physical life, whilst clothed in the physical body, the physical body that you are doesn't cause any separation from your soul and spirit body. When you receive Divine Love in your physical experience, your attention may well be situated in your physical context, but the Loving Spirit and Divine Love are acting upon your soul that then energises the systems of your spirit body. If you were only to receive a thimble full of Divine Love in your physical life, this will not be sufficient to cause your soul to energise and transform into its perfect natural love that then is experienced in your spirit body. But with the continued receipt of Divine Love over many years, be this for a small amount of time every other day, gradually you may feel the effect from the Divine Love received flowing through your spirit body, which then covers your physical attributes. Some men and women today have experienced this. It is the ultimate of earthly realised spirit energy experience.

I will not write more. What a splendid day this has been receiving from Rose, Ronald and Luke; I have loved sharing with you again, My love always, Saleeba

112

Hello; my name is Andrew Kershaw. I have been living here since late 1998. I remember the extent of my physical life with absolute clarity. I lived a usual social life, nothing was out of the ordinary. I was well educated, lived in the city of Melbourne enjoying all that Australia had to offer. I travelled overseas as many Australians do, I spent my holidays on the coast, I had a good job working in a law firm. I was engaged but not married. I died in what would be described as a usual event from an illness that had no cure. One day I didn't feel so well and my blood pressure dropped. Following the diagnosis, within six months I passed into my spirit life. I had no idea about what was to follow!

As I adapted I came to accept the fate of my life. I felt unfulfilled. That is to be expected when relatively young as I was born in 1962. As I adapted to this new experience it was easy for me to believe that the environment I lived in was one infinite plane of existence. I had no idea that there would be different environments existing at the same time; these are the spheres that have been identified to you. As time passed, the reality that I was never to return or experience anything physical again began to gain more solid form in my spirit-mind. I was told that this was the scenario but it takes a little time to adjust to the conclusive nature of being a spirit.

I have remained to the environment that I feel comfortable in, which is where I arrived. I haven't moved on although I have been informed that there are other circumstances that I could engage with; I don't feel ready to receive Divine Love. I like how I am, where I am and the way I am living my social spirit life. I don't know anything about the way I see those other brighter spirits living. I am not interested in living with God. I have been permitted to speak to you to provide an honest word about my present life. The idea about any involvement with a medium when I lived in my physical life would never have crossed my mind. I had no comprehension or interest in this sort of thing at all. Not because I feared it, but because I was never exposed to it, nor did I have any interest in this subject matter. I had a good mind, a productive mind and I was a good person; I am a good person now. I have been told that to embrace the Divine Love involves God. At this time in my spirit life, I like living the way I do without feeling any interest involving God therefore, I don't participate with Divine Love, but I know about this Love and Its availability - we all do here, but for myself I am not embracing my spirit life by living with this Love at this time. There is so much evidence of It existing in those who are living with It that we see all the time. I never saw this on Earth. I am grateful that I could speak to you at this time as I like feeling back in contact with the world I left behind. I do keep in touch with current events that shape the earthly world such as the bushfires in the state of Victoria and around Australia. I still have this strong connection with the social earthly life. This has got something to do with not missing out and feeling connected to important social things. I like this feeling as it causes me to enjoy the memories of my life. These memories make me feel connected with my personal history. I don't want to give this up.

Well, I thank you. Enjoy your summer. AK

113

Hello; my name is William Shakespeare. I reside in the Celestial Heaven. My experience living my spirit life has been purely an experience of love. I will not convey to you a chronological history of my earthly life, or how I intrinsically described social relationships through verse and drama. That part of my life remains to its history to the present day and into the future for the stage!

As I progressed in my spirit life I was aware that my linguistic skills were unique and highly developed. I knew a lot more language than most. What I didn't know or have that was innately within me, were the words that could communicate the true Immortality of the mortal soul. Like everyone else, I had to learn what this was by living it. The only way to live it is to begin receiving that which makes the soul of a mortal, Immortal. Needless to say as I progressed my linguistic skill, able to incorporate the narrative of soul-life. I am as skilled in this as I was with my inherent earthly communications. I was impressed with the Celestial teachers who had such a command of a spirit-soul perceptual language. I sought to develop this myself. It is one thing to communicate on the nature of the social human compared to the real nature of the mortal soul as God has formed such nature to be.

As you know, I have lived here for quite some time. Living in my Immortal life is not a new thing. I am aware, though I am a resident living in the Celestial Heaven, that my fame has spread worldwide and increases as time goes by. Many individuals contributed to an earthly vocation whose fame has continued or been unearthed and circulates the world today. It is an unusual experience living away from Earth in the

Everlasting

Celestial Heaven, knowing that a contribution made that was the action of the day is being re-energised all the time by new generations. Some of these individuals who reside in the Celestial Heaven achieved vast wealth through their life experience along with their fame. Though they are living in the Divine Love in the Celestial Heaven, they are aware that the contributions they left behind are still generating vast sums of money.

I have a teaching role in my spirit life which is to assist those coming through the spheres progressively in Divine Love, as I can explain much about this experience by the use of my vocal skill. I very rarely write any more, as there is a form of literature here, but it is nothing like the materials utilised on Earth. Everything is living here. This is a substantial difference that defines so much that contrasts between an earthly and spirit life.

I did have an attuned sense for the romantic. Just about all high forms of creative and artistic involvement do. Romance is aligned with expressions of natural love that communicate among other things, a sense of hope that love wins the day and is the fabric of life.

I like that I can communicate verbally with individuals who have problems sharing how they feel. I am a ready-made communicator. Receiving the Divine Love and experiencing how this Love transforms the soul and spirit attributes is so dynamic that a lot of individuals are unable to express exactly how they feel as they are advancing through this experience. The energy that the Divine Love is - is so real - bringing change into the individual life. Living through this, most are without as I once was, the internal vocabulary to describe the change they are living through. I like being of service in this way.

I am not permitted to convey to you the intimate details of my writings. The reason for this is that I am a public figure in human culture and that history has been lived and realised with my contribution well completed. For me to convey to you a long detailed account of my relationship with my writing would alter the historical context which is not required. My experience differs than other spirits you have received as I have left behind a legacy that is studied the world over. Other individuals have shared details of their human life to a greater or lesser degree. For me to convey to you a long narrative about the writing of my plays would bring history into another convergence.. This could reopen history leaving a far-distant past exposed for reinterpretation, which I will not do. I hope you understand this, that it is a condition that involves the exchange of information between spirits and mortals.

Everlasting

Imagine if another individual who left a valuable contribution behind wrote from here at great lengths on their personal interpretation which would change the future and alter the perceived historical context. I have changed so much, as all of us do who receive Divine Love progressing to the Celestial Heaven. On Divine Love, I am free to write, free to speak and free to express this perfect gift.

As I experienced Divine Love, my understanding of my own soulful nature came to life. It happens this way. There were many before me and many after me and many at the same time involved in their living with this Love. One person's legacy might be that they were pleased to leave such wonderful children behind. For another, a piece of music, a love song or a heartfelt poem, it might be the garden one established or funds to assist others. For me, it was that I contributed works that men and women could participate with. I like that my works are studied toward an enriching experience. Like so many, as I progressed in Our Father's Love the objectivity of my life gained a greater perspective. I lived a long time ago; I am present to this day and do not live in the past. The Divine Love is an all-embracing spirit life experience for me. How this Love enters the soul then brings about change that results in progression is an outstanding insight. Never by personality alone or by the spirit body acting on its own volition can the soul progress to the Celestial Heaven in its own essence. We simply require God's Divine Love to change and progress here in the spirit life. This progression has been highlighted to you before, but it astounding when you consider how movement happens here in spirit life. This kind of movement is not seen by the physical human eye among the peoples of the Earth. This is why it is so astounding as it is seen here and lived all the time. I see individuals being changed in front of my eyes just as I changed in front of other spirit's eyes. The change that happens is a subtle experience, never demanding too much from us. I know that you will not see this change on Earth. You may not experience this sense of change as you receive Divine Love in your physical life, but this does not mean that we are to prevent ourselves who have lived through this change not to communicate this to you as these changes define spirit life. We are able to measure the difference of change here in spirit life by what changes or does not change. Those individuals residing in their perfect natural love have changed due to their natural love being perfected, but once perfected, no further change transpires. God's Divine Love then becomes the measure of difference, the substance of change.

I have met a lot of the actors who had roles in my plays. I have met individuals who have studied my collected works and people who have read my works. They have asked me questions that I have gladly answered as I have become an established figure in the earthly world of literature and drama. I was gifted with the ability to see the social nature of man, but as I said, I had a romantic voice like a musical note that I heard when I wrote. As it has been conveyed to you, individuals are able to meet history here, a history that is living in the present! Like all of us here who are aware of the Divine Love and what this Love represents to all of mortal life, we are so glad that James Padgett was able to receive the teachings that he did which brought forward a beginning that is slowly moving throughout the world that introduces the scope of this Love and what It brings to the soul. I must say here, that even with all my skill, I did not possess the same ability that James Padgett did and that you both are working with now. That is why there are gifts of fate that have their timing that each bring forth.

I will stop now. WS

114

Saleeba speaks:

It has taken you a little time to settle, but I can connect with you now. Your perceptions reaching out to see if we were present informed you that we were. You have had a busy day so far and, we needed the Father's Love to cover your souls so that our connectivity for communication would be uninterrupted. You both know that this happens from time to time having had so much experience receiving from us. You are aware that this can happen and how drawing close to the Soul of God brings you back into rapport for this kind of communication.

Individuals have conveyed to you their experience of living with Divine Love in their spirit life. The Divine Love is true, consistent, and the same non-evolving form of energy that each individual receives. God's Divine Love acts the same way in each finite soul causing the same effect in the finite soul, the unique spirit body, and ultimately maturing the individual personality to its perfect form in attributes. The Divine Love as a form of energy never changes. Our Father has created this energy to be in its existence, changeless for all eternity. What this means is that you will never hear from spirits teaching or telling of their experience with Divine Love in a different context such as, "And now receiving Divine Love the Divine Love became a different thing unknown to me."

What I desire to say here involves your experience on Earth. Your social experiences evolve and change, sometimes quite rapidly or drawn out over a long extensive time. One day you are doing this and the next day you are doing that. One day you are single the next day you have fallen in love. One day you travel, one day you go for a walk. One day you are introduced to Divine Love, and the next day you are teaching all about it without much experience of It at all. There have been individuals who have received Divine Love and who have read The Padgett Messages. They have held an interest in the spirit world and have spoken about some of the Truths. But, their social life sharply contrasted toward anything other than living examples of their good, natural love. This potential exists among men and women in physical life ... that is, to be aware of Divine Love yet to live in contradistinction to any evidence of living a loving empathetic life has to be mentioned as it is an actuality in the world today. There was a man who was introduced to the Divine Love, read some truths then proclaimed himself to be Jesus reincarnated. Such deception creates compensation. This man's portrayal of being Jesus is an error, untrue and a fictitious lie. No such truth as this individual portrays exists. Therefore, such an error comparing oneself to other people that they are Jesus damages their soul stagnating any progress or improvement until such error is retaught to all who he has deceived

There have been some people who have treated other people who are also aware of the Divine Love with complete disrespect breaching The Golden Rule. We have conveyed to you how loving we become in our spirit life as our natural love is perfected by the inflowing of Divine Love, and as we progress into the Celestial Heaven. This is true, but from your perspective you may be experiencing and socialising with anything other than individuals living as shining examples in their natural love due to the Divine Love and Its influence in their soul. It is important to mention this aspect of humans living in their physical life aware of the Divine Love and to mention that and receiving Divine Love, may not automatically make a bad person good or a good person better. The social evidence based on over a hundred years of The Padgett Messages being present on Earth so far reveals that being aware and receiving Divine Love remains to the social individual, social diversity, and estranged relationships. This is nothing new among the social cultures of the world. I lived in a day where people were traded as slaves and death was their only freedom. Here in spirit life, their souls and spirit bodies were free to activate into living pure independence and obtain their individuality.

The Divine Love is an individual experience. No man or woman or spirit can wilfully determine another to actively receive the Divine Love. Each individual is to decide for themselves to participate in this change. We would like to think that by being aware of Divine Love and in receiving Divine Love, a better more improved quality of living may eventuate in the life of the individual. Over here, we are with that visibility that reveals a consistency of truth so there is no error taught about the involvement with this Love and Its origins. The way that the truths relating to the natural and the Divine Love that comprises the Padgett Messages are reaching into the fabric of humanity and how these truths are interpreted will be the subject of much social discussion, opinion, judgement and love offset by the beautiful immediacy of the individual able to receive Divine Love in the quietness of their own speed and time.

Again, this is a wonderful experience having these exchanges where the Divine Love is central, openly discussed and celebrated. My love to you all, Saleeba

115

Luke speaks:

Whichever way you look at it, the recognition that a unique form of energy exists that we can individualise with direct participation is a dynamic that is conclusive. You can look at this energy any which way, but the evidence at how this energy works in the soul is consistently conclusive as seen, known, experienced and lived here in spirit life. During earthly experience, there are always going to be things that you find yourself enthralled with. For some it might be their study of the vision that the Divine Love portrays as being the dynamic that all convergence of change hinges on and comes into contact with. Physical life begins in the physical world, transition happens and that person begins their spirit life in the spirit world. This is a change that is an inevitable consequence involving physical human life, but it is without the dynamic that the Divine Love brings as the real change of human

Everlasting

life. People transition into their spirit life adapting to their spirit life and experiencing the greatest change of all, yet they are living without any awareness that the Divine Love exists. In the spirit life, the dynamic of change is brought about by receiving the Divine Love into your soul. This is the real change that results in the individual understanding what the nature of mortal life is all about insofar as understanding what change in social human life is. The dynamic of transition is with inevitable consequences. As soon as the soul incarnates and acquires the physical attribute and spirit body, it becomes part of these natural and inevitable consequences. What is not inevitable is the involvement with Divine Love. This, the individual is to voluntarily participate with initiated in either their physical life or their spirit life. This means that the dynamic of Divine Love is a dynamic that exists outside of the normal evolving consequences of human life. The soul that you are can begin receiving Divine Love now in your physical life but you will still live through the change of inevitable consequences. In the spirit life, you can begin receiving the Divine Love or continue receiving what you delightfully received in your physical life and then through the spheres you will proceed. If you remain in your natural love in your spirit life, without accepting the Divine Love as a voluntary choice of change, then you will be subject to another inevitable consequence that involves the stagnation of your soul by remaining in its natural love even if you are living perfect natural love.

In your physical life, an attraction to experience Divine Love might well be founded in a desire to learn more about the spirit world or spirit guides and spirit life. It might be that you wish to believe that such a substance exists and that it is comforting as your social or antisocial life experiences continue. It might be that you don't know why, but you are compelled to let this Love join in your soul. There are myriad reasons why in a physical life a person may feel inclined to participate with this Love once they are aware of Its existence without even making a solid choice to voluntarily establish their relationship with God. If one begins receiving Divine Love, are their souls looking for God? Are they looking for a confirmation that this perceived being exists? Here in the spirit life, we begin teaching about involvement with Divine Love in a context that involves the soul-life with the Soul-Life of God. God is never excluded from the outset of an introduction to Divine Love. The individuals here have a different perspective on life as they are living in the spirit world having survived physical death, so usually their beliefs about life have significantly readjusted into an alignment of an inevitable consequence realised. The best outcome is to believe in the existence of God and to include this in your soulful acceptance of Divine Love. It is from this position that the inevitable consequences of life happen. What was once external to your life - being the Divine Love - now forms part of your internal soulful nature which comforts and provides sustenance that might otherwise have been sought for but never found.

You have received my teaching well. Your friend, Luke

116

Luke speaks:

As you have heard, there is quite a difference receiving an individual's account of their spirit life when that individual has spent limited time living their spirit life. How an individual conveys their experience living with Divine Love and advancing to the Celestial Heaven having transitioned from their earthly life, sounds different than communication that you have received from an individual who transitioned hundreds or thousands of years ago. From my perspective, substantial workings from the Father involving the soul-life are conclusive, known to me, and well-lived. I have lived with the knowledge about the true Immortality that the Divine Love brings to the soul for two thousand years. Jesus taught us about this and other vital Divine Truths when we were men living with him on Earth. How does the experience of Immortality sound when conveyed by an individual who has only recently taken up their experience receiving Divine Love having recently transitioned? Understanding the duration of time with experience will place your context for experience involving living with the Father's Love into a perspective of speed and time. Some individuals that receive Divine Love early in their spirit life can fathom their subjective experience. They live through their changing spirit condition offset by the vision that being aware of this Love establishes the potential that all mortal souls can participate with this Love. Many individuals who receive this Love advance through the spheres and reside in the Celestial Heaven personalised and individualised in their soulful relationship with the Soul of God. They are empathetic to their socialisation among other spirits whilst retaining their singular approach to their involvement without connecting with the vision potential that this Love in all Its existence, potentially provides.

Everlasting

As I received the Love in my spirit life, part of my natural love with its perfection provided me with vision. This vision gave me the truth that showed me how available this resource of energy was, why It had been made, and how inclusive It is. But most importantly, what it is like to live without It in the spirit life! There are billions of human souls who have never received Divine Love for they are unaware of Its existence. Earthly humanity is unaware that such a form of energy exists. If you are unaware, then how can you be aware and choose to participate with It? Part of the reason why I have spent much of my spirit life socialising with other spirits about this Divine Love in the natural spheres involves how this Love brought to life my vision that involved potential. The more I received Divine Love, the more my natural love connected with the Truth of the Love. This compelled me to serve the Father by assisting other individuals with their progression in the Love, and also to be the living example to those individuals in the natural spheres that a potential for soul-life and its inclusion to advancing love and experience is an existing potential. Some individuals when connecting with the Father understand the nature of the gift of Divine Love feeling an internal desire to make known this potential. It has to be like this. It is like this. Why? If all of those residing here received Divine Love without anyone ever feeling compelled to share the potential for this Love, then no one other than Jesus would ever know that such a Love exists.

The essence of my teaching is to convey that some individuals, upon receiving Divine Love experience the vision of Its potential and may feel inclined to elaborate on this potential so that others may understand that such a resource of loving energy exists. I am not by any measure of means asking that anyone receiving Divine Love in their earthly life become missionaries of the word. This does not work, and quite often is in breach of The Golden Rule bringing all sorts of calamity to the experience. It is important to acknowledge that some of you, by receiving Divine Love will absorb the compelling vision of this Love yet you may live much of your human life in silence. As William Shakespeare said to you, he assists individuals progressing in the Love for he has the linguistic skills to help vocalise what others may be feeling or experiencing. It is partly why these communications are vastly important so that the reader can silently relate and participate with the potential of vision that is seen in your own soul-spirit-perception that involves all the Divine Love.

Your friend and teacher, Luke

117

Luke speaks:

As this new year 2020 settles in, I have been with you both listening to your discussions these past few weeks that have involved your personal history, your public history and your life experiences that have involved being aware of the Divine Love. This has included: your experience being involved with receiving spirit communication, learning about introducing the Divine Love when the timing has called for this information to be shared, your introduction to the communications James Padgett received, and how you have individually related your attributes to the Father. You have both lived a life aware of the Divine Love for over 30 years. I have listened as you have discussed why individuals are interested in the experience of Divine Love and why they are not. You are both in a unique experience as a few other people are. You are all aware of this Love, Its significance and ramifications involved with a social life where most that you meet every day are unaware and showing no interest at all in any degree of spirit truth. You have both held an enduring relationship with the Soul of the Father learning as much as you can about being aware of the Divine Love with Its extenuating cause in a human life. This has extended toward the vision at how the spirit world and the spirit life in this world resides and progresses in the Love. I mention this again as you both have a terrific resource of knowledge that is factually lived, truthfully ascertained and lovingly embraced. Years ago you understood that a spirit truth or working that involves the Divine Love is a working that is consistent and never changing and that this Love requires no further addition to It. You both understood that nothing in mortal or Immortal man could change the outcome of this Divine Love set in motion by the Soul, God. You understood that to identify a spirit truth relating to the Divine Love and our soul-life is a foundation of truth that is consistent for all who experience this Love in real-time and have the potential for all souls to receive It.

Receiving the communications that we have conveyed to you has involved revealings that layer upon layer intricately reveal an image in a solid form that involves the soul living with the Divine Love in an earthly experience or in the spirit life. Layer by layer, the communications that we have conveyed to you over these years have brought forward an entirely new way for the individual to identify a whole experience of life that has never been revealed with such love or exacting truth - from an evolving experience in the Earthly life to a non-evolving experience here in the spirit world. The identity of human evolution is changed by the inclusion of a non-evolving form of energy introduced to the natural love of the mortal soul.

I am not elevating your ego at this point, I am merely pointing out what has happened. The reader who desires to advance their human knowledge about the structural fundamentals about human life, the spirit world, spirit life, God, the Spirit-Verse and the Divine Love to name a few, will be grateful that such knowledge has been brought forward in the way and example of love in the living.

As it has been conveyed to you, other than the messages James Padgett received, there didn't exist anything of any real substance that you could both read that would advance your knowledge about the form of energy that the Divine Love is. You have both sought for this to answer the questions that you have both asked and that others have asked you in your social and public interactions. You have both been aware of what you were doing while you were doing it. By contrast, James Padgett was unaware of the Divine Love and the consequences that this Love brought to the life of the mortal soul at the time he began receiving spirit communications from his wife Helen.

I would like to say again at this time, that for all that is truly remarkable about the existence of man, both earthly and spirit, God's Divine Love is the *only* form of energy that is the real dynamic of causal change that a mortal can participate with. If you can grasp this, then the Divine Love becomes the causal link that substantiates the soulful reality of man in all its reach. I know that we have conveyed this to you before, but we must never leave the single platform and foundation of spirit truth that began with the life of Jesus those years ago, and the life of the First Parents before Jesus.

Lastly, there are real solid structures comprising the spirit spheres. We interface with these structures, such as the structures that comprise the First Natural Sphere. Every human that transitions into the spirit world never arrives at an environment void of any spirit structure. So much care is taken by those caring souls who reside here to facilitate beginnings as most haven't a clue about this real part of their life that they find themselves awakening into. It is astonishing that ever since the First Parents died, generation after generation has passed into their spirit life without any real idea of what to expect or how the human lives in this environment. This even more incredulous since earthly life is brief compared to the permanent spirit life one will live. The more aware you are when living with Divine Love in your earthly life, the more Spirit of Truth you will perceive and you will see how incredible it is that you live among a vast population that perceives nothing at all. Even those who are receiving Divine Love can be looking in an erroneous direction.

As we have said, we could write forever on why men and women will not be interested in the real truths that involve the Immortal life. We can write forever on all those errors, wrongs, transgressive actions and stagnated causes and disappearances, for there is nothing better than a good story or drama that begins with an error to captivate the imagination where truth and love is missing. What is positive, is that the Divine Love - that wonderful resource of energy - isn't missing, and that a vast majority of spirit humanity are righted as they progress toward the Spirit of Truth, and that people today on Earth are slowly finding their way to a resource of knowledge that will never be manipulated by mortal personality.

There are those times when real truth needs to be spoken and heard, such as I have conveyed to you recently. For some hearts that are near broken in life can now be mended by hearing and seeing, feeling and knowing that which has been sadly lost. Other hearts that are shining can draw upon the Spirit of Truth as a teacher and guide.

I will withdraw back to my home in the Celestial Heaven. Stay close in your attunement with the Love and I will return soon. Your friend and teacher, Luke

118

Luke speaks:

When I revealed teachings that involved the nature of the human soul, the natural love and the Divine Love to James Padgett, the other teachers and I were aware that we were introducing beginnings. The beginnings of a new language, interpretation of life, vision relating to the nature of man and the nature of the spirit world. Above all and singularly the most important thing, we were beginning to lay down new insight into the nature of God. We had to do this through the somewhat limited means utilising the service of a man and the pencil and paper. This was an experience involving a form of communication the likes of which the earthly world had never seen, read or heard before. We were aware that when bringing our experience and knowledge, our insight, wisdom and the real workings that elaborated the nature of man as being the soul that it is, that such a beginning would involve limitations. James received a vast array of information, but he was limited in his experience of living with the Divine Love that we were introducing as an available resource for the human soul. Fortunately, we have been able to bring a substantial weight of information to you now because you both have received unlimited Love as you were well aware and involved with Divine Love before our beginning to communicate works that extended all that was introduced to James.

I use the word 'limit' poignantly. The existence of Divine Love can be perceived as an unlimited supply of pure energy that the mortal soul can receive for all eternity. If 'supply and demand' be a common phrase, the demand of the human soul for living with the Father is the supply of Divine Love that equals the mortal demand. This relationship between supply and demand is of real economy for never will the demand exceed the supply, nor will the supply exceed or be diminished by demand.

The Divine Love is unlimited. It will never be limited as Its origin is the unlimited energy of the Soul, God, the existence that defines all mortal life in its true soulful nature. It is unlimited as it will never be taken away from the soul receiving this Love. But it is existing with a limit. This is a teaching about perspective. The Divine Love is limitless as It reflects Its origin, but it is with a limit as It never changes, is non-evolving and cannot continue to redefine us of Its own accord in terms of acting with an evolution in our mortal soul.

Jesus and other individuals have been receiving Divine Love a long time now, as you know. What hasn't happened to those of us living with the Father a long time, is that we have received this Love only to experience an unlimited evolution in our soul and spirit attributes creating a whole set of dynamics that set in place unlimited evolution which leads us into limitless random or internal chaos about our state of existence and potentials in personality morphing, spinning out of control due to equilibriums become destabilised in the formed personality situated through the entire spirit body and its characteristics.

The spirit body is a real living body comprised of its systems, many of which we have already identified. Just as many of you are, you live in your physical body without really understanding all its dynamic and systems as you socially move about. Much like walking, you are not meant to think about each step. The body performs its voluntary and involuntary functions as your personality experiences colour and life. Some people investigate the internal dynamics of the human body to its nth degree looking at it in the sum parts of the whole as people specialise in certain parts of the anatomy. It would be a very interesting image if all the information known about the body today was comprised in a single image of a male and female by the best in the world in their knowledge in a singular virtual profile. The accumulation of this knowledge demonstrates the unlimited capacity of certain individuals to seek out how a form of creation functions. Not everyone living in the Celestial Heaven knows their full internal dynamic as they walk each spirit step. Just like on Earth, some spirits specialise in the cohesive image of the spirit body and its function and how personality relates as it is situated in the spirit body. Personality moves your body around on Earth, and likewise it moves the spirit body around in the spirit world.

I recently touched on potential, how individuals such as myself living with Divine Love see and feel Its potential for all mortal souls to receive. There is a limit to this. Only the individual prevents themselves from participating in their active soul-life aware of living with Divine Love. This prevention is situated in the God-factor. To engage with an unlimited source of energy that realises your potential involves God. There is no way to circumvent this truth or negotiate your way into understanding that the Divine Love is separate from - or from another source entirely - than God. Every single individual residing in the Divine Love Spheres, the Celestial Heaven and Universal Spheres accepts in their soul, the source and origin of this unlimited resource of Love.

When we conveyed our teachings to James Padgett, we knew that what we were living was well established. This very teaching I am conveying to you now was known and taught by Jesus, then by myself from our earliest moments in the spirit world. We knew that what you would be hearing, reading and praying for was brand new! This sense of the newness remains always present among the peoples of the Earth. Our responsibility conveying our experience from the spirit world is to liberate information and not to place limits, boundaries and conditions that prevent you from embracing this Love before you have even started. As so many have said when they are in the Seventh Sphere, 'How could I have ever lived without this Love being part of my life?"

You have received my teaching well. Your friend and teacher, Luke

February

119

Aman speaks:

I am here in the spirit environment, close to you both as you are in good condition to receive me. Some time ago, you heard from my soulmate, Amon. Throughout the spirit communications that you have both received, Amon and I have communicated experiences of our life to you. You both became aware that we had lived when you read the messages James Padgett received. A lot of people have read the communications that Amon and I conveyed at that time, those years ago when James was new to his Divine Love experience. The very concept, idea and reality that we existed is a new experience when introduced to the realm of spirit universality. Let us be truthful here. It is not every day that people around the world are thinking about us, as we have introduced ourselves through the messages that James received. Amon and I are an unknown in the everyday life of any modern-day reality. Amon and I began with Our Father. Our story has now been told through the messages James received and the messages you have both received. I haven't revealed to you what the weather was like when Amon and I walked our first steps upon the planet Earth or exactly the place, location or a date relative to the last Ice Age. We haven't told you of our intimate thoughts, how we reproduced our offspring, the dialect we spoke or what we thought about as we set about our life purpose with the Creator. We haven't given you any personal details about how we received the Divine Love or about our relationship with the Originator of this Love, or how we communicated with other non-evolving super-formed personalities who would visit us regularly in the time before our separation from the Father. It is incredibly difficult to afford you incremental detail that has such little relevance now. Our life on Earth was lived and is over. Jesus came and now resides here. We are all living and receiving the Divine Love set to our purpose here in the spirit world. This is what is important today.

The kind of effort, energy and soul condition required for you both to sustain the intense energy levels that bridge us together so I can speak to you has its effect in your physical life. You know this to be true, for over the years you have had physical ailments and have tried to receive. These experiences have provided you with a context for your understanding that you need your physical bodies to be in good shape, your soul well-tuned and your mind well-rested. What is vitally important is that a vast amount of information that elaborates on the Divine Love and other soulful related themes have been forthcoming so that in the future the reader and avid studier of the soulful life with Divine Love can be attentive to the present without reading reams of spirit information situated only to the past. The Divine Love doesn't have a time limit! It is not a form of energy that has a past or future. It is as Its Origin is, constantly present. But this present is constantly attuned to the present that the Soul-life of God lives and resides in. This explains why it can be so difficult to perceive the actual imaging of the Love Itself as in Its form while in your physical life. What you are looking at - or trying to see - is a form of energy existing in the spacial timing limit of Its Originator, and since the Divine Love does not originate from any mortal handiwork or planetary environment, the timing of the Divine Love is only subject to Its Originator.

The timing of the availability of the Divine Love and Its relationship with the now aptly named, Loving Spirit, has been explained to you sufficiently. Enough for you to see that the Love and Spirit, which were available when Amon and I arrived, then became unavailable due to our separation from Our Creator, then was reactivated with the life of Jesus to present day. Amon and I can recall our memories of our far-distant mortal life. What I desire to reveal about our mortal life is that we lived an Immortal life in our mortal life when living on Earth. It was only after our actions that resulted in our loss of access to the Loving Spirit that we were then subject to the evolutionary ageing process that transpires to all mortal physiology. Our souls remained transformed as the Divine Love that we had received with abundance was never displaced or extracted by any working of the Father from our souls. Much about our lives in the spirit world after our human life ended in normal death has been conveyed to you. The Celestial Heaven remained closed to us for we could not progress through the Divine

Love Spheres to reside in the Celestial Heaven as it required the Loving Spirit and Divine Love to be involved in this progressive process of delivering us closer to the Father. We remained in the Perfect Natural Sphere helping to establish the natural spirit spheres as humanity gained momentum. This was part of our compensation. And here I am today, speaking to you with all the availability of the Loving Spirit and Divine Love available, with all our history and the history of Jesus lived in our memories. Here we are today, teaching about the soul-life, living with Divine Love and enjoying an expansive experience about the most enduring and everlasting Love gifted to the soul of mortal man.

In our communications to you, we have always been inclusive of the messages James Padgett received. We have purposely done this, for the experience that the Divine Love provides for the individual soul is always in a context of living in the present. Even though James Padgett received messages 100 years ago, the reality of the information relating to the Divine Love and the natural love isn't situated to living historically in or through the words of a book or manuscript. This will be the same for the communication that you have both received 100 years from now and well beyond. The messages that you have both received and that James received will always remain current to the daily experience as individuals are introduced to the availability of Divine Love. Humankind may pursue with interest in learning how to live a mortal life with the knowledge and experience of receiving Divine Love. This is what is so incredible about this form of literature. It is all derived from living experience and not a pathos for the heart to never realise the joy of living with Love.

As I said, my life was lived out on Earth a long time ago. And my experience receiving God's Divine Love with Amon remains truthful to today. The Divine Love that we had both received and later that Jesus received while he lived as a man, along with the Divine Love received by individuals today, is working toward the same outcome in the soul ... to experience perfect natural love and the gift of an Immortal life. This truth is irrespective of the involvement of the life of unique personalities such as Amon and I, Jesus and the experience James Padgett and his friends Eugene and Leslie lived at that time. This brings us back to the fact that since Jesus arrived in the spirit world individuals have been experiencing the Divine Love, including Amon and I and many of our offspring, along with the vast humanity living in the present and no longer subject to their earthly history. In this I am conveying to you the sense and feeling of timing. In your earthly life history is so relevant, which infers a past that confirms the truth about the present. With the Divine Love, we are teaching about a form of energy that has only ever been a form of energy living to Its own present and relating to Its Originator and never subject to a dusty history or a past that substantiates Its existence in the present and outcomes of the future. The Divine Love is the perfect convergence of all timing - past, present and future. This convergence of timing is why it is so necessary for us to have a unique form of energy. It is so that as we reside in our spirit life, we are with a structural component that provides us with a context of time for our soul and spirit perceptions so that we can perceive the existence of: spirit attributes, the Divine Love we have received, and the Origin we have received It from.

The reality that the Divine Love is a non-evolving form of energy specifically created by the Soul, God, fits perfectly with the understanding that the nature of the mortal soul and the spirit body are formed into existence without being subject to any physical or planetary evolution. The attribute that you are, a soul with the attribute of a spirit body that clothes the soul, is formed by the specific workings of the Father. This brings such life into existence that is harmonious to each other soul and spirit body but are without an evolution to bring them into existence.

The attribute of the soul is formed without any Divine Love within it. This is the same with the spirit body. Although the soul and spirit body formed without any evolution, they are perfectly situated to receive the Divine Love into your soul via the Loving Spirit. The Loving Spirit covers your spirit body so that the Divine Love can become infused into your soul which, causes the change that then follows throughout from your soul and into your spirit body.

You have understood that natural love can be perfected and that the spirit body reflects this improved condition. The natural love is a good love and is beautiful in its living; this is seen in the Perfect Natural Sphere. What this also describes to you is that without the inclusion of Divine Love, the attribute of soul and spirit body that you are, is with its limit to evolve and subject to the forming personality which begins at the commencement of conception. You are physical and with forming personality. Unaware that you are soul and spirit body, your physical life evolves largely subject to the environment of the planet that shapes all evolutionary species.

Everlasting

All life on planet Earth and everything that planet Earth represents is the same thing, as all species have their origin from the planet and the planet forms part of their innate instinctive life. Humans are the same, or so we're led to believe! But this is not true. Humans are comprised of a physical body with a forming personality, a physical body subject to its biological relationship with its planet and its light source. But you also have two highly advanced attributes that were formed into existence at your time of conception without any planetary evolutionary influence.

The creation and forming of the human individual involves God. This has been illustrated to you before, but now that the Divine Love has been expanded to the degree and reach that It has, placing the attribute of soul, spirit body, and the forming personality with its physical attributes in context with a non-evolving form of energy, provides the clarity to see the life of a human with greater vision, especially in the outcome of a spirit life.

I will stop now. Aman

120

Luke speaks:

Throughout this time of our communicating to you both, we have emphasised what evolves with what does not evolve. This has been a priority of ours so that the reader may gain insight into the greater spirit vision that exists rather than the social human relationship that is immediate. A person may experience Divine Love in their physical life, for they feel attracted to this Love for reasons personal to them. Another person may be responsive to the Love purely from a faith experience or a confirming experience that such a Love exists and that God exists. These are very good reasons as to why one may choose to receive the Love in their physical life. Then ***progressively,*** there are substantial realities that exist that are of 'spirit' and exceed the relationship with evolution which mortals participate with a social context. Having been introduced to the existence of Divine Love, for example, is to be introduced to a non-evolving form of energy.

Amon introduced the reality of the attribute of soul and spirit body that contributes toward forming the human being and which originates without evolution being involved. This is true. It is so true in fact, that in the spirit life individuals embracing their soul-ship with God experience the Divine Love which acts upon the soul in an environment where evolution is absent in the spirit spheres. We have had to emphasise this dynamic relationship between what does and doesn't evolve in order to grasp a more complete understanding of the soul-life living with the Father.

It could be said that individuals beginning their spirit life are always learning new things. To progress in your natural love through the spheres with Divine Love is to progress with new information as new spirit life experiences advance your condition. With these new experiences the individual can interpret this as a form of individual evolution in a personal sense. But what is evident is that such progression or perceived evolution is being generated by an alternate source of energy that sparks and generates the attributes of the soul into activity. As you look around in your physical life, you are seeing men and women being generated by influences other than God's non-evolving form of energy. Here in the spirit world, what you only see are humans still living this way in the natural spheres, or humans living their life experience generated by God's non-evolving form of energy, the Divine Love.

I will leave you now, your friend and teacher Luke

121

Luke speaks:

The identification involving evolution is extensive. Ultimately looking at evolution is identifying how species originate, why they originate and the characteristics and social interactions that develop. Most of all, evolution is a lineage of survival. In the human species, like many other planetary species, light plays a significant role in evolution and survival. In the human species survival has selected that the average gestation period of the female is nine months. Myriad circumstances are fixed to the mutable evolution that happens involving planet Earth, but these myriad possibilities for the survival and evolution of a species are of a fixed nature due to the limit that happens naturally involving the source of energy that the planet provides from the sun. In the spirit life, the spirit body is the principal body with its own characteristics for survival. The survival of the spirit body with its characteristics ensures the survival of the soul and its nature in the spirit world. Without a physical body and its subsequent evolution, the individual personality is subsequently subject to another form of life experience that excludes all previous physical evolution and survival. I have taken a lot of time to clarify this so that the reader will have a clear perspective about the nature of progression in the spirit world involving Divine Love compared to the nature of experience with Divine Love lived in physical life on Earth. I guide you toward this understanding so that you might have a clear indication about the structural context that happens in the physical life when introduced and coming into contact with this non-evolving form of energy which in the spirit life is perfectly suited for the progression that the spirit body experiences as it is no longer being subject to any form of spirit body evolution or spirit sphere evolution for its survival.

In the messages that James Padgett received, we introduced the attribute and use of soul perceptions to identify a soulful life. Soul perceptions on their own are not enough to perceive the existence of this teaching about the evolving with the non-evolving nature of God's Divine Love. It requires 'spirit perception' along with soul perception so that the individual has a more extensive context to evaluate this intricate convergence that takes place within the realm of their own soul.

Hopefully, the individual is desiring to feel like they are in contact with 'spirit' in their life by receiving the Divine Love. The individual may see evidence of their spirit attributes being generated into a more active life that reflects how it is that individuals progress here when involved with receipt of the Divine Love. Hence, confirming the experience and expression, 'Living spirit on Earth'. Unfortunately, there are very few examples of this active experience so yourself become your guide. If you always retain the Soul, God, as your central source, then your independence and luxury are to explore the wonderful attribute of your acumen of spirit nature that exists in your spirit body. It must be stated that God is Soul and Spirit, but does not live clothed in a physical and evolving body.

You have received the stillness of my message well in an otherwise noisy world. Your teacher and friend, Luke

122

Luke speaks:

Several days have passed since I last spoke to you. I was present listening as you both discussed how your 30 years being aware of Divine Love has progressed. You speak about this from time to time, and as time goes by you are able to evaluate your experiences having the Father in your lives. The amount of information that you have been exposed to involving the soulful life presents a human horizon that has not been looked at before. We have conveyed so much information about the soul-life, and all that it involves while living with the Divine Love active in your lives, that an expansive understanding about your personal humanity and what it means to be human has advanced. It is important to acknowledge your participation as there will be other people who benefit from what you share so readily. Like yourselves, there will be individuals who will perceive being human with a complete spirit interpretation. In other words, like yourselves, these individuals will understand a whole new context for being the individual that they are while living in ongoing humanity that is mostly concerned with social beliefs that have very little to do with anything that involves the real nature of the soul. I must say this for there will be - as there are now - individuals living aware of Divine Love who understand the importance of their soul and life everlasting.

At face value in the physical life, individuals will become advanced humans in their personification of the Divine Love as real living energy causing an effect in their earthly physical life so that the personality relates with 'spirit' as much as it does with physical life and mortal conditions and beliefs.

What would be the point of receiving and being aware of the Divine Love if everything were to remain the same?

Throughout the extensive teachings that we have conveyed to you that involve living the soul-life, the word 'living' defines the energy that the Divine Love is. We have explained to you that the Divine Love is a non-evolving form of energy, but this teaching must not be misconstrued with the idea that the Divine Love is inert because as a form of energy it doesn't evolve. The energy that this Love personifies is living! It is living with so much life that it is this livingness that causes change in our soulful experience resulting in all the things that we have revealed, taught and explained to you. It is the catalyst for change as nothing else permeates the soul to bring about the kind of change that takes place in the soul and spirit attributes to generate progression. There are everlasting realities that involve our living with Divine Love, exploring God's Divine Love as a non-evolving form of energy brings new vision into our relationship that appears to evolve as we receive this truthful Gift.

Your friend and teacher, Luke

Contents

Foreword and Dedication 5

Everlasting - The Book of Spirit and Love - 6

March 2019 6

May 2019 6

2. 6

3. 7

June 2019 10

4. 10

5. 13

6. 18

7. 19

8. 22

9. 27

10 28

11 34

12. 39

13 45

14. 49

15. 52

July 2019 55

16 55

17 59

18 61

19 64

20 66

21 69

22 71

23 78

24	80
25	81
26	83
27	85
28	86
September	90
29	90
October	93
30	93
31	94
32	96
33	97
34	100
35	102
36	104
37	105
38	109
39	111
40	112
41	114
42	115
43	115
44	116
45	117
46	119
47	124
48	126
49	128
50	129

51	131
52	133
53	134
54	136
November	138
55	138
56	140
57	141
58	141
59	141
60	142
61	142
62	145
63	146
64	148
65	149
66	151
67	152
68	153
69	155
70	156
71	158
72	160
73	163
74	166
75	167
76	170
77	172
78	173

December	175
79	175
80	178
81	180
82	182
83	184
84	188
85	192
86	194
87	197
88	198
89	199
90	202
91	204
92	207
93	209
94	211
95	212
96	214
97	214
98	215
99	215
100	216
101	216
January 2020	217
102	217
103	219
104	222
105	224

106	226
107	228
108	230
109	231
110	232
111	235
112	236
113	237
114	240
115	242
116	244
117	246
118	248
February	251
119	251
120	255
121	256
122	257

www.ingramcontent.com/pod-product-compliance
Lightning Source LLC
Chambersburg PA
CBHW060352080526
44583CB00012B/283